Care Practice
for S/NVQ3

Care Practice for S/NVQ3

Edited by Janet Miller

Written with
George Baker
Susan Gibb
Doris Graham
Ellen Lancaster
Peter Laverie

HODDER
EDUCATION
AN HACHETTE UK COMPANY

Orders: please contact Bookpoint Ltd, 130 Milton Park, Abingdon, Oxon OX14 4SB.
Telephone: (44) 01235 827720. Fax: (44) 01235 400454. Lines are open from 9.00 - 5.00, Monday to Saturday,
with a 24 hour message answering service. You can also order through our website www.hoddereducation.co.uk

If you have any comments to make about this, or any of our other titles, please send them to
educationenquiries@hodder.co.uk

British Library Cataloguing in Publication Data
A catalogue record for this title is available from the British Library

ISBN 978 0340 88933 6

Published 2005
Impression number   10 9 8 7 6 5 4
Year   2009

Typeset by Servis Filmsetting Ltd, Manchester.
Printed in India for Hodder Education,
an Hachette UK Company, 338 Euston Road, London NW1 3BH.

*In recognition of all
people who experience
discrimination and oppression*

CONTENTS

CHAPTER 4 INTERPERSONAL SKILLS AND COMMUNICATION Ellen Lancaster

CHAPTER 5 HEALTH AND SAFETY Doris Graham

CHAPTER 6 PROTECTION FROM ABUSE Janet Miller

CHAPTER 7 INTRODUCING PSYCHOLOGY AND SOCIOLOGY Susan Gibb

CHAPTER 8   A PERSON-CENTRED APPROACH TO ASSESSMENT AND CARE PLANNING   Sylvia Brewer and Janet Miller

CHAPTER 9   IMPLEMENTING CARE PLANS – APPROACHES TO HELPING AND THE PROMOTION OF WELLBEING   Janet Miller, Sylvia Brewer, Margaret Crompton and Robin Jackson

CHAPTER 10 SUPERVISION AND PROFESSIONAL DEVELOPMENT   Peter Laverie

CHAPTER 11 THIS CARING BUSINESS   George Baker

FIGURES

FOREWORD

People using services put a high value on the support which they receive from care workers. The work we do is essential in enabling many people to improve their lives, for others to keep safe, and for some, literally to stay alive. We now know a lot more than we did in the past about what turns a routine into a quality service. It is not simply what we do, but how we do our jobs that is very important for people using services. There are expectations that we will be reliable and skilled in the activities we do, but it matters whether we show respect, whether we listen to what people are saying to us and take account of their preferences. These are the things that give the service we provide its quality. This fact is the same whether we are new to care or are very experienced. For those of us who have worked in care for some time, it is essential that our own knowledge and expertise are recognised when we are trying to develop best practice. We also need to be ready to learn to use new ways that will improve the experience of people using services.

When there is a lot of change it is very easy to think that what we have contributed over the months and years counts for nothing any more: that all that matters now is pushing a piece of paper rather than actually doing the job day in and day out. When feeling like this, it is worth remembering that the national occupational standards were built from the expertise of people doing caring jobs like ours. What they thought was necessary to be able to do and to know about for good practice shaped both the skills and the knowledge that are set out in the Standards. While as a whole there seems a mountain to climb, it is less daunting if taken in smaller steps. This approach is also more likely to fit into our busy work and family lives. This book can be dipped into in ways that link with the different parts of our job, or when we cannot work out what is going on or how to cope with a particular situation. Everyone, those new to care practice, experienced workers, qualified or not, becomes stuck from time to time. We, like everyone else, need time to think through or reflect on what is happening, or why what usually works is failing this time. Care work is different each day and never boring – challenging, yes, but never dull. That is why we need to keep on learning, however long we have been around. Supervision is one way of doing this, but having books that set out the theories and methods used in social care is another resource for us.

This book has the advantage of being very focused on linking what each of us knows and can do with the knowledge that underpins the national occupational standards in Health and Social Care, BTEC and other NVQ, SVQ and HNC Awards. It can be used flexibly. There is the opportunity to read through to get a sense of the whole territory, the values and methods of social care. Equally, it is possible to dip in to check out different terms and ideas when we have the time, the energy or urgency. The beginning of each chapter sets out how the knowledge relates to different qualifications and standards (NVQ, SVQ and HNC units), which helps when we are searching for the underpinning knowledge for our portfolio. A list at the end of each chapter gives ideas about further reading that can be used either now or in the future.

Finally, for those of you who, like me, are always on the move, the fact that the book can be carried around is important. Adult learners usually have too much to do and not enough time to do it in; but that does not mean that we are any less committed to improving our practice and keeping up to date.

Daphne Statham CBE
President of the Social Care Association
December 2004

ACKNOWLEDGEMENTS

We have received help from many people. Service users and carers are the reason for the existence of this book and they have contributed significantly to its content. This has included contributions from people from Carers Scotland, Parkhouse Centre, Waverley Care, and at various consultation meetings held throughout the UK. Without the long, unpaid hours that Joyce Hanna spent word processing and creating diagrams, the book may never have seen the light of day. Several people contributed accounts, diagrams and/or suggested significant ideas. These included Phil Baron, Ursula Corker, Senga Crighton, Gary Dickson, Christine Grant, Stephen Jennings, Campbell Marjoribanks, Marion Miller, Jimmy McIntosh, Laura Steckley, Claire and Theresa. The publications of SHS Ltd and the Social Care Association provided sound guidance. We thank our colleagues at the Scottish Social Services Council, Cardonald College and James Watt College for their support; also Matthew Smith and Colin Goodlad at Hodder Arnold.

Many thanks to other significant contributors:
Sylvia Brewer to Chapters 8 and 9
Margaret Crompton to Chapter 9
Robin Jackson to Chapter 9
Robin McLean and Andrew Parry for the cartoons.

We could not mention everyone individually who gave us ideas, comment and time, but thank you everyone for the part you played.

The publisher would like to thank Phil Baron for Figure 0.1 (© Phil Baron 2004).

INTRODUCTION

> **Imagine a society in which everyone can flourish.**
>
> (SHS (2003) based on a statement by Aristotle (384–322BC))

We did not want to produce a stuffy textbook or a patronising guide to care practice. You are the person doing the job and know more about your job than we do. What we have set out to do is to present some values and principles, skills and knowledge, some of which are vital and others that may be useful in your practice, while at the same time asking you to examine everything you do. Use questioning, imagination, be creative, take a risk or two where this is likely to benefit and will not be harmful to service users, think around corners and across boundaries. Do not ever presume that you are the expert. Neither are we. We are simply trying to improve things with and for people who, for whatever reason, use care services. This book is one way of contributing to this. Let us know how you think it can be improved.

Figure 0.1

The thinking in the book has been greatly influenced by the social model of care, explained in Chapter 1, and ideas about person-centred planning, which places the emphasis firmly where it belongs, on the people who use care services. Being person-centred is not just a fad, an alternative approach or just another way of going about things. It is central and vital and involves a partnership with service users. Being person-centred includes:

❑ listening to people
❑ respecting their dignity and privacy
❑ recognising individual differences and specific needs, including cultural and religious differences
❑ enabling people to make informed choices, involving them in all decisions about their needs and care
❑ providing coordinated and inclusive responses
❑ sharing power
❑ involving and supporting carers when appropriate.

You should be able to feel the relevance of this book in your day-to-day job. We hope that it will stimulate you to want to learn more and to improve your practice. It attempts to provide a road map with lots of possible routes, with flexibility about the ones that you take according to the needs and wishes of service users. You should be able to adapt the content of the book to develop practice that is *your* practice, which has your own special contributions, and uses both your gifts and those of service users and carers.

The book is divided into 11 chapters. These chapters discuss the values, knowledge and skills for units and modules of care qualifications, including the reviewed NVQs and SVQs in Health and Social Care available from the beginning of 2005, and HNCs in Care and Social Care. The content is also relevant to a range of other care qualifications, including BTEC and SQA awards. Guidance is given at the beginning of each chapter to indicate which units and modules relate most closely to the chapter. The division into chapters is somewhat arbitrary since all of the chapters are linked to one another, and in the end come back to providing the value base, knowledge and skills which are needed to work with service users. The relationships among disciplines are emphasised, and it is hoped that the reader will be able to appreciate these relationships to gain an integrated and 'holistic' approach to care practice. A summary of each chapter follows in order to give the reader an idea of the breadth of material covered.

In **Chapter 1**, entitled **Care Practice: Content and Context**, the meaning of 'care' is examined. Accounts are given of service users and care workers to give you an idea of the people behind the words. This is followed by a consideration of the contexts of care, including history, ideology, social policy and demography. The regulatory role of the Care Commissions and Councils, and statutory, voluntary and private provision of care services are discussed. The chapter ends with considerations of the social model of care, institutionalisation, and the way forward through being more imaginative and inclusive about the ways in which care is provided.

Principles for Ethical Practice are the subject of **Chapter 2**. The emphasis is upon the importance of a value base, with two core values and a set of principles as the foundation upon which ethical practice is based. Consideration is given to applying the value base, and a set of values and principles is described. Two fundamental values are outlined: respect for persons and the right to social justice and welfare. From these derived a set of principles for practice which include the promotion of the rights to equality, choice, privacy, and protection from danger, harm and abuse. The discussion of ethical thinking and ethical dilemmas begins to tackle the complexity of putting the value base into practice. The second half of the chapter gives attention to anti-discriminatory and anti-oppressive practice, seen both in terms of the application of the principle of equality, and also as a means of practising in a person-centred way.

Chapter 3, Service Users and Carers – Include Us, is of central importance to the spirit of this book. It stresses the vital significance of including and seeking the views of service users and carers, and recognising their diversity. The 'Service User Statement of Expectations', from the reviewed Health and Social Care NVQs and SVQs, is reproduced, since this gives an account of what is expected in the words of service users and carers themselves. A section on good practice in including service users and carers looks at the factors outlined by SCIE (Social Care Institute for Excellence), and some useful guidelines are given for organising meetings that include service users and carers. Finally some examples of good practice in relation to service user and carer involvement are outlined.

Chapter 4 considers **Interpersonal Skills and Communication**. Effective communication is essential to forming caring, valuable relationships with people. It rests upon the value and knowledge base but also requires that bit extra, what is referred to as 'oomph'. The meaning and different forms of communication are considered, and emphasis is given to the importance of listening skills. Recording is also part of communication, and guidance is given in relation to this at the end of the chapter.

Chapter 5, Health and Safety, covers content for one of the core units of many care qualifications, including NVQs and SVQs. Everyone's responsibilities in relation to health and safety are emphasised, together with some of the dilemmas that occur sometimes between promoting individual rights, and health and safety requirements. A great deal of attention is given to monitoring and promoting health and safety, including minimising and managing risks, and your role in this as a care worker.

Chapter 6 tackles the sensitive and difficult subject of **Protection from Abuse**. The meaning of abuse and forms and signs of abuse are discussed so that you are in a position to recognise when abuse has occurred or is likely to occur. Some factors that occur more often among people who abuse than those who do not, are considered. These include stress and stressful environments, lack of love and attachment, and learned negative behaviour. Ways of responding to and preventing abuse are discussed. Inquiries into failures to protect people, including the Victoria Climbie inquiry, are looked at in terms of the lessons that can be learned from them.

Chapter 7, Introducing Psychology and Sociology, explains key ideas, perspectives and theories from these disciplines. The main perspectives considered are the psychodynamic, behavioural, cognitive and humanistic in psychology, and functionalism, conflict, symbolic interactionism and feminism in sociology. All of the perspectives are illustrated by applications to care practice, with a final examination of poverty to demonstrate psychology and sociology in action.

Chapter 8, A Person-Centred Approach to Assessment and Care Planning, begins by examining a model of care based upon assessment, care planning, implementation, evaluation and a person-centred approach. The section on assessment looks in detail at the concept of need and the importance of a needs-led approach. Two models of care planning are considered: the exchange model and person-centred planning. The importance of person-centred planning for people who wish to make changes in their lives is emphasised, and a chart is given illustrating what person-centred planning is moving from and towards.

Implementing Care Plans – Approaches to Helping and the Promotion of Wellbeing is the subject of **Chapter 9**. This chapter provides ways and tools of helping that are available to workers depending upon the outcomes of the assessment and care planning process. Promoting wellbeing can be tackled through creating positive care environments, dealing with people's emotional and physical pain, developing networks and circles of support, building resilience and promoting spiritual wellbeing. Consideration is given to the importance of team work and collaboration. Some further methods of helping are outlined including cognitive behavioural work, task-centred work, group work and advocacy.

Chapter 10 looks at **Supervision and Professional Development**. Supervision is considered to be everyone's right and covers a wide range of activities. It is seen as having managerial, educational and supportive functions. The qualities of 'good' supervision are emphasised including being planned and regular, recorded and evaluated. You are encouraged to examine your own experiences of supervision. Supervision is closely linked to professional development and contributes to it. The themes addressed in the section on professional development include lifelong learning, dealing with stress, personal growth, and the learning process.

Chapter 11 is an exciting final chapter that looks critically at **This Caring Business**, and invites you to expand your horizons through developing habits of critical thinking and reflective practice. There is a return to examining the passion and power associated with care work. Finally the importance of relationships and the framework of value base, knowledge and skills, are revisited.

CHAPTER 1

CARE PRACTICE: CONTENT AND CONTEXT

Janet Miller

> The words 'caring' and 'to care' are some of the most heavily freighted in the English language. Like magnets they attract the most noble images and concepts. Like veils, they conceal the most complex confusions and illusions.
>
> (Gordon, S 1996)

By the end of this chapter, you should be able to:

- ❑ examine care from different viewpoints
- ❑ recognise the diversity of service users and care workers
- ❑ examine the overlapping contexts of care
- ❑ know about the relevance of history, ideology, social policy and demography
- ❑ know about the providers of care
- ❑ know about the regulation of care in the different countries of the UK
- ❑ understand different models of care: medical, psychological and social
- ❑ understand the meaning of institutionalisation and moves from institutional care to inclusion and community care.

The content of this chapter provides underpinning content and context for all care qualifications including NVQs and SVQs in Health and Social Care, and BTEC, SQA and other Health and Social Care qualifications, including HNC Social Care. It relates especially to the following units:

NVQ and SVQ Level 3 Core Unit HSC34 and 35: Promote the protection and wellbeing of children and young people; Promote choice, wellbeing and the protection of all individuals

HNC Social Care Unit: Social care theory for practice

BTEC National Unit: Equality, diversity and rights in care work.

INTRODUCTION

The meaning of care

Care gives scope for providing service in all sorts of ways: with imagination or routinely; inclusively or exclusively; by doing with or doing for; creatively or cursorily; equitably or unfairly; with choice or a lack of it; in partnership or not. It is not a straightforward word for straightforward activities but a developing, evolving concept with a range of interpretations and possibilities. 'Care' presents an opportunity to improve the way you do things and to get things right with the individuals with whom you work. It requires not only values, skills and knowledge but energy and a willingness to think beyond the obvious, what Ellen Lancaster (Chapter 4) calls oomph. You have to be crazy about people while also remaining sane, irrational about the possibilities while also being rational about what could be achieved, outrageous in your thinking and humbled by the thoughts of others.

But what, actually, does 'care' mean? In reality it means lots of things. The Concise Oxford Dictionary gives the following definition of care:

> The provision of what is necessary for the health, welfare, maintenance and protection of someone or something.

The Chambers paperback dictionary simply says 'to provide (for)'.

The Social Care Association (SCA 2002) regards care as a balancing act of meeting physical needs at the same time as respecting the feelings of

ACTIVITY 1.1

What does the word 'care' mean to you?

Identify three different kinds of care and outline what each one involves.

others, and addressing social, intellectual, emotional and cultural needs, responding to strong emotions and dealing with difficulties in behaviour and relationships.

One care worker said 'care is about working with people and sharing responsibility'.

In Activity 1.1 you may have chosen to write about any of the following: community care, palliative care, through care, residential care, day care, social care, child care, health care or another kind of care with which you are familiar. Whatever you wrote about, there are some things which are common to all kinds of care and care setting. It is these factors that will be the focus of this book, emphasising a holistic, generic and social model of care, while also recognising that everyone is different and that care should be provided according to a person-centred approach.

Who are the service users?

There is ongoing debate and controversy about the 'best' terminology to refer to people who use care services. The aim is to use terms that do not discriminate and that avoid being patronising and confusing. The term 'people' is fine for most purposes, but where there is a need to identify those who use services, the term 'service user' has been adopted. It is the term in current usage and avoids stigma, implications of possession, dependence or patronising overtones. It is not, however, universally liked and in some circumstances the terms 'client', 'resident' or 'customer' may be preferred.

Every service user is an individual and it is absolutely impossible to generalise about who they are, any more than it is possible to generalise about who is a school pupil or a footballer. The only generalisation that can be made is that service users need assistance to meet some of their needs some of the time. 'They' are often 'us' at various times in our lives. Here are a few examples. For reasons of confidentiality, names have been changed except where people have given permission for their own names to be used.

Jimmy

Jimmy McIntosh (his real name) was a resident/patient in Gogaburn long-stay hospital from 1956 until 1983. He was placed there because of his physical disability. In the book 'Gogaburn Lives' (Ingham, N 2003) there is a detailed account of aspects of his life there. The paragraph quoted below reflects some of Jimmy's campaigning:

> In the early eighties Jimmy McIntosh and Alec Greenhill, key individuals in the Patients Committee and the campaign to win voting rights, became married men. Both were patients at the time, Alec marrying Marion, a fellow resident, while Jimmy got married to Elizabeth who lived outside Gogaburn. These weddings took place in an institution which not long before had separate male and female locked wards, operated a punitive regime of sexual segregation, and still employed staff who were sympathetic to such practices. Their ground-breaking actions were closely followed by Alec, Marion, and Jimmy leaving Gogaburn as soon as their respective houses were ready.

Jimmy has written the following account for this book.

'I am Jimmy McIntosh, I am 65 years old and I am a very active person. I campaign for disabled rights and I am a board member of various committees including Sticking Up for Your Rights Group (Edinburgh) and Partners in Advocacy and on the board of the Scottish Social Services Council (SSSC).

One of the most important things in my life is my work promoting awareness of disability issues. My greatest achievement to date has been securing the job of council member of the SSSC as it was my first proper, paid job.

I sometimes become frustrated about the way in which disabled people are portrayed in the press. I am treated differently because of my physical disability, even though there is nothing wrong with me mentally. Another thing which frustrates me is the lack of benefits which personal assistants (p.a.s) receive. They are not entitled to travel allowance and do not receive a higher rate of pay for working late.

I use direct payments from the social work department to employ my personal assistants. They accompany me to meetings and help me with shopping and getting about. I do not use personal assistants at home as I live with my wife and she also helps me.

My ideal p.a. should have a good understanding of disabled rights or be interested in learning more about them. I like to build up a friendship with each p.a. so that we can work well as a team.'

Claire

Claire has written about her life in a secure unit.

'My life in a secure unit is okay but there is some stuff I do not like about it. Well, I really miss my mum and dad; they know I am safe in secure care because at my old school I kept on running away.

The staff are here to look after me. I like my school, I like art and English. Maths is okay. I do not really like my room because I have to be locked in at night, but I have to for my security. I will be in secure care maybe till the end of December or the start of December. At my last hearing I got another three-month order and I hated it. I was shouting and screaming because I did not want to come back, but it is not as bad as I thought it was. It is good at times, like you get your full privileges and walks and outings. I will be getting my one-to-one walks and I am happy about that because I am managing my behaviour for once. I have to really put my head down and get on in secure care.'

Stephen

'Stephen, my son, has cerebral palsy. I have been his main carer for 35 years, though my second husband and the care workers we employ with Stephen's direct payments also play their part in his care. It was not until he was 11 months old that Stephen's disability was confirmed. He was then labelled "spastic". In spite of this label and severe physical disability, Stephen has maintained a determined personality and has achieved some remarkable things.

Stephen attended a special school for children who have physical disabilities in Liverpool, where one of his main interests was making life as difficult as possible for his teachers and in particular the headmaster. He would team up with one of his friends who has now sadly passed away and they would, using their wheelchairs, barricade the class doorway by pushing chairs and desks against them, the staff having to climb up the fire escape chute to gain entry and "rescue" them. Stephen enjoyed school and demonstrated the obstinacy and self-determination which have remained with him to this day.

It was while at school that his communication skills started to show a vast improvement, through the introduction of the Bliss Symbolics system. Prior to this, as he could not talk he was sometimes unable to express himself in an understandable manner. He still uses his Bliss Board but in the main uses a Delta Talker, which speaks for him, albeit in an American accent.

Stephen now attends a purpose-built activity and resource centre which primarily caters for people who have a learning disability, although there are a number like Stephen who have a multi-disability. Over the years he has enjoyed a range of options at the centre such as pottery, craftwork, photography and horse carting. In recent years the options for him have changed due to a greater emphasis on educational interests, which are of little interest to him.

Despite his disability, Stephen has shown his determination by winning a prestigious regional photography competition using a specially adapted camera, and has also won the District's Disabled Sportsman annual award twice for his achievements in sailing in a specially adapted Challenger boat. He has also been caving and abseiling. Who else would agree to be lowered down a cliff in a wheelchair? That is Stephen.'

Who are the care workers?

As with service users, there is an infinite variety of care workers with differing functions, differing approaches to their work and different titles ranging from support worker to senior practitioner. 'Care worker' provides an all-embracing term to cover all of these. A few examples should suffice to give an idea of this variety.

Teresa

'I am a residential social worker. I work in a secure unit for young people between the ages of 11 and 17. Young people from all over the country are placed in the secure environment that we provide. We offer stability and security for young people who find themselves involved in increasing anti-social behaviours that may harm themselves or others.

My early shift starts at 8am. The team meet in the unit office as all the young people are still sleeping. We usually have a cup of tea and discuss the forthcoming day's events. We may have young people who need to attend meetings with social workers, and some may need to attend hearings or court in their local areas. As a staff group we need to make sure all the travel arrangements and cover for these meetings have been made and the appropriate people informed.

By 8.15 we are wakening all the young people in order to allow everyone time to be showered and dressed, ready for school. At this time the team leader goes to the morning meeting, which all the other team leaders also attend with senior management; here the daily diaries are discussed and coordinated to allow for efficient use of staff and to spot any oversights.

During the education day, a member of staff from each unit remains in education to offer support to the young people to remain in class should it be needed. The other staff go back to the unit and are able to write reports for their keychild, should one be required for a hearing, LAC review or court appearance. The daily paperwork is completed at this time and filed appropriately. Staff also keep the relevant social workers and family up to date on any issues that may have arisen for the young person.

As a staff group, we are always aware that we use ourselves as role models for our young people. We use a lot of negotiation skills to de-escalate conflict between young people. The job is very demanding, it offers many challenges to all staff, but it is also a very rewarding job, with positive relationships being built up with the young people and the staff.'

Marion

'I am a support worker for a group of women with severe learning disabilities, and the majority of my work is carried out in their own home. There are seven women who are tenants in the unit, which is separated into two houses joined by an office and laundry room. Six of the women living here spent most of their lives in an institution. The youngest is 53 years old. Five years ago, the institution closed and all of the people who lived there were rehoused in the community. Three women live in one house, four in the other, with space for one more.

It was a huge change to go from a very restricted life where a ward was shared with 24 other people, to having a small house where everyone has their own private bedroom; not to mention the increased range of activities, which the tenants now have access to, and all the new people they are able to meet through these activities.

In the morning, a shift starts at either 7.30 or 8am. On arrival, staff are required to check the communication book, which passes on any important information from previous shifts, and the diary, which lists the appointments for the day. We greet everyone, talking to them as we give the first lot of medication at around 8am and assist with bathing and breakfast. There is always a lot to do, and not enough time to do it in, but we undertake the tasks in a caring way that respects the dignity of the people we are working with. The women and the staff appreciate the routine which enables us to be ready for the rest of the day.

At 10am, day activity staff come in to accompany the women to their activities. These vary and are sometimes on a one-to-one basis, and other times in small groups, with two or three support workers. One of the group classes that the women attend is a music and movement class where they have the opportunity to communicate through movement. None of the women has verbal ability, and it is therefore vital that they have exposure to other ways of expressing themselves.

Not all of the women like to participate in the group activities. I think these are beneficial in integrating them into society, but also limited sometimes to activities in 'service land', where instead of mixing with the general public, the women find themselves mixing with other people with learning difficulties.

I really enjoy my job, and it is so rewarding to see the women do new things and enjoy them. It is hard work, and very tiring, as a good proportion of the day is spent in practical tasks, though we do try to have plenty of time left over to spend with the tenants. The project always runs smoothly when there is a full complement of staff, but unfortunately the staff turnover is high, and at the end of the day it is the tenants who suffer.

It is important to remain patient and understanding regardless of the situation, and despite any challenging behaviour. Although the job can be stressful, a smile or a sign of appreciation more than compensates for the difficult side, and is a reminder that it is all worthwhile.'

Christine

'I work with offenders in a residential unit. As a staff team we try to support and encourage service users to make changes in their lifestyles that will break their offending behaviour and enable them to live more fulfilling lives. The service users who stay here must be 18 years old or over, have a social worker and be on an order, e.g. probation or parole. Our unit is staffed 24 hours a day, 365 days a year. At the moment all of the service users are men, though we do accommodate women if they are referred to us. I am keyworker to two of the men, but also work with everyone in the unit when I am on shift. I interact with the service users, spend time with them and try to build up supportive relationships. This enables me to be able to encourage them in their interests, help them in their search for employment, voluntary work or access to college courses, and also to develop skills associated with everyday life such as cooking and budgeting. I use humour and banter with them from time to time, but only when appropriate. I also spend time interacting with them, which can include the following: watching television, listening to music, chatting and, most importantly, listening to their worries and concerns.

We have inhouse programmes on the following subjects: drug awareness, alcohol awareness, anger management, assertiveness, stress management, victim awareness and loss and bereavement. Each service user is asked to choose two inhouse programmes to work through during their time with us, and their keyworker will take them through the programmes. We also do group work once a week and we encourage service users to attend this, although it is optional. For those who are unsure about the group work, I'll say "If you don't give it a go, you'll never know." Often when they do participate they find it very useful, it helps them to make changes in their lives and they are proud of the certificate they gain at the end of the six-week programme.

It is sometimes quite hard trying to motivate people. There's a real sense of achievement though when people start to do things for themselves that they have never done before, even if it is a quite small thing that most people take for granted, like putting clothes in the washing machine and ironing them afterwards.'

Campbell

'I am a frontline manager at a day centre for people with learning difficulties, and am responsible for running the centre. I have to make sure the staff team works well and that service users are receiving the service they want and need. The day centre provides a stimulating, pleasant and safe environment for people to mix with their friends and peers, and also provides the practical care that some of them need.

Although I am responsible for the day-to-day running of the centre, staff and service users play a large part in decision-making about what will happen on a daily basis. We have a mixture of activities from art to cookery to carpet bowls, and service users assist with running the coffee bar. The service users have their own decision-making committee led by an advocate, which staff do not attend. At the centre we try to do anything that the service users want, or would do usually.

I have been involved in frontline management for 25 years, and suggest below some of the things that I think are important in the job. It is necessary to:

❏   be a good listener and sensitive to the situations facing both service users and staff

- ❏ be good at assessing risks: calculate potential dangers, try to minimise risks, but still take them, without succumbing to the fear of litigation
- ❏ be honest about situations, never procrastinate, and deal with things as soon as possible
- ❏ accept responsibility and do not take criticism personally
- ❏ be able to prioritise while being able to juggle a number of problems at one time
- ❏ be prudent with budgets and deal well with administration
- ❏ cope with being piggy in the middle sometimes, where headquarters managers may have a different agenda from that of service users and staff.

Most importantly, you do not have to be crazy, but you must have a great sense of humour!'

Senga

'I am a residential child care worker. I began this line of work four years ago. My first experience with children and young people was working for Community Education as a youth worker at night. I enjoyed this very much.

I then secured a full-time job in a local factory, and because of shifts, I had to give my youth work up after six years. After 11 years in the factory, I felt like a robot. I really missed the young people. I was in a position to be able to take redundancy, and took a Community Education course at the local college. While I was at college, my placement was at a residential school. I loved it and, after working on a sessional basis, managed to gain a full-time post in a residential school following my course. I now work in an intensive support unit at the school, which currently houses four boys aged 13–16. This unit has a focus programme:

F   Family problem-solving
O – Outdoor, planned, personal achievement
C – Cognitive development milieu
U – Unique recognition of the individual
S – School education services.

The unit provides a safe, secure and friendly environment. This is for young people who may need more support than in other units. The staff ratio is higher than other units as well. We try to empower the young people (who have emotional and behavioural difficulties) on their journey to adulthood, and give them skills for life.

Young people engaging with the focus programme reside in the unit which has four single rooms. A high staff ratio provides the opportunity to leave behind the 'group' mentality of larger, less well-supported residential units. Young people can pursue their personal needs and choices throughout the week rather than via the group decisions. There are two keyworkers for each young person, which offers greater continuity, a wider skills base and more intensive input. Time, another enemy of the larger unit, is more available for collaborative design and maintenance of unique and effective care plans. Special consideration and support are given to the young person's exit plan, regardless of where their next placement may be.

I am always aware that I am a role model for the young people. The job can at times be very challenging, but if you speak to the young people on their level and not down to them, treat them with respect and give them a chance to trust you and build a good relationship, then it is a rewarding job. As you know, you cannot be given respect, you must earn it. You receive a lot of training in this job, but your own personality does not change. Training makes you more confident at what you do and offers a better service. I am glad I came into this line of work; it is very rewarding and I would not change it for anything. If you are thinking about a career change, I would say 'Go for it, you will not regret it'. It is good to know you have changed a young person's life forever by just doing something you enjoy.'

ACTIVITY 1.2

Use one of these accounts to identify what you see as the personal attributes and qualities of a good care worker.

In Activity 1.2 you may have identified some of the following or different things:

- ❏ honesty
- ❏ reliability
- ❏ warmth
- ❏ good sense of humour
- ❏ knows what to do
- ❏ good communicator and listener
- ❏ enthusiasm.

Once you have done this, draw a four-box chart, labelling the boxes as follows: knowledge, skills, values/principles, qualities/attributes.

Knowledge	Skills
Values/principles	Personal attributes/qualities

From the case studies above, identify what you see as the knowledge, skills, values/principles and personal attributes/qualities that contribute to good, competent care work, and list these in the appropriate box. When you have finished working through this book, go back to your chart and see if you want to make any additions or changes. These are areas that continue to be developed throughout the career of a care worker.

THE CONTEXTS OF CARE

Introduction

Many factors have influenced and continue to influence the ways in which care is practised today. Just as the person you are is influenced by several things, including your childhood, your genetic inheritance and the society in which you live, so care is influenced by varying mixtures of history, ideology, social policy,

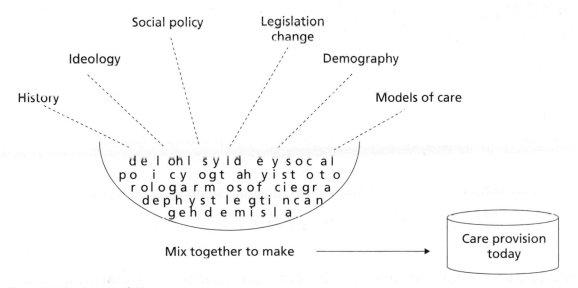

Figure 1.1 The Context of Care

legislative change, demography and different models of care. All of these factors are both a cause and effect of one another and, rather like the ingredients of a cake, when you put them all together they make something completely different from the individual components.

History, ideology and social policy

For as long as there has been recorded history there is a history of care: care of travellers, care of the sick and dying, care of children who have been orphaned or abandoned, care of poor and elderly people. Care can be provided formally, by paid care workers in organisations in the statutory, private or voluntary sectors, or informally by carers who are unpaid and often unappreciated. Even in the twenty-first century, it would cost billions of pounds to pay for the informal, unpaid care provided by family, friends and 'the community'.

Some historical examples of care provision

Workhouse – in 1848, conditions in the Huddersfield township workhouse were appallingly cramped and unhygienic, with up to ten children sharing a bed. The inmates' diet was miserable even by workhouse standards. Conditions in the infirmary were even worse – a living patient occupied the same bed with a corpse for a considerable period after death, and the sick were left unwashed for days on end.

Childcare – between 1868 and 1930, 100,000 children 'in need' were migrated from the UK to Canada, and today over 10 per cent of Canadian families are descended from these children.

Disability – Following World War Two, Group Captain Leonard Cheshire introduced a new element into the care of people with physical disabilities: participation in decision-making.

(Source: Heatherbank Museum of Social Work: www.lib.gcal.ac.uk/ heatherbank/contact.html)

Some of the care provided historically has been given with concern and respect for the dignity of the individual; some of it though, seems to have been designed to punish and demean, while still meeting some basic human needs for food and shelter.

ACTIVITY 1.3

Read the account below of Thomas Fretwell's entry into a workhouse orphanage in 1918 following the death of his mother. State the ways in which you think the care provided differs from care practice today.

> The Orphanage, which was a very big building, was surrounded by three walls but was still within the grounds of the Workhouse. We all slept in hospital type beds: the boys on the first floor, the girls on the second. Here I just became one of many and had to stand up to bullying from the older children. There was a big playground surrounded by high walls where we played . . . The longer I stayed the less I liked it and was glad when I was eventually moved to Ashley House, a Catholic Orphanage just off Park Road near to my old home. It was a big house with the name Ashley House stencilled in faded gold lettering over the front door with two large iron gates to the wide drive. This led past the side of the house into a huge playground, which was surrounded by two high brick walls. . . .. Friday nights were bath nights. Immediately after tea we were given a good scrub with the brushes the girls used on the floor. . . Then we were lined up in front of the Matron who gave us a dose of brimstone and treacle, then off to bed.

(Quoted from: http://users.ox.ac.uk/~peter/workhouse/Barnsley/Barnsley.shtml)

The history of care reflects to a certain extent the ideologies of the age in which it was practised. **Ideology** refers to the beliefs held in society at any one time, particularly dominant beliefs that affect society, its institutions and policies. Different ideologies have influenced the provision of care throughout history and, in turn, historical factors have influenced ideologies. **Social policy** refers to courses or principles of action which deal with issues that the government of the day regards as needing attention. It changes with both history and ideology and, therefore, it is also considered here.

There have been some key historical factors that have played a part in the history of care provision, which have had ideological and social policy implications. The industrial revolution that tore through Britain and Europe in the eighteenth and nineteenth centuries was undoubtedly one of the most important of these factors. In pre-industrial society, care was practised by many people: family, friends, priests, healers. Churches and monasteries provided residential care through almshouses, infirmaries (for the care and treatment of sick people), hospitals and hospices (for poor people, especially those who were old or infirm, and for travellers who needed temporary shelter). The Poor Law Acts of the seventeenth century authorised parishes to levy taxes to pay for services for people in need, 'the impotent poor' as they were called. The able-bodied poor had to fend for themselves or suffer punishment.

But with the industrial revolution came problems on a much larger scale as people were concentrated in large cities, often living in deprived and unhealthy conditions. They were seen as a potential threat to the more wealthy members of the population, and the ideology of the day prescribed the 1834 Poor Law Amendment Act. This made a distinction between the deserving and the undeserving poor, though in practice the dividing line and the difference in treatment were hard to distinguish. The 'deserving poor' (e.g. sick and disabled people) received help from charitable and voluntary organisations where it was available and they could convince the governors of their need. Everyone else was forced to turn to the state, where the only form of poor relief was the workhouse. Charles Dickens's novel, 'Oliver Twist', tells of the conditions that prevailed in many workhouses. Oliver is nine years old when he enters the workhouse. After asking for more porridge he is placed in solitary confinement for a week. His experience of this is as follows:

> Let it not be supposed by the enemies of 'the system', that, during the period of his incarceration, Oliver was denied the benefit of exercise, the pleasure of society, or the advantages of religious consolation. As for exercise, it was nice cold weather, and he was allowed to perform his ablutions under the pump, in a stone yard, in the presence of Mr Bumble, who prevented his catching cold . . . by repeated applications of the cane. As for society, he was carried every other day into the hall where the boys dined, and there sociably flogged . . ..

The workhouse was meant to put people off being poor and dependent on the state, to the extent that they would do anything to get out of these circumstances. To their credit, many people did, or tried to, but others could not. They did not have a place in an industrial, capitalist, competitive society. They may have been mentally ill or with learning difficulties, or old and frail, or young and orphaned, or traumatised or a whole host of other things that did not make them deserving enough to be the 'deserving poor', but which incapacitated them enough to be unable to play a part in paid employment.

ACTIVITY 1.4

From the account given in this chapter, identify the prevailing ideologies and social policies of the industrial revolution.

In the nineteenth century, a great deal of philanthropic, charitable activity attempted to alleviate the lot of needy people, but it was often patronising and not based upon any concept of what people really needed. It was often well-meant though, and did sometimes keep whole families out of extreme poverty and from dying of starvation.

In the mid-twentieth century, the Welfare State emerged after World War Two with an ideology aiming to conquer the five giants of 'Want, Disease, Ignorance, Squalor and Idleness' (HMSO 1942). Welfare State policy resulted in statutory provision on a massive scale: the National Health Service; National Assistance; education; pensions, local authority children's departments, welfare departments and health departments. Margaret Thatcher's Britain in the 1980s began to dismantle all of this in favour of a much freer market economy. In 1991 The National Health Service and Community Care Act put in place a policy of a 'mixed economy of care'. Caring for People, the white paper that preceded the Act, defined community care as follows:

> Community Care means providing the services and support which people who are affected by problems by ageing, mental illness, mental handicap or physical or sensory disability need to be able to live as independently as possible in their own houses or in 'homely' settings in the community.

> (Department of Health 1989, Caring for People, para 1.1)

Although the Act received Royal Assent in 1990, it was not 'fully' implemented until 1993. In fact, truly full implementation is unlikely in the light of resource limitations. The key objectives of the legislation are set out in the White Paper as follows:

- ❏ To promote the development of domiciliary, day and respite services to enable people to live in their own homes wherever feasible and sensible
- ❏ To ensure that service providers make practical support for carers a high priority
- ❏ To make proper assessment of need and good care management the cornerstone of high quality care

- ❏ To promote the development of a flourishing independent sector, alongside good quality public services
- ❏ To clarify the responsibilities of agencies and so make it easier to hold them to account for their performance
- ❏ To secure better value for taxpayers' money by introducing a new funding structure for social care.

These objectives indicated some changes about thinking in relation to social care, for example the stated objective of promoting the independent sector. This was part of a policy of providing the mixed economy of care referred to above, where local authorities were no longer the main providers of care but were able to buy in services from private and voluntary agencies. The fact that support for carers, theoretically at least, received high priority, recognised that carers are an invaluable resource, especially if their interests are attended to and support is given before crises are reached. The promotion of domiciliary, day care and respite services was designed to enable more people to remain in their own homes for much longer and so reduce the demands upon the residential services which could then focus upon those in greatest need of them.

And now we have a devolved Britain under the current Prime Minister, Tony Blair, full of contradictions, as most societies are, and with the four countries within the UK sometimes pursuing different policies from one another. There are policies to tackle exclusion and discrimination, but a ruthless capitalist economy that excludes millions of people from an 'average' lifestyle; there are benefits to assist people in need, but a pensions crisis that means that many people must choose between a poor old age or ongoing employment; for others there is no choice in an era that promotes the right to choose; there is an exciting multi-cultural society but ongoing discrimination even at institutional levels; there continue to be policies that promote an increasingly mixed and private economy of care, while at the same time regulating care more centrally in efforts to protect vulnerable people; there are campaigns to promote a positive image of care, but care workers continue to carry enormous responsibility for the most vulnerable people in society, often incompatible with their low salaries and status.

Demography and social care

Demography can be defined as the analysis of the size, structure and development of human populations. An understanding of demography and demographic change is of major importance in understanding society, and contributes to an understanding of the changing care needs of the population.

	1971	1981	1991	2001	Percentage change from 1971 to 2001
Males					
65–74	7.4	8.3	8.1	8.1	9
75–84	2.6	3.4	4.1	4.6	77
85 and over	0.5	0.5	0.8	1.1	120
All aged 65 and over	10.5	12.1	13.5	13.7	30
Females					
65–74	9.6	10.1	9.5	8.7	−9
75–84	5.0	6.1	6.7	6.6	32
85 and over	1.2	1.6	2.2	2.7	125
All aged 65 and over	15.9	17.8	18.4	18.0	13

(Source: Arber, S and Ginn, I 2004)

Figure 1.2 Proportions of older people: by sex and age, 1971 to 2001 United Kingdom

One major demographic factor is that Britain has an ageing population with a higher proportion of the population over the age of 65 than ever before, and a rapid growth in the proportion of people over the age of 85 (see Figure 1.2).

This undoubtedly has an impact on the number of people in this age group who need support. A direct link between an ageing population and increasing levels of dependency and the need for care is, however, sometimes called 'apocalyptic demography', a story of doom and gloom which is perhaps unnecessarily pessimistic. Although there is an increasing number of older people, in general they have never been healthier or more active. This is with the exception of some groups unjustly likely to be more disadvantaged than others: some ethnic groups, those in receipt of income support, those on a low income who do not qualify for income support or other benefits, and disabled and ill people.

The over-65 age group contains the largest number of carers as well as the largest number of cared-for people, and also provides immense amounts of practical and financial support to younger members of the population. This support saves the taxpayer billions of pounds annually. The 'burden' of the old is not all that it seems and in future years it is likely that more older adults will continue to contribute more than ever before economically through paid work, and practically and financially through transferring money from one generation to another. Arber and Ginn (2004) point out that it is the last year of life that is the most expensive, at whatever age it occurs; also that the quite dramatic rise in the population of over 85s is more of a concern because in this age group a larger percentage of the population is without a supportive partner, with 23 per cent of women and 12 per cent of men in this age group living in communal settings.

Care Councils, Commissions and Sector Skills Councils

Contributing to the changing context of care and resulting from concerns about the provision of an optimum service, Care Councils, Commissions and new Sector Skills Councils have emerged in the four countries of the UK. Care Councils and Commissions vary in the four countries, though they share the aims of protecting service users through a registration, qualifications and training agenda for the workforce, promoting codes of practice for employees and employers, and inspecting services against a background of service standards (national minimum standards and national care standards). There are several relevant Sector Skills Councils for the UK, including Skills for Care and Development, Skills for Health and Skills for Justice, charged with developing the workforce and planning for the future through an understanding of the sectors' structure and training needs. Each of the Care Councils and Commissions has been set up under different legislation in the four countries. Figure 1.3 shows the names of the Councils and Commissions in the four countries of the UK, the legislation under which they were set up and the location of the Care and Development Sector Skills Council functions for each country.

ACTIVITY 1.5

For the country or area in which you live and/or work, find out what the Care Council and Commission do and where they are located.

Country	Relevant legislation	Council	Commission or Inspectorate	Sector Skills Council functions (UK Skills for Care and Development Partnership)	Other Relevant UK Sector Skills Councils
England	Care Standards Act 2000 + Health and Social Care (Community Care & Standards) Act 2003	General Social Care Council (GSCC)	The Commission for Social Care Inspection	Skills for Care (Formerly Topss)	Skills for Health, Skills for Justice, Skills Active, Lifelong Learning UK
Scotland	Regulation of Care (Scotland) Act 2001	Scottish Social Services Council (SSSC)	Scottish Commission for the Regulation of Care (known as The Care Commission)	SSSC	
Wales	Care Standards Act 2000	Care Council for Wales (CCW)	Care Standards Inspectorate for Wales	CCW	
Northern Ireland	Health and Personal Social Services Act (Northern Ireland) 2001	Northern Ireland Social Care Council (NISCC)	Four Local Health and Social Services Trusts (proposed Northern Ireland Commission for Social Care Inspection)	NISCC	

Figure 1.3 Care Councils, Commissions and Sector Skills Councils in the UK

WHO PROVIDES CARE

Formal care is provided by three sectors: the statutory, voluntary and private sectors. Increasingly there is emphasis upon these sectors working in partnership to provide the best possible service to people in need.

The statutory sector

The care referred to includes all kinds of care. Statutory agencies include local authority social services and social work departments, education departments, sometimes separate children's and community care departments, housing departments and health boards and trusts, in varying combinations and partnerships.

Statutory services are those services provided or resourced under various pieces of legislation to meet the needs of individuals, their families and carers. The services may be directly provided by a statutory agency or commissioned using statutory resources. They are provided because various Acts say that they must be provided, though there is scope for a great deal of variation in how provision is made and resourced. The statutory agency can be the provider of services or can buy services from other organisations in the voluntary or private sector. Some statutory agencies provide substantial services themselves; others buy in as much as 85 per cent of provision from elsewhere. The services provided or purchased range from home care to residential, including nursing home care, and care for diverse groups including children and young people, people with disabilities and older people. One exceptional service is Forces Help Social Work Service (SSAFA) established in 1963 to offer social work support to service personnel and their families overseas and an advisory service to the military chain of command. SSAFA is a voluntary organisation, providing a statutory social work service underpinned by UK legislation, on behalf of the Ministry of Defence. It is also registered as an adoption agency.

The voluntary sector

> **The amount of work that voluntary and community groups do with very limited resources is frankly amazing.**
>
> (Leeds project)

Voluntary organisations often provide exciting opportunities to meet need in creative, innovative ways. They may also be in a position to comment on and challenge existing services and policies.

The voluntary sector consists of non-statutory independent organisations operated on a not-for-profit basis. Most voluntary organisations have developed in response to unmet or inadequately met needs experienced by a group of people, often in broadly similar situations or with broadly similar areas of need, e.g. people with mental health difficulties or families with a child with disability. They have often changed and evolved through time in response to changing needs and philosophies, so that many of them are dramatically different from their original manifestation. The examples of Age Concern and Barnardo's below illustrate this point.

Some voluntary organisations are registered charities, some are limited companies, while others are both charities and companies. Voluntary organisations such as neighbourhood associations operate on a self-help level and may be neither charities nor companies. Many include service users and carers in their management. Organisations in the voluntary sector often operate independently of each other, although they also often work together when it is appropriate

The fact that an organisation is a voluntary one does not mean that all the people who work there are volunteers. Most organisations have grants and funding to employ paid staff. For some organisations this may mean one worker, for others it may mean hundreds of workers. Funding may come from many sources, ranging from local authorities who buy in services as part of a mixed economy of care, to money in trust or raised through fundraising and donations.

The work of the sector is perhaps best illustrated through a couple of examples, though the variety in the sector means that there is no such thing as a typical or representative voluntary organisation.

Age Concern

From small-scale beginnings at the end of World War Two, when it was known as 'The Old People's Welfare Committee', Age Concern has become the UK's largest voluntary organisation working with older people. It provides vital local services as well as influencing public opinion and government. Age Concern supports all people over the age of 50 (hardly 'old') in the UK, aiming to ensure that they get the most out of life. It provides services on a local basis such as day care and information. It also campaigns on issues like age discrimination, and works to influence public opinion and government policy about older people.

Age Concern initiatives include 'Opening Doors', which aims to raise awareness about specific needs of older lesbians and gay men, and working with and for black and minority ethnic elders in the UK. The Age Concern website is a treasure trove of information for older people and those involved in their care and support.

Barnardo's

Many people when they hear the name 'Barnardo's' think of the former Dr Barnardo's orphanages housing thousands of children. This was the original nature of the organisation. In 1870 Thomas Barnardo, a doctor from Dublin, opened his first home for boys in Stepney. This resulted from an encounter with a boy, Jim Jarvis, who attended a ragged school that Barnardo had established. Jim took Barnardo around the East End of London, showing him children sleeping on roofs and in gutters. The encounter so affected Barnardo that he decided to devote himself to helping destitute children.

By the time Barnardo died in 1905, the voluntary organisation he founded ran 96 homes caring for more than 8,500 children, which is an average of nearly 100 children per home, with some homes really monumental in size. One home for girls had 1500 residents. At this time residential care emphasised the physical and moral wellbeing of children and young people, rather than their emotional wellbeing. Some children experienced warm and caring environments but for many the memory is of harsh and distant staff.

Today Barnardo's has changed beyond recognition, in line with changes in the way in which people think about the care of vulnerable children and young people. The formal 'Dr' has been dropped from the name and there are no longer any Dr Barnardo's orphanages. Although the aim to help children and young people in the greatest need remains the same, services range from community projects that assist children and young people who have been sexually abused, to work with children with disability and their families, and work with former Barnardo's children to help them to trace their records and to find out about their past. Fundraising and purchasing by local authorities play a significant role in the way services are funded. One example of the scale of this funding is a cheque for £2.5 million presented by a large supermarket chain that made Barnardo's their charity of the year in 2003.

The private sector

The private care sector is an expanding and changing sector. Sometimes also called the independent sector, this sector can be run either on a for-profit basis or, as in the case of one of the largest private providers, as a Provident Association, having no shareholders but reinvesting any money made in providing improved care. Care is bought for at least the price that it costs to provide it; or rather, that is theoretically the case. Many care home owners have for a long time complained that the payment they receive from local authorities who buy their care for service users is insufficient to cover costs. Provision in this sector ranges from enormous organisations with hundreds of care homes and thousands of staff members to individuals who own one or two residential homes on a for-profit basis. The private sector has been much maligned for putting profit before care, sometimes justifiably so, but it also has some excellent provision, equalling or improving upon that of the other sectors. The private sector has the potential to provide for choice, attracting investment and responding quickly to plug gaps in service provision. It also, unfortunately, often fails in such an imaginative response. The Audit Commission's latest report confirms that it has the lowest salaries and makes the minimum investment in training. In April 2001 only 17 per cent of residential home places for older people in the UK were provided by the statutory sector, compared with 70 per cent in the private sector.

THE SOCIAL MODEL OF CARE

There are different models or ways of looking at care that make a tremendous difference to the care context and the way in which care is delivered and practised. What happens in reality is usually a combination of approaches containing aspects of different models, but with more emphasis on one than another. The models usually considered are the medical model, psychological models and the social model. These models originated in the disability movement, but can be used to look at the provision of all kinds of care. The medical model focuses upon looking for the causes of problems and their solution within the individual person's body, so that disability or old age, as well as illness, are viewed medically, susceptible to medical solutions.

Tony, for example, is unable to walk following a car crash. Within the medical model, his inability to walk is treated as much as possible; he has physiotherapy for a few months, is given tablets for his physical pain and is sent home. He does need the medical treatment but does it necessarily have to be given within a medical model that places all the emphasis on treating only the physical individual? Within the medical model, medical and care staff see Tony's disability first rather than Tony the person; his dysfunction and abnormality are the main focus of attention. Gradually this is how Tony comes to see himself and since other people insist on doing things for him all the time he forgets how to do things himself, loses the energy to assert himself, learns to be helpless and dependent and to see all the causes of his problems within himself. He is well on the way to institutionalisation, which receives further consideration below, whether he is living in hospital or living at home.

Without going into the detail of different psychological models, dealt with in more detail in Chapter 7, these focus upon the individual's *mental* response to impairment, disability, illness or life stage. As with the medical model, the focus is on treating the individual. The focus for Tony in this instance is on coming to terms with his disability and the loss experienced through not being able to walk and do the things he used to do. The problem and the solution are seen within Tony. This approach is helpful to some extent: Tony's psychological state does need to be considered. But, as with the medical model, there is a tendency to see disabled Tony rather than Tony the whole person in his social context. The consequences are similar to those of the medical model, except that at least some attention has been paid to Tony's psychological state.

In contrast to the medical and psychological models of care, the social model sees that many of the causes of problems for people who are ill, disabled, old, young or psychologically disturbed at any age lie not in themselves but in society, in their environments, in the attitudes of other people and in discrimination. The primary emphasis is upon the whole person and the context in which they live. Tony is Tony first, living in a society that makes the independent, working and social life he would like to lead very difficult for him. The focus of care is to find ways to enable and empower Tony so that his needs and dreams can be met in ways that he chooses. The Union of Physically Impaired against Segregation (UPIAS) presented one of the first accounts of the social model in 1976. An important distinction was made between impairment and disability. They were defined as follows:

> **Impairment**: lacking part or all of a limb, organ or mechanism of the body
> **Disability**: the disadvantage or restriction of activity caused by a contemporary social organisation, which takes no or little account of people who have physical impairments, and thus excludes them from participation in the mainstream of social activities. Physical disability is therefore a particular from of social oppression.
>
> (UPIAS, 1976, p.14)

The social model is now seen as not only useful in looking at the circumstances of people with impairments, as defined above, but of people experiencing any kind of problem. It is society that aggravates impairments or problems, through the ways in which it is organised and treats people. Society turns impairments

ACTIVITY 1.6

Before you look at the chart below, draw two columns with the medical and psychological models on one side and the social model on the other. Write in each column the essential aspects of the models and their consequences for individuals.

Medical or psychological model	Social model
Focus on individual dysfunction	Focus on society as primary cause of problems
Difficulties seen as direct result of individual's impairment	Difficulties created by society
Solution is to treat the individual's dysfunction	Solution focuses on how society turns impairment or problem into disability
Medical or psychological treatment provided according to diagnosis	Assessment of need is starting point, with whole person and social context as the focus for intervention
Concentrates on negatives	Concentrates on positives
Treats conditions that are not medical as medical, e.g. old age	Begins with this person, not that problem
May result in dependency, learned helplessness and institutionalisation	Promotes independence and empowerment
May result in guilt and shame if not 'cured'	Engenders confidence and pride
Treats this person's body or mind, but often disregards this person as a person	Aims to promote justice, full citizenship and equality in society

Figure 1.4 Models of care

and problems into disabilities. Impairments may need medical or psychological interventions, but these can be provided within a social model of care, which locates many of the solutions within society itself. People can be enabled to gain confidence and pride through maximising their abilities in environments that promote access and full participation. Tony can work, shop, use his brain and qualifications, have relationships and be a full participative member of society if only people fully understand the social model and put it into practice. Society has made a start, at least we have the model, but there is still a long way to go. Your practice is very important in promoting this approach. Person-centred practice, discussed in subsequent chapters, has its basis in the social model of care.

INSTITUTIONALISATION

The importance of institutionalisation lies in the efforts that care workers need to make to avoid it, both for service users and themselves. Institutionalisation is a state of being which often results from residence in long-term institutional care, although it does not necessarily arise as a result of living in an institution; nor is it a feature resulting from residence only in large, total institutions such as long-stay psychiatric institutions. It can occur in people who spend even quite short stays in care unless efforts are made to counter its causes and effects. It often results from the application of medical or psychological models of care.

What is institutionalisation?

Erving Goffman, in his book *Asylums* (1968), has presented one of the best-known expositions of the concept and, although written some time ago, it remains the classic analysis of institutionalisation. Goffman was particularly interested in total institutions, of which he identified five broad groupings. The terminology is his and may seem somewhat dated. The groupings are:

1. Places which care for people such as the old, the blind and orphans.
2. Places for people seen as a threat to society, e.g. mentally ill people, people suffering from TB etc.
3. Places which protect people from perceived dangers, e.g. prisons, prisoner of war camps and concentration camps.
4. Places which allow limited access and have a functional use, e.g. barracks, ships and boarding schools.
5. Places designed as 'retreats' from the world, e.g. monasteries and convents.

One of the main features of these institutions, according to Goffman, is that a person's self-concept is changed and 'taken over' by the institution. In the outside world, a person's self-concept is built up and maintained through his or her social world, including relationships with family, friends, work colleagues etc. Once inside a total institution, however, this world is to a large extent lost. The processes of admission and institutional life contribute to the breakdown of the person's former self-concept, and individuality is denied. This breaking down of self is sometimes referred to as the 'mortification of self' and some things that contribute to this are as follows:

- ❏ role loss
- ❏ undressing and wearing regimented clothing
- ❏ hair cutting
- ❏ fingerprinting
- ❏ expected cooperation and/or obedience
- ❏ deprivation of clothing, name and possessions
- ❏ expected verbal responses
- ❏ humiliation and/or ill treatment
- ❏ keeping of personal details on record open to others
- ❏ regimentation which means deprivation of personal decisions and daily routine
- ❏ work organisation often disguised as 'rehabilitation'.

I went recently to see 'The Magdalene Sisters', a harrowing film (directed by Peter Mullan, 2002) based upon the story of three young women who were sent to a Catholic laundry to live and work because they were considered to be too immoral to be 'allowed' to live in the outside world. The laundry was a prime example of how the self can be mortified: uniform brown clothing, hair cutting used as a punishment, severe punishment for even the slightest disobedience, humiliation, regimentation, loss of freedom of speech or to go out, lack of privacy, boring repetitive work. These laundries existed in Ireland until the 1960s to house women who had committed what were considered the dreadful sins of pregnancy out of wedlock, flirtatious behaviour or being the victims of rape.

It does not even take all of the above 'mortifications' for a condition labelled 'institutional neurosis' to set in. This has the following characteristics:

- ❏ apathy
- ❏ lack of initiative
- ❏ loss of interest

- ❏ submissiveness
- ❏ lack of interest in the future
- ❏ inability to make practical plans
- ❏ deterioration in personal habits
- ❏ acceptance that things will go on as they are
- ❏ occasional aggressive outbursts
- ❏ characteristic posture.

In some understaffed, unimaginative homes for vulnerable people, these characteristics can be observed, not back in the 1960s, but in the present day. The characteristics that seem to contribute most to this pathetic state of affairs are:

- ❏ Few, if any, efforts to maintain contact with the outside world.
- ❏ No activities, a lot of empty time and enforced idleness.
- ❏ A large distance between staff and service users, with staff in uniforms behaving in an authoritarian way.
- ❏ Working to a medical model ('You are sick and I am making you better . . . my way').
- ❏ Hardly any prospect of ever going out of the establishment, either temporarily or permanently.
- ❏ A lack of respect for the dignity of individuals, demonstrated through belittling expressions and no regard for privacy.
- ❏ An almost total preoccupation among staff with the practical aspects of the job – meals, baths, cups of tea, visits to the toilet at set times – with no thought given to possible improvements in the quality of life for service users.
- ❏ Staff immensely interested in their own affairs and talking to one another as if the service users were not there.

You can live in enormous or small residential settings, or even your own home – and still be institutionalised. Wherever you live, the workers (residential and non-residential) can make all the difference, transforming your experience for both good and bad. I have seen examples of individuals who had previously been written off as having 'profound handicaps' or 'challenging behaviour', having their own home, developing their abilities and living a life few would previously have thought them capable of, with appropriate resources, sensitive support and imagination.

(Peter Beresford, *Community Care* 8–14 January 2004. Published by permission of the editor of *Community Care*)

ACTIVITY 1.7

Describe five ways in which institutionalisation is or could be avoided in a care setting that you know.

Peter Beresford in the above article points to some of the ingredients necessary to avoid institutionalisation: 'appropriate' resources, sensitivity and imagination. How can you learn to be more imaginative? Here are a few suggestions:

- ❏ Ask questions: What is the situation now? What is right with it, what is wrong with it from a service user standpoint?
- ❏ Put yourself in the service user's shoes.
- ❏ Look at the resources and possible resources.
- ❏ Think outside the box – even ridiculously.
- ❏ Look at dreams and nightmares as well as facts.
- ❏ Ask everybody questions – see what ideas everyone concerned has – you may find areas of skill, imagination and knowledge you did not know existed.
- ❏ Do not accept the status quo.
- ❏ See if there is any research/literature you can draw on.
- ❏ Consult constructively.

Figure 1.5

SUMMARY

In order to practise effectively as a care worker, you need to understand the context in which care work takes place. This chapter has examined that context through looking at the meaning of care, and the relevance of history, ideology, social policy and demography. A consideration of different models of care practice and of institutionalisation has set the scene for the development of a person-centred approach.

FIVE KEY POINTS

1. Care is an evolving concept that has changed and developed through time. Emphasis is no longer on doing *for* but on doing *with* people, including them in decision-making and empowering them to determine how they will lead their own lives.
2. The context of care and the way in which services are delivered are influenced by varying mixtures of history, ideology, social policy, legislative change, demography and different models of care.
3. Care provision is regulated through Care Commissions and Councils in the four countries of the UK.
4. Care services are provided by three sectors: statutory, voluntary and private.
5. The social model of care emphasises that many of the causes of the problems that people experience lie in society, the way their environments are structured, and the attitudes and discrimination of other people.

THREE QUESTIONS

1. What do you think are three of the most important qualities that service users would like to see in their care workers?
2. Identify three historical factors that you think have played a part in the way in which care services operate today. Are these factors positive, negative or a mixture of these? Give reasons for your answer.
3. If you are setting up a care service, identify three things that it is important to establish, right at the beginning.

RECOMMENDED READING

DALY, M. (ed) (2001) *Care Work: the quest for security*. Geneva: International Labour Office. Quite a challenging book to take your thinking further in relation to conceptualising what care really means.

KAHAN, B. (1994) *Growing up in Groups*. London: National Institute for Social Work. Although this book was written mainly for residential childcare workers, it is a wonderful resource for all care workers. It deals with the complexity of care work and is full of relevant examples.

Community Care magazine. Haywards Heath: Reed Business Publishing. A weekly magazine for care workers with examples of good practice, contributions from service users, discussion of current issues, news and jobs.

CHAPTER 2

PRINCIPLES FOR ETHICAL PRACTICE

Janet Miller

My underlying philosophy is that everyone matters a lot.

(Kohler, T 2000)

By the end of this chapter you should be able to:

- ❏ understand that the value base underpins everything that the care worker does; care practice is meaningless without it
- ❏ explain the meaning of values, principles, ethics and rights
- ❏ examine your own value base
- ❏ understand the content of the main values and principles that underpin care practice
- ❏ examine values and principles in the context of National Service Standards, Codes of Practice and Codes of Professional Conduct
- ❏ understand the practical implications of the value base, including anti-discriminatory and anti-oppressive practice.

The Chapter is divided into two parts:
Part 1 – Values, principles and ethics
Part 2 – The promotion of equality through anti-discriminatory and anti-oppressive practice

The content of this chapter provides underpinning content and context for all care qualifications. It relates especially to the following units:

NVQ and SVQ Level 2 Core Unit HSC24: Ensure your own actions support the care, protection and wellbeing of individuals

NVQ and SVQ Level 3 Core Units HSC 34 and 35: Promote the wellbeing and protection of children and young people; promote choice, wellbeing and the protection of all individuals

HNC Social Care Unit: Social care theory for practice

BTEC National Unit: Equality, diversity and rights in care work.

PART 1

VALUES, PRINCIPLES AND ETHICS

Sound structures are built upon firm foundations. Care work means nothing without its foundations, the value base from which sound, ethical, professional practice has developed. Discussion of a value base leads to a consideration of terminology. Various words are used in relation to the value base: among these are values, principles, ethics and rights. Consideration is given here to the meaning of these terms and, although there are no universally accepted definitions, an attempt is made to sort out and clarify the issues surrounding them and possible approaches to their meaning.

Introduction

There are choices to be made: values and principles can be seen as the same thing (values are the ethical principles upon which care workers base their practice); or values can be seen as having intrinsic worth as good things (the word 'value' comes from the French 'valoir', to be worth, worthy, valuable) and principles (from the Latin 'princeps' meaning first or chief) can be seen as the practical manifestation of these values. While both interpretations are valid, it is predominantly the latter that is developed in this chapter. Principles can be seen to be based upon two core values: respect for persons and the promotion of social justice. From these can be derived all of the principles for ethical care practice. These values and principles constitute social care's value base, with principles derived from one or both of the core values. For example, equality, choice and confidentiality are all encompassed within the promotion of respect for people and social justice in society. These values and principles are each discussed separately (respect, justice, choice, confidentiality etc.), though in practice they overlap in their meaning and their application, and are not separate entities.

Ethics, similarly, can be seen in different ways. For example, ethics is a branch of philosophy that studies morality, moral problems and moral judgements; it looks at and analyses moral terms such as good, bad, right, wrong, moral, immoral. Ethics can also be interpreted as standards of behaviour, based upon values and principles, against a background discussion that attempts to answer ethical questions about what is considered to be 'moral' or 'right'. Ethical conflicts occur when a difficult choice has to be made between conflicting principles, where no single principle is clearly the 'right one'. Codes of ethics are really about standards derived from the value base. Standards guide care work, distinguishing sound ethical practice from unsound, undirected, immoral practice. For example, the UK Codes of Practice, national service standards (called variously national care standards or national minimum standards) and Codes of Professional Conduct for Health Care are based upon principles, and emphasise everyone's right to be treated according to these.

Also fundamental to any discussion about values, principles and ethical practice is a consideration of rights. Are some rights more important than other rights? What happens where there seem to be conflicting but equal rights and a choice has to be made one way or the other? According to Feinberg (1973), a right is a valid claim. A valid claim in care practice can be seen as to be treated according to the care value base, underpinned by the UN Charters of Human Rights and the Rights of the Child, and the provisions of the law. Barbara Kahan (1994) makes the distinction between 'rights of action' which include the freedom to choose whether or not to do something, and 'rights of recipience' which are rights to receive particular services, e.g. the child's right to education or the vulnerable person's right to health care.

A consideration of rights also involves a consideration of responsibilities. Some rights are absolute and do not involve reciprocal responsibilities, e.g. the right of everyone to protection from abuse; other rights carry the expectation that certain responsibilities will accompany them. Parents, for example, have rights in relation to how they will bring up their children, but they also have the responsibility to do this in such a way that children are nurtured and protected. If they fail or are unable to undertake these responsibilities, it is likely that their rights as parents will be curtailed or lost. Ethical practice involves the promotion of rights. It also sometimes involves dealing with ethical dilemmas, where aspects of the value base conflict with one another, or your own personal beliefs about an issue conflict with those of the person you are working with. Further consideration is given to ethical dilemmas later in the chapter (see page 50).

ACTIVITY 2.1

During one week, keep a chart that describes situations you have encountered and/or dealt with that have involved making an ethical judgement or decision. List the beliefs, values, principles or thoughts that influenced you and state the outcome. At the end of the week look at the chart and state anything that could perhaps have been done differently. Try to discuss this with a colleague or your supervisor.

Situation	Ethical judgement or decision	Belief, values, principles or thoughts	Outcome	What could have been done differently

The preceding account has attempted to clarify terminology while at the same time giving a flavour of the complexity of ethical practice. Before entering a discussion of the values and principles, it is worth taking a little time to become more self-aware about the ethical basis of your own practice and thinking.

THE ETHICAL BASIS OF GOOD PRACTICE

Respect for persons

In every country that has a care profession underpinned by a value base, there is a value or principle that equates to respect for persons. It is variously defined but, whatever the definition, it incorporates respect for the dignity, individuality and uniqueness of all people, irrespective of who they are or their attributes and status.

This value has been influenced by Kantean philosophy, and to some extent derives from it. Kant was an eighteenth century German philosopher who became famous fairly late in life. One of his themes was respect for the individual person as a self-determining being, to be treated as an end in him- or herself and not as a means to someone else's being.

This may sound complicated, but can be illustrated by a couple of examples. A care worker steals money from a service user who has a learning disability. She justifies this by convincing herself that the service user never spends very much and probably does not understand what money is all about. The service user is seen as a means to an end (obtaining money through stealing), and not as an end in herself. She is kept in a state of subjection and ignorance through the crime and misuse of power of the care worker. A second care worker sees it as her task to enable the service user to make the best use of her money, as independently as possible. In this instance this involves setting an example about how to budget, providing information about spending, saving and keeping money safely, and communication about what the service user would like to do with her money. Here the service user is seen as an end, not as a means to an end, and is respected for her intrinsic worth as a human being and as this human being in particular. Another way of putting this theme is that no one should become a pawn in your game of life. We are all major players in the same game.

The underlying ethos of the value of respect was further developed by Father Biestek (1961), a Catholic priest who set out seven principles of practice. Although he did not name 'respect for persons', his principles are underpinned by it and include individualisation, the recognition of the individual's unique qualities, based upon the rights of human beings to be treated not just as a human being but as this human being, and acceptance of people, their innate dignity and personal worth.

Some definitions based upon the principle of respect for persons, both nationally and internationally, are given below.

> Implicit in care practice is the recognition of the dignity and value of every human being.
>
> (Social Care Association, 2002)

> You have the right to be treated with dignity and respect at all times.
>
> (National Care Standards, Scotland, 2001)

> Respect the patient or client.
>
> (Code of Professional Conduct, Nursing and Midwifery Council)

> Protect the rights and promote the interests of service users and carers.
>
> (GSCC, 2002, Code of Practice for Social Care Workers)

When asked about what should be included in the care workers' value base, service users and carers said the following in relation to this principle:

A good care worker is someone who respects you as a person.

The promotion of social justice and welfare

> **Injustice anywhere is a threat to justice everywhere.**
> (Martin Luther-King, 1963)

Respect for persons is a good beginning, but it is not enough on its own to underpin care practice. Respecting people for who they are, accepting them and their dignity as human beings, is a fine beginning, but for people living in poverty, experiencing pressure or coping with crisis, indeed for all people whatever their circumstances, the other side of the coin is the promotion of social justice and welfare. Social justice refers to fairness, equity and supporting the rights of individuals in society. It includes enabling people to exercise their civil rights, e.g. the right to vote, to receive what is their right in law and morally as a member of society. The promotion of welfare refers to enabling people to experience wellbeing and their rights to certain fundamental entitlements such as adequate housing, food, health care and income to meet their needs.

ACTIVITY 2.2

Read the account below and explain how the lack of a travelcard fails to promote both social justice and John's welfare.

John, who lived in a 'long-stay' hospital for the largest part of his life, was discharged from hospital to live in the community. He has now lived in his own house with support from paid support workers for almost a year. John enjoys going into the city to shop. However, because of the expense of bus travel, he is limited to how often he can do this. When the student support worker realised John's plight, he made inquiries about why he did not have a concessionary travelcard. Alas, this possibility had been overlooked by the support workers.

You may have mentioned that the negligence had caused John to be deprived of his leisure pursuits and had limited his trips into the city. Social justice gives him the right to receive the concessionary travelcard, and this should have been available to him when he originally moved into his own home. The support workers involved in this situation were failing to ensure that John's welfare needs were being fully met or that he was living his life to the full.

Although these two core values give rise to what is generally seen as the principles of care, there is a further more radical agenda that emphasises the fundamental place of the principles of equality and empowerment of service users and carers. This agenda is examined both in the section of the chapter that relates to principles and in the consideration of anti-discriminatory and anti-oppressive practice.

The right to equality

Equality is not to be confused with sameness and uniformity. Promoting equality does not mean treating everyone the same. If you promote real equality, equality in the sense of everyone having equal rights under the law and the right not to be unfairly discriminated against or oppressed, then you also promote difference. The opposite of equality is inequality, not difference. Equality as a principle involves a redistribution of power so that people are not only treated fairly, but are enabled to exercise power over their own lives to the maximum extent. They are also fully included in decisions that relate to them, and included in the mainstream life of the society in which they live. A much fuller explanation of this principle and its practical manifestations is presented at the end of this chapter in the section on promoting equality through anti-discriminatory and anti-oppressive practice.

The right to choice

Vicki Farnsworth has learning difficulties. She works at the 'Rotherham Speak Up' project and has participated in a Commission for Health Improvement (CHI) investigation. She said the following about choice.

> I make my own decisions and look after myself but the people I saw can't because they need someone to help them. I expected that they would have choices but often they didn't. They were not being treated as equals.
>
> (Farnsworth, V 2003. Published by permission of the editor of *Community Care*)

Choice begins with this person in this situation. It is the foundation of person-centred planning, discussed in Chapter 8, and is closely linked with dignity, equality, normalisation and empowerment.

ACTIVITY 2.3

1. Think of a care workplace and give three examples of how choice can be promoted for service users.
2. How is choice linked with dignity, social justice and empowerment?

Much has been said about increasing choices for people, but choices must be based upon what people need and wish for. Often our thinking mistakenly begins with the notion of services and shortage of service provision. For example, government is proposing that if the number of residential care places is increased, then people will have more choice, but they will only have more choice of residential care establishments. What is needed is a much more imaginative approach to choice than this, provision of services based upon plans developed *with* service users, not *for them*, that detail their choices about what they would like for themselves and meet need in ways that people choose. This may not be the most expensive option either, and it is quite unlikely that it will involve an increase in 'traditional' services that are often paternalistic, institutional and costly. Choice is not absolute for anyone. We all have notions of what we would like if we had absolute choice, without financial or other constraints. And so for service users there will be limitations to choice too; but this should not be curtailed in ways that are any more limited than for other people. It is up to care workers and others to facilitate maximum choice, promote options and provide information to empower service users to participate fully in the choices they can make in their lives.

Choices can be about the big things in life, major life changes and decisions, and about small things: what to have for dinner or where to go on an outing. Care workers can maximise the information available to service users about the choices they have. They can always offer a choice when one is available, and promote choices where these have not previously existed.

The right to privacy

If we respect people, it follows that their right to privacy should be preserved. Everyone has a right to privacy, to have his/her own space. It is not difficult to imagine how it would feel if someone accompanied you to the bathroom and insisted on staying, or barged in without permission when you were in your own bedroom, or listened in to your telephone conversations, or discussed your financial affairs with you in front of others. If you consider the

Example

A student on a placement in a nursing home had to assist a care worker one morning in waking up residents and then helping them to wash and dress. The student was horrified when the care worker boldly walked into each resident's bedroom without knocking, switched on the lights and proceeded to help them out of bed. The student did not follow suit. She knocked on the doors first and then, when told to enter, went up to the resident and spoke kindly to her before switching on the light, allowing time for the resident to decide when she wanted to get out of bed. The student was given a 'ticking off' for her actions by the care worker, and told that they did not have time for this. Realising that this was common practice in the home, the student discussed her concerns with her supervisor. The supervisor, without hesitation, discussed with all staff this practice and it was agreed that in future this type of practice was not acceptable. It is only by not accepting poor practice and by good example that long-standing 'Well, that is the way that we do it,' poor practice will change.

humiliation and embarrassment this would cause you, then you will appreciate the need for care workers to give service users the privacy that is their human right.

The right to confidentiality

Confidentiality may appear at first sight to be fairly straightforward. When people give you information that they do not want to be passed on, you do not pass it on . . . or do you? Understanding confidentiality can, in fact, be rather complex. Confidentiality in a care context is an extension of the principle of privacy, relating to promoting the service user's right to the privacy of information. It means protecting information from misuse, and only passing on information where it needs to be passed on, only to those who need to know it and with the consent of the service user wherever possible. It does not necessarily mean total secrecy. In fact, sometimes keeping secrets is not helpful to good practice. Although personal information should be regarded as confidential, there are occasions when information **must** be shared, e.g. in relation to the disclosure of child abuse, or where information is required as evidence in court proceedings. There are other occasions when information should be shared in the interests of good practice. Agency policy regarding confidentiality should be explained to the service user. There should be a negotiated agreement about its limits and boundaries, so that the service user understands how information will be used, as well as what is confidential and what is not.

Some further guidelines may help to clarify an understanding of confidentiality:

❏ Information supplied for one purpose should not be used for another.
❏ Information supplied should not be disclosed without the person's consent other than in exceptional circumstances. There should be an explanation about when exceptional circumstances apply.
❏ All records should be kept under lock and key when not in use.
❏ Access to records should be limited to the service user and 'approved' others.
❏ Service users and carers should not be talked about behind their backs or to others who are not members of the care team.

A conversation overheard on a bus was brought back to me by a student. Two care workers were discussing a service user, known to the student, in a derogatory and judgemental way. This disregarded both the value of dignity and the principle of confidentiality. A similar example concerned a student whose mother was being discussed by two members of staff in the home in which she was on placement. They were talking about the relatives of the service user, judging them to be uncaring because they had allowed their mother to be placed in a home. The student who overheard this discussion was extremely distressed and felt betrayed by her colleagues. They knew nothing of her mother's choice or the stressful circumstances which had surrounded her admission to care. Again, they breached confidentiality in unnecessary discussion and were discriminatory about people about whom they knew little or nothing.

The right to protection from danger, harm and abuse

Individuals in society have a right to feel safe, secure and protected from danger, harm and abuse. For people who need care services, this principle is especially important since one reason for their need for care may be their vulnerability and/or abuse by others or themselves. Any kind of abuse or threat can be oppressive, unequal and harmful. The whole of Chapter 6 examines issues in relation to harm and abuse. Here protection as a principle is considered. Although people must have a right to be protected, they also have a right to be self-determining. Protection can sometimes come into conflict with this. In the field of mental health, for example, many people feel that they have been over-protected from risk and harm to the extent that their freedom to act independently has been unnecessarily curtailed. A care programme/care management approach has been developed to overcome some of these difficulties, and is more fully discussed in Chapter 9.

The right to be enabled to reach potential

Everyone has potential, everyone has gifts, and everyone has an equal right to flourish, to achieve all they can and to make the most of their lives. This belief and faith in the potential of everyone is one of the bases of person-centred planning and care practice. Part of the care worker's job is to facilitate ways of achieving this. Included within this principle is the right of every child to receive an education that promotes and encourages their potential.

Example

Research (NCH website, 2004) has shown us that looked-after children and young people (i.e. who are being cared for by a local authority because they cannot live with their families) have very poor academic achievement records, and are much more likely to be homeless in later life than other children and young people. They have very often lacked the opportunities to reach their potential through lack of encouragement, frequent moves and the interplay of many negative factors in their lives. Care workers may have a mountain to climb in enabling looked-after children to reach their potential, and need skills, knowledge and commitment to work in partnership with children, families, educators and others to make this happen.

In May 2002, Cathy Jamieson, then Minister in Scotland for Education and Children and Young People said:

I want to see every child get the opportunities to reach his or her potential. Looked-after children are amongst the most vulnerable young people . . . and we have a particular responsibility to meet their needs. Our eventual aim is that all looked-after children perform as well as their peers at school . . . [and] can successfully make the transition to independent adult life.

(Scottish Parliament, 2002)

> **Example**
>
> Many people with disabilities lose motivation in their lives, not because of their own limitations but because of the limitations placed on them by people's preconceptions and the way in which institutions in society operate. As less seems possible, less is achieved and a vicious circle of less leading to less sets in. A process of person-centred planning can enable people to find ways of breaking the circle and moving towards reaching potential. Sometimes the solutions are not too complicated, though they may require the 'right' resources, e.g. a wheelchair, a circle of support, a computer, together with some more complex changes in attitudes and access.
>
> Professor Stephen Hawking, who has motor neurone disease, is assisted in reaching his potential through using a single switch and a computer with a speech synthesiser, both on his desk and built onto his wheelchair, to write his books, to converse and order his lunch!
>
> (Source: www.bbc.co.uk)

The right to expect care workers to act professionally

- ❑ As a social care worker, you must uphold public trust and confidence in social services.
- ❑ As a social care worker, you must be accountable for the quality of your work and take responsibility for maintaining and improving your knowledge and skills.

(GSCC 2002 Code of Practice for Social Care Workers)

This is a pretty tall order, but the least that service users can expect. All care workers in social services organisations are expected to work to UK codes of practice. With registration of the care workforce comes further expectations and requirements of professional practice. Once registered, care workers should work towards qualifications and continue their professional development. In this way, care workers can begin to provide what service users deserve, and workers can begin to gain the status and regard that they deserve as professional people providing a professional service.

Breaches of professional ethics and practice have been the basis of many inquiries into poor practice in residential settings. It is not just what care workers do, but also what they fail to do that is at issue here, as illustrated in the example below.

Sir Ronald Waterhouse (2000) reporting on child abuse in children's homes in North Wales named and criticised almost 200 people for either abusing children or failing to offer them sufficient protection. There were clear breaches in the professional practice of these workers. Clear Codes of Practice, registration of care workers and the appointment of Children's Commissioners in the countries of the UK will go some way towards remedying this situation, but individual workers must take responsibility for their own practice for all of this to work.

ETHICAL THINKING AND ETHICAL DILEMMAS

The key purpose identified for those working in health and social care settings is to provide an integrated, ethical and inclusive service, which meets agreed needs and outcomes of people requiring health and/or social care.

(Skills for Care and Development, 2004)

When decisions have to be made in care practice that relate to values and principles, and especially when two or more principles conflict with one another, the care worker is faced with an ethical decision which involves a moral judgement about what to do. Some examples are given below to illustrate the kinds of decisions that have to be made when there is an ethical dilemma.

The first example is that of Lil Scholes, a 72-year-old woman who lives alone. When a community care worker visited her, she found Lil living in a corner of one room of her house; other rooms were stockpiled with rubbish. Lil looked undernourished and mobility problems prevented her from shopping. A friend who regularly shops for her was away on holiday. The worker offered Lil a home care package of care, including shopping, until her friend returned, but Lil wanted nothing to do with social services and refused to accept all forms of help.

What are the considerations here and which principles are involved? Lil is mentally alert but physically frail. She has a right to choose how she leads her life. On the other hand, she is at risk of becoming very ill or even dying if she does not receive adequate food. She is already undernourished. The community worker feels that she must protect Lil, but at the same time she does not wish to force Lil to receive help against her wishes. The dilemma was put to a panel

---

ACTIVITY 2.4

What would you do in this situation? How do you think the ethical dilemma could be resolved?

---

that had varying views. The first member felt that if the worker perseveres with the relationship and can win Lil's trust, Lil may accept help. But what if she does not? Another member raised the possibility of invoking legislation, e.g. The National Assistance Act 1948, which allows the compulsory admission of a vulnerable person into supervised care even if it is against their wishes. Unfortunately deaths are common following such orders and it is never an action that a care worker would take lightly. A member of Knowsley Older People's Voice acknowledged the frustrations for the care worker but felt that Lil was only exercising her rights. Sensible suggestions were made to explore all avenues to enable Lil to remain in her own home while at the same time receiving the food she needs. It was suggested that a voluntary agency could be approached and may be more acceptable to Lil than social services; also that there should be some discussion with Lil's friend when she gets back from holiday, since she may not realise the extent of Lil's dependence on her or the availability of additional support. (Source: *Community Care* (2004) 'She won't let us help her'. Published by permission of the editor of *Community Care*)

The second example concerns another pensioner (Witcher, S. 2004. Published by permission of the editor of *Community Care*). He sold his house well below the market value then proceeded to spend £8,000 in two months on a prostitute. At this point social services intervened and put an end to the party. Yet all he was doing was spending his own money and doesn't he have the right to spend his money in any way he chooses? The dilemma is again about choice and protection. But this time resources are also at issue. This man needed social services' help. He could make a contribution towards paying for this help if he did not spend all his money on enjoying himself. What do you see as the ideal resolution?

In these situations it is not enough to know the values, principles and standards, since these alone do not provide all of the answers or ensure that the best decisions are made. For this, the worker needs to develop a habit of ethical thinking, based on a process of reasoning that is morally guided. This thinking needs to take into account the unique complexities of every situation. It can be developed through reflective practice, examined in Chapters 10 and 11 of this book, and through discussion of difficult decisions with colleagues, supervisors and others.

PART 2

THE PROMOTION OF EQUALITY THROUGH ANTI-DISCRIMINATORY AND ANTI-OPPRESSIVE PRACTICE

> Please understand that we are absolutely serious when we talk about the need for change. We will not accept present discrimination. When we say all children must be included, we mean all children. All does mean all.

> (Murray, P and Penman, J 1996)

Especially related to equality, but underpinned by all of the above values and principles, are the linking themes of anti-discriminatory and anti-oppressive practice. They have a place in this chapter because they are so closely allied to the value base and to an ethical approach to care practice, yet they belong equally in a discussion of person-centred practice and will be referred back to at intervals throughout the book.

Introduction

Before any discussion of practice can take place, it is necessary to clarify terminology. Anti-discriminatory practice means to act against any kind of discrimination, whatever its basis. **Discrimination** can be defined as the unequal and unfair treatment of an individual or group. It may take place because of a person's class, ethnicity, race, gender, religion, sexual orientation, age, disability, impairment or any other perceived difference from whoever is doing the discriminating. Discrimination is based on **prejudice**. Although prejudice, the pre-judging of someone, can be positive or negative, when used negatively it results in negative discrimination. Prejudices are based on learned behaviours and result in biased and intolerant attitudes that often fly in the face of reason. They may lead to **stigmatising** whole groups of people, labelling them all in a negative way, so that the needs of individuals are ignored.

> I am still surprised and upset to find the word 'psycho' and other offensive terminology casually used by the broadcast media and press . . .. This erroneous hijacking of psychiatric terminology, which is used out of context in a misleading fashion, further confuses a public already unsure of what mental health problems really entail . . .. My history of psychiatric illness is something I am often reluctant to reveal.

> (Waddell, H. 'Unspeakable episodes'. 28 October 2004. Published by permission of the editor of Community Care)

The example above illustrates some aspects of discrimination. The media, which have enormous influence on the views of millions of people, are stigmatising people with mental illness. This makes it very difficult for people with a mental illness to be seen as individuals. Fear is created about the response they may receive at the hands of other people, and irrational fear is created in the general population about the nature of people with mental illness. This in turn can lead to discrimination against people with mental illness in many walks of life; e.g. in employment, education and recreation.

Anti-oppressive practice means to act against any kind of oppression. It may not seem very different from anti-discriminatory practice, especially as one of the main outcomes of discrimination is oppression. However, to discuss its relevance is important since it places an emphasis on empowering people who are not only discriminated against, but also made powerless by the treatment they receive. Oppression has two meanings in the dictionary, both of which illustrate what usually happens when people are discriminated against. It is defined in the Oxford Dictionary as 'to keep in subjection and hardship' and also 'to cause people to feel anxious or distressed'. There are aspects here both of social position and feeling, so that what is being tackled in anti-oppressive practice is not only people's place in society, but also the feelings they have about their treatment. Anti-oppressive practice not only tackles discrimination but also works with individuals to enable them to have the confidence and the power to assert their rights in what should be an equal society.

LEVELS AT WHICH DISCRIMINATION TAKES PLACE

In order to enable you to understand what actually happens when discrimination and oppression occur, a model illustrating levels of discrimination is explained. This model identifies three different levels of discrimination: the individual, institutional and cultural.

Individual discrimination

This occurs when an individual or group of individuals is singled out and treated unfairly because of prejudice. You may also be contributing to individual discrimination if you could, but do not, stop it from occurring. Here are some examples:

> Stephen Lawrence, a black teenager, was murdered on 23 January 1993. The inquiry into his death stated that his murder 'was simply and solely and unequivocally motivated by racism'.

> (Macpherson, W 1999)

My sin is that I have a gender dysphoria, having been born as one gender but feeling more aligned to the other. When I declared this to one of my directors, I was informed that I should look elsewhere for employment before the decision to do so was taken for me.

(*Community Care*, 'Viewpoint', 28 October 2004. Published by permission of the editor of *Community Care*)

A black woman is verbally abused by a white shop assistant. No one in the shop offers any support to the black woman. The shop assistant is discriminating, but so are other people in the shop by not saying anything or taking any action.

Institutional discrimination

This practice occurs when discrimination is embedded in the rules, regulations and practices of an organisation.

Simon Heng, a service user, found that the abuse of vulnerable people was often embedded in the practices of care establishments. This is a form of institutional discrimination. He writes:

I wasn't prepared for the variety and intensity of abuse that has been meted out to those who could not speak out for themselves, particularly older people and those with learning difficulties.

(*Community Care*, 29 July 2003. Published by permission of the editor of *Community Care*)

Sir William McPherson in his investigations into the death of Stephen Lawrence found not only individual discrimination on the part of his murderers, but institutional racism on the part of the police force investigating the murder. This hampered the murder investigation, and probably caused the lack of any conviction for Stephen's murder. The police were slower to respond and took less trouble about resolving cases involving black people. They made incorrect assumptions based upon prejudice and these became embedded in the practices of the police force.

Cultural discrimination

This occurs when a whole culture promotes discrimination through passing on prejudices, and through the way in which people are socialised and educated. People see the world through their culture, which reflects the way in which things are done in society. They often form views about other cultures and groups based upon ignorance.

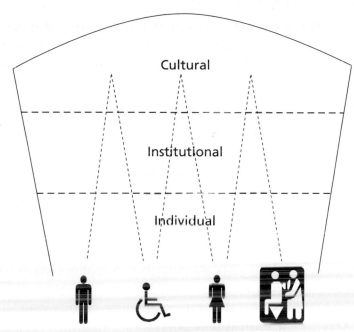

Figure 2.1 Levels of discrimination: how they interact and influence individuals in different ways

In 1996 The Commission for Racial Equality set up an exhibition called 'Roots of the Future', which aimed to change cultural stereotypes about Britain's ethnic minorities through showing how they had enriched Britain's culture. The Commission ran workshops for schoolchildren, who made the following comments: 'I didn't know that curry didn't come from here'; 'I didn't think there could be 20,000 black people in London in 1787'; 'I've always related Jews with the holocaust, never back to the Norman Conquest'. Lack of knowledge about the variety of groups in society enables discrimination to continue, even though based upon irrational and unfounded assumptions.

The three levels of discrimination are not separate entities. They are inextricably linked, and can be both cause and effect of one another. This is illustrated in the above diagram (Fig. 2.1).

TYPES OF DISCRIMINATION

As well as different levels of discrimination, three different types of discrimination can be identified: direct, indirect and unconscious.

Direct discrimination

This occurs when someone knowingly treats someone unreasonably or unfairly because of some characteristic. For example, a man who is gay is beaten up because he is gay, a black woman is gang raped because she is black, a boy who has learning difficulties is bullied at school, a man who has learning difficulties is not served in a pub or an elderly woman is given poor service in a shop when everyone else is served well.

Indirect discrimination

This is less obvious than direct discrimination, but is nevertheless just as damaging and effective. The best way to understand it is through a few examples.

All of the information leaflets produced by a social care agency are in English, even though more than 30 per cent of the local population are Asian, half of whom do not speak or read English. Although the leaflets state that the agency does not discriminate on any grounds, people who do not read English do not see that, and cannot understand the leaflet anyway. In this way they may be excluded from a service through the indirect discrimination resulting from publishing the leaflet only in English.

A childcare agency has steps up to the front door. Although there may be a sign on the door saying that everyone is welcome, it is difficult for mothers with small children in prams or pushchairs to enter, and virtually impossible for a carer with a child in a wheelchair. Statsitics for use of the service are very low for families with a child with disability because the agency makes it so difficult for them to gain access.

Unconscious discrimination

Sometimes people discriminate and just do not know that they are doing it. It requires insight and questioning of all the things you do to overcome some behaviours that have become so much second nature that they are not even performed at a conscious level. People who always talk to the person pushing the wheelchair and never to the person in it, people who assume that a person with a speech difficulty cannot talk so always ask their carer the questions, carers who always answer on behalf of the person they are caring for, may not realise what they are doing, or that what they are doing is unconsciously discriminating. They may also be perpetuating discrimination through some of the processes well known to augment it: infantilisation is when adults are treated like children. Many people treat older adults in this way, often at an unconscious level.

Marginalisation leaves some people out on the margins of society. Separated people are often not invited to social occasions by their married friends,

> ## ACTIVITY 2.5
>
> Think of three ways in which each of the above forms of discrimination could happen in the provision of care. What could you do in two of these situations to prevent discrimination from happening?

unemployed people are shunned by people in employment, people are patronised and put into dependent situations, when what they need is to be enabled to meet their needs themselves. Although these actions can result from all kinds of discrimination, they may also occur at an unconscious level.

The way in which language is used can perpetuate unconscious discrimination. Aiming to counter unconscious sexism through the use of more equal language, Glasgow City Council (1997) stated the following in its leaflet 'Language Matters: A Guide to Good Practice':

❏ Don't assume it is acceptable to address women by endearments such as **dear, pet** and **love** when you would not address men in such a way.

❏ Some words and phases such as **manpower** and **man the office** exclude or ignore women. Use inclusive terms like **staff** or **workers** and **staff the office**.

WAYS TO COMBAT DISCRIMINATION AND OPPRESSION

In practice, there are several ways in which you can promote equality through practising in an anti-discriminatory and anti-oppressive way. These include:

❏ increasing your knowledge and self-awareness
❏ promoting people's rights through legislation
❏ redressing power imbalances and empowering people
❏ inclusive practice.

Increasing your knowledge and self-awareness

Unless you understand the meanings and implications of equality, anti-discriminatory and anti-oppressive practice, it is impossible to move forward in your work with individuals. It is important to be aware of your own attitudes and behaviour, and to be prepared to change them if they affect other people negatively. You can start this process by doing the exercise below, but take care to broaden your thinking and experience through practice, reading and gaining

ACTIVITY 2.6 Ways to increase self-awareness

Here are three different ways to improve self-awareness.

❑ **Today**
Write down or discuss your thoughts and impressions of the last piece of care work you were involved in. This may have been at work or informally with a member of your family or network. Ask yourself whether you discriminated in any way, either in your thoughts or your actions.

❑ **Within a month**
Keep a log in your workplace, placement or other relevant setting of the ways in which you have ensured that people have been fairly treated. Write about one situation in detail to show how your thoughts and actions promoted equality.

❑ **Within a year**
Attend a training course, conference or workshop that relates to promoting equality and anti-discriminatory and anti-oppressive practice.

Example

A care worker applied for a post with a voluntary agency and was delighted when she was offered the job. She was however dismayed when she found that she was going to work in a small, homely setting for four women who were labelled as having profound learning disability and no verbal communication. When she had been in the post for a while, she realised how short-sighted she had been to be dismayed. She examined the views that had led to her dismay and found that they were founded upon discrimination. She did not realise that she had stereotyped the people she was going to work with, or that she carried an unconscious prejudice against people who could not speak. Once she had been able to see the women as individual personalities with individual rights and needs, she was able to work positively with them. Here were four women who may not have much speech but could certainly communicate. The worker learned their various ways of communicating, read up the notes about their histories (they had all spent long years incarcerated in a psychiatric hospital), discovered their interests and their very different personalities. She valued their diversity and in doing so enhanced her life and theirs.

knowledge in any way you can. Participation in workshops, training, conferences, discussion groups and the supervision process can all help you to work in an anti-discriminatory and anti-oppressive way.

Promoting peoples' rights in legislation

The issue of rights has already been discussed to some extent in the discussion of social justice. Equality is inextricably linked with justice and rights. People have a moral, legal and social right to expect just, fair and equal treatment in society, and this is backed up by legislation. Examples of legislation and documents that support peoples' rights are summarised in Figure 2.2.

To illustrate the link between rights, equality and the law, three pieces of legislation are taken as examples: the Human Rights Act 1998, the Disability Discrimination Act 1995 and the Race Relations Act 1976, as amended by the Race Relations (Amendment) Act 2000.

The Human Rights Act

This Act (HMSO, 1998) was implemented in the UK in 2000 to provide, wherever possible, recourse to justice in British courts, rather than the European Court of Human Rights in Strasbourg, in relation to the rights and freedoms guaranteed under the European Convention of Human Rights. The Act is mainly intended to protect people from the misuse of state power. The rights that are protected are the right to respect for private and family life, freedom of thought, conscience and religion, and Article 14, prohibition of discrimination. This last clause states that 'The enjoyment of the rights and freedoms set forth in this Convention shall be secured without discrimination on any ground such as sex, race, colour, language, religion, political or other opinion, national or social origin, association with a national minority, property, birth or other status'.

The Disability Discrimination Act 1995

This Act (HMSO, 1995) aims to end the discrimination that disabled people face in relation to employment, accessing goods and services and buying or renting land

Scope of legislation or document	Examples of legislation and documents	Brief summary of each piece of legislation or document
International	Declaration of human rights 1948	All human beings are born free and equal in dignity and rights. Describes basic rights and freedoms in detail.
	International covenant on economic, social and cultural rights 1966	Defines the right to freedom of expression, highest standards of physical and mental health and the right to education.
	International covenant on civil and political rights 1966	Defines the right to freedom of opinion, the right to life and freedom from torture and violence.
European	Treaty of Rome 1957	Article 119: Each member state has to apply the principle of equal 'pay' between men and women of work. 'Pay' covers more than just wages.
	Directive on equal treatment 1976	Guarantees men and women the same conditions of work. Can be used to challenge sexual harassment.
	Directive on health and safety of pregnant workers 1993	Provides the right to maternity leave, to return to work afterwards and to health and safety considerations while pregnant.
	Recommendation on promotion of positive action for women 1984	Suggests measures from raising awareness to practical measures to achieve equality.
British	Sex Discrimination Act 1975	Direct and indirect discrimination on the basis of gender or marital

Figure 2.2 Legislation and documents that support people's rights

		status was made illegal. Certain exemptions to this were allowed, if gender was considered to be a 'genuine, occupation qualification'. The Equal Opportunities Commission was set up with powers to monitor and implement the Act.
	Race Relations Act 1976 as amended by the Race Relations (Amendment) Act 2000	Direct and indirect discrimination on the basis of race was made illegal. Certain exemptions to this were allowed, if race was considered a 'genuine occupational qualification'. The Commission for Racial Equality was set up to implement and monitor the Act. The amended Act also protects against institutional discrimination.
	Disability Discrimination Act 1975	Defines disability and encourages employers, transport providers and others to make reasonable efforts to respond to the needs of people with disabilities.
	Children Act 1989 and Children (Scotland) Act 1995	Clearer definition of children's rights and parents' responsibilities, protection of children and young people.
	Children Act 2004 and The Commissioner for Children and Young people (Scotland) Act 2003	Establish a Children's Commissioner to ensure a voice for children.
	Data Protection Act 1998	Gives people the right to see personal information held about them.

Figure 2.2 (continued)

	Education (Scotland) Act 1981	Children over two years with 'specialeducational needs' are to have a record of needs established and resources to implement it. This enabled these children to attend mainstream schooling.
	Human Rights Act 1998	Brings UK legislation on human rights into line with Europe – mainly to protect people from the misuses of statutory power.
Local Authority	Community care plans	Outline the council's plans to provide and finance care provision. Written after consultation with users and providers of care services. Funding for services is often dependent on having an equal opportunity policy and good practice.
	Other policies and strategies	For instance, Equal Opportunity statements on treatment of staff and on how they will provide a service to the community.

Figure 2.2 (continued)

or property. It aims to put an end to 'blatant and gratuitous' discrimination made through ignorance. A person is considered to be disabled if they have a disability (medical, physical or sensory) which makes it difficult to carry out normal day-to-day activities. The disability must be substantial and have a long-term effect, i.e. it must last or be expected to last for at least one year. Employers of more than 20 people (except of the uniformed services, of people on board ships, hovercraft and aeroplanes) have to take reasonable measures to make sure they are not discriminating against people with disabilities. It is illegal to refuse to serve someone who is disabled, or offer them a service which is not as good as the service offered to other people. The act allows the government to set minimum standards for new public transport vehicles (trains, buses, taxis) so that people with disabilities can use them more easily. Schools, colleges and universities are required to provide information for parents, pupils and students, e.g. about their arrangements for students with disability, to ensure that they will be treated fairly.

The Race Relations Act 1976

This act (HMSO, 1976), as amended by the **Race Relations (Amendment) Act 2000** (TSO, 2000) makes it unlawful to discriminate against anyone on the grounds of race, colour, nationality (including citizenship), or ethnic or national origin. The original act concentrated on discrimination by individuals. The amended act also imposes duties on many public authorities to promote racial equality. It is a direct result of the Stephen Lawrence Inquiry conducted by Sir William McPherson (1999). The amended act imposes a general duty on all major public bodies to promote equality of opportunity and good race relations. It applies to jobs, training, housing, education, and the provision of goods, facilities and services, including the police.

Redressing power imbalances and empowering people

Power, imbalance in the distribution of power and the misuse of power are at the root of inequality, discrimination and abuse. It is a central theme at all levels of discrimination. Power has been variously defined. The Oxford Dictionary gives several definitions of power that include: 'the ability to do something or act in a particular way'; 'the capacity to influence the behaviour of others, the emotions, or the course of events'. It involves the exercise of control over people, things or circumstances. Thompson (2003) says the following about power: 'one common theme is that of the ability to influence or control people, events, processes or resources'.

Power can be a positive or a negative force. When used negatively it is oppressive, discriminatory, abusive and very destructive. Lukes (1974) identified three levels of power. Although he did not compare these with levels of discrimination, they can in fact be seen to equate to different types of discrimination:

- ❏ Level 1 – what is done – decisions made, steps taken. In terms of discrimination, this equates with direct discrimination. There is a misuse of power that is both obvious and open.
- ❏ Level 2 – what is not done – decisions that may be avoided, not taken or subverted. In terms of discrimination, this may equate with indirect discrimination which occurs when a condition is applied that limits the opportunity for some individuals or groups to comply (subverted decisions), or no decision is taken, resulting in some individuals or groups having an unfair advantage (avoided decisions or decisions not taken).

❑ Level 3 – this third aspect of power refers to the level or context in which power is exercised. In terms of discrimination, this refers to the individual or institutional levels of discrimination, and the cultural and structural factors that influence what takes place.

It is especially important that care workers understand the meaning of power and the potential for the misuse of power in their own role. It is only in this way that they can begin to work towards empowering service users. As a principle, empowerment means enabling people to take control of their lives, having the power to make decisions and choices. As a method of care practice, empowerment seeks to enhance the power of people who lack it.

Empowerment is fundamental to person-centred practice and assessment, and requires creative thinking in relation to its promotion. It is not enough, in this model, to accept things as they are in society. If barriers exist to meeting service user need for maximising the life chances and wellbeing of individuals, empowerment attempts to look at how services users can optimise their own part in the care process and their own choices about how care is provided.

It goes beyond providing choices, however, in that it means putting the individual in a position where these choices can be made, not just at a practical level but at a psychological level. It involves maximising the inclusion of service users in decisions that concern them and facilitating their participation in the exercise of power over all aspects of their lives. It is very important in caring, since many service users may have spent many years in a situation of powerlessness. The process of institutionalisation is a prime example of a process which disempowers people and deprives them of their ability to make decisions. Overcoming the effects of institutionalisation and avoiding it in the first place are both aims and effects of empowerment.

For example, John, who had been in long-term hospital care, was astonished to find that in the hostel in which he went to live he had the choice to close the toilet door if he wanted to – even to lock it – and he did not have to ask permission to do so. He also had the choice to go outside or to stay in. Taking these decisions, however, was not as easy as making a simple choice because John had forgotten, or had never learned, how to make choices.

So empowerment is sometimes also about unlearning helplessness, and learning at a thinking level that choice and decision-making are not only a possibility but that, in the end, they provide a reward in terms of fulfilment and satisfaction with life. Empowerment may be a very slow process, where the care worker is placed in an educational role of showing what is possible, and offering encouragement and support to people who have not been used to exercising power in any area of their lives. Once the process is under way it is a continuing one, as Stevenson and Parsloe have pointed out:

> Empowerment is an evolving process and has no clear end point, which may explain the reluctance with which it is sometimes regarded.

> (Stevenson and Parsloe, 1993)

Inclusive practice

This is underpinned by the promotion of equality. If you believe in equality, it follows that all people must be included in planning for services, taking part in the planning process and also ensuring that services meet their needs and not just the needs of some people at the expense of others. Additionally, all people must be included as much as possible in plans for their own care.

Inclusion is applicable to everyone. Together with empowerment and a person-centred approach, inclusion is central to the philosophy of this book and encompasses the principle of equality and experiencing mainstream rather than marginalised services. It is a multi-dimensional concept, embracing a variety of ways in which people can be enabled to participate in society, to exercise their full and effective rights of citizenship in the civil, political and social spheres. There is an underlying emphasis on active participation by people to improve their living conditions and to bring about change.

Here are some examples of policies and projects that have set out with inclusion as their aim.

- ❏ Government social inclusion and modernisation agendas that emphasise the need for interdisciplinary and cross-sectoral collaboration, community participation and citizen involvement.
- ❏ Person-centred planning, developed initially as a revolt against a medical model of planning where 'experts' diagnose and treat, emphasises an empowering approach that seeks to mirror the ways in which 'ordinary people' make plans. It seeks to avoid this:

When I got my plan typed up, the four things I wanted had been left out, but some of the things staff wanted were there.

> (Sanderson, H 1997)

❏ In Glasgow, a project to support users of services and carers from black and ethnic minority communities to participate in planning, development and delivery of services which will meet their needs in an accessible and appropriate way. One part of this project was the establishment of a group of Asian women carers. Through the group, Asian women grew in confidence both individually and collectively, and many now participate in other community activities, including leisure and health classes.

❏ James and Nicola learn to cycle as part of a new Wakefield Council scheme to boost the confidence of children with disabilities and behavioural problems and increase social inclusion. The cycling days in schools are a joint initiative with the Wheels for All cycling project. (*Community Care*, 5–11 August 2004. Published by permission of the editor of *Community Care*)

❏ A series of informal meetings aimed at gaining the views of service users and carers in Kincardine. One such event was memorably called 'Blether over yer denner'. A comment from one person who attended was as follows:

The format of the 'Blether' meetings was really good – those people who probably would never have gone to the council office or faced up to someone who was an official went along and had their say . . . Public meetings are intimidating for people to speak at but in the 'Blether' format we could make our point or ask a question over a cup of tea.

(Barr, A 2001)

Where did thinking about these principles of empowerment and inclusion come from? Ideas about normalisation have played an important part, with empowerment and inclusion going beyond this in their greater emphasis on the use and misuse of power, and the need for structural change as well as change in care practice.

NORMALISATION

Ideas about normalisation were initiated by Wolfensberger (1972) in relation to people with disabilities, and were further developed by many theorists and practitioners.

Normalisation set out not only to combat the negatives of institutionalisation, but to go much further than this through enabling people to lead 'normal' and fulfilling lives in ways that are also socially valued. 'Normal' is a controversial

---

ACTIVITY 2.7

From the above accounts of empowerment, inclusive practice and normalisation, how do you think you can work more inclusively to promote equality?

---

term. What is normal, after all? Is anyone leading a 'normal' life? 'Normal' is not seen as a particular way of life, it just means having the freedom to exercise the choices and to make the decisions that are the right of every citizen and human being. One of the dangers of normalisation, though certainly not intended to be its interpretation, is that normalisation is translated into what particular workers or organisations unquestioningly think service users should be doing to be 'normal'. These ideas often conform to a particular view and take little account of ethnic and cultural diversity, for example.

One clear and creative explanation of normalisation is contained in *Beyond Community*, edited by Shulamit Ramon (1991), in which she emphasises the necessity for attitudinal change:

> In particular the approach challenges the perception of people with disabilities as inferior to those without them, as passive recipients of charity and professional wisdom, as having nothing to give but only to take, as needing care but unable to care for themselves or others. In so doing, the accepted divide between professionals and users, between the givers and those in need is threatened.

How can care workers be inclusive in their work?

Some suggestions may be by:

- Finding out what people want and need, e.g. through chatting informally over lunch.
- Ensuring that decision making and power are in the hands of the service user as far as this is possible.
- Providing information.
- Campaigning for improved resources, for mainstream services to be accessible to everyone.
- Ensuring that if people need help to express their needs and views, this is provided, e.g. bilingual staff, translation services, group facilitation that includes the use of pictures.
- Building on what exists already by knowing what is available.

- Preparing for the tasks to be undertaken, and aiming for equality of opportunity and access.
- Using a holistic approach.
- Facilitating user involvement in creative ways, e.g. use groups; use pictures where communication is difficult; involve families and friends.

Figure 2.3

SUMMARY

In this chapter an account has been given of the values, principles and ethical considerations that underpin care practice. Some of the complexities associated with ethical practice have been outlined, emphasising the need for self-awareness and ethical thinking. The second part of the chapter explored the promotion of anti-discriminatory practice and anti-oppressive practice. Consideration was given to levels and types of discrimination and to methods of combating discrimination and oppression.

FIVE KEY POINTS

1. The value base is the foundation of care practice.
2. Two core values underpin the principles of ethical practice. These are 'respect for persons' and 'the promotion of social justice and welfare'.
3. Decisions in practice are often complex and require workers to develop ethical thinking.
4. Equality is promoted through anti-discriminatory and anti-oppressive practice.
5. Discrimination and oppression can be combated through:
   - increasing your knowledge and self-awareness
   - promoting people's rights through legislation
   - redressing power imbalances and empowering people
   - inclusive practice.

THREE QUESTIONS

1. How does an understanding of ethics help your practice?
2. What do you consider to be the guiding values and principles of your practice?
3. Do you think you have any prejudices that may affect your ability to work with some people? What will you do about these?

RECOMMENDED READING

ADAMS, M. *et al.* (2000) *Readings in Diversity and Social Justice.* New York: Routledge. A fascinating, enormous tome of readings about racism, anti-semitism, sexism, heterosexism, ableism, classism – something for everyone.

BRAYE, S. and PRESTON-SHOOT, M. (1995) *Empowering Practice in Social Care.* Maidenhead: Open University Press. The chapter entitled 'Values in Social Care' looks at what are referred to as 'traditional values' and 'radical values'. It challenges your thinking.

THOMPSON, N. (2003) *Promoting Equality*, 2nd edn. Basingstoke: Palgrave. A really useful text which makes you stop and examine the way in which you do things.

CHAPTER 3

SERVICE USERS AND CARERS – INCLUDE US

Written with contributions from service users and carers

> **Don't talk about us without us.**
>
> (Service user statement)

By the end of this chapter you should, in relation to service users and carers:

- ❑ understand how important it is to include them and seek their views
- ❑ recognise their diversity
- ❑ know what they have said about the values, knowledge and skills that they think care workers should have
- ❑ know what they have said about and what they expect from managers
- ❑ learn from what they say about their experiences
- ❑ know about some useful ways to gain their participation and views.

This chapter provides underpinning content and context for all care qualifications.

INTRODUCTION

It is inconceivable to think that there was once a time when service users and carers were routinely provided with care services without being consulted about what they wanted, what kind of service they would like, where they would like the service to be provided and by whom. Neither were they consulted by agencies or the government about policies that related directly to them. Unfortunately this still happens far too often, though we are journeying along a hopeful path of encouraging the participation of and listening to service users and carers. When one local council made a presentation to local councillors about including service users, one councillor said the following:

> Let me get this clear, you are introducing an approach that finds out what is important to people so that we can make sure that services are responsive to them? You mean to say we don't do that for everyone already!

(Ritchie, P et al., 2003)

To ask why service users and carers should be consulted may seem like an invitation to state the obvious, but since this has not always happened, it is worth examining why it is so important.

Why include us?

1. It is everyone's right

Inclusion and participation are, first and foremost, everyone's right. Inclusion in decision making is written into codes of practice, national service standards,

---

ACTIVITY 3.1

Imagine that you need a care service because, after a long illness, you are unable to manage at home without help. A care manager comes along and tells you what you need and arranges everything, without asking you about what *you* think you need.

- ❏ How do you feel about this?
- ❏ How would you like decisions to be made about what you need, without anyone even asking your opinion?

national occupational standards and the UN Convention on the Rights of the Child.

> As a social care worker you must promote the independence of service users.
>
> > (Codes of Practice for Social Care Workers and Employers, GSCC and other Care Councils, 2002)

How can you promote people's independence if you do not include them?

> You or your carer are encouraged to express your views on any aspects of the care service at any time.
>
> > (Scottish Executive, 2001)

This quotation is from Standard 11 of the national care standards (care at home), the service standards in Scotland for care at home, addressed to the service user.

> Relate to and support individuals in the way they choose. (HSC24a) Develop supportive relationships that promote choice and independence. (HSC35a)
>
> > (Skills for Care and Development/Skills for Health: Health and Social Care national occupational standards 2004)

Promoting choice and independence are impossible to achieve without including people in decisions that relate to them.

> The child's right to express an opinion, and to have that opinion taken into account, in any matter or procedure affecting the child.
>
> > (Article 12 of the UN Convention on the Rights of the Child, the child's opinion (Participation))

2. It is empowering

Some of the feelings which service users have experienced in relation to needing a care service can be attributed to feelings of powerlessness, a dislike of dependency and a fear of losing independence. A whole range of negative emotions may be experienced by the initial recognition of the need to accept help. And yet the intention is that care services will make positive differences to people's lives, minimising any negatives and optimising the positive. Inclusion in the decision-making process can make the difference between a negative and a positive experience.

> We want to think about what we want for the future and get things together ourselves before we involve other people. I want to meet, sit and talk with my keyworker and I will say what I want.
>
> (Sanderson, H 1997)

> Yeh, I did get asked but felt that with the people it just went in one ear and out the other.
>
> (Who Cares? Scotland 2003)

These quotations emphasise that including service users must be seen to be genuine and not just tokenistic. People must *feel* included.

3. It is practical

Including service users and carers is also very practical. Your work is far more likely to be successful if service users and carers have participated in decisions that relate to them.

> . . . people with dementia are not consistently given their diagnosis or the information and support they need afterwards. Knowing the diagnosis can have huge benefits for patients and carers in decision making, planning and quality of life. Organisations have developed good practice models of social support and information after diagnosis, and involved staff and service users in high-quality dementia service development.
>
> (Pearl, J. 'Be Honest with Me'. 26 August 2004. Published by the editor of *Community Care*)

Why are service users and carers involved? Because it works. Retired teacher, Betty, who lives with her husband Arthur, was diagnosed with dementia. Workers involved Betty and Arthur fully in giving information about Betty's condition and about possible sources of help. This has enabled Betty to be fully included in a plan of care that enables her to develop those things that she can do, such as going shopping with Arthur, but avoids other activities that are dangerous, such as driving a car. Her full inclusion has had positive practical and psychological outcomes. Arthur's inclusion has meant that he has been able to say what support he needs.

4. It recognises people's experience

The words of Peter Beresford sum up the essence of this point, in an address he made to the Shaping our Lives conference in 2003. He said:

> But there is one thing we can all agree about. That when we have had those bad experiences – of prejudice, of not having enough money, of being excluded, of being seen as useless or defective, of having our rights ignored, or our needs not met as we would want, we have certainly found out a lot of things. We have learned a lot – the hard way. We have gained an enormous amount of knowledge from our experience. We know what it is really like to be treated like this, to have these experiences; to undergo such things. It is this first-hand experience that we have as service users that is what we have in common, that unites us as service users and which is the basis for what we know. And now this experience is beginning to be recognised as important.

STATEMENT OF SERVICE USER AND CARER EXPECTATIONS

As part of the review of the N/SVQs (National/Scottish vocational qualifications) in Health and Social Care, service users and carers were invited to contribute views about what their ideal care worker is like and what values, skills and knowledge they thought care workers and managers should hold. It is the intention that everyone undertaking a VQ in Care should read this statement and take on board its content in their practice developments. Below is a summary of what was said from the perspective of service users and carers.

The ideal care worker

This is what we said we wanted of care workers:

> A good care worker is someone who listens to you and takes you sincerely and puts what you have said into practice.

> Ideal care workers go out of their way for you, try to understand what it is like for the service user and carer; they are happy and interested in their work and knowledgeable about their jobs and sources of help. As people they are friendly, diplomatic, interested, patient and

responsible. They are good communicators who listen and do not try to follow their own agenda.

Children and young people emphasised that:

> Ideal care workers are people you can trust, who listen to you and explain things, get involved in your life, are there for you and stand up for you. They help you with your homework and talk to you.

Values

These are the values we expect care workers to hold and what we said about them.

Respect

Show respect for the dignity and privacy of the individual; place value on the person:

> A good care worker is someone who respects you as a person.

> . . . someone you can trust who will be honest with you . . .

> They show that they care for you, not treating you like an idiot in a wheelchair.

> I felt worth something and that I could make a difference.

> It's my house, not your house.

Choice

Provide realistic choices:

> They tell you what choices you have got. They would sit down and tell you what one thing would be like and the other . . . It's fair – you know what can happen.

> They let you choose things, your clothes and that.

> What is a choice?

> It is important to us to be able to choose things for the unit.

Being non-judgemental

Do not judge people; avoid making assumptions about them:

They listen to me and are non-judgemental.

If you see behaviour that you think is difficult, there could be lots of different causes. Do not label it 'challenging behaviour', look for why it is happening.

Keep an open mind.

Inclusion and empowerment

Involve and empower service users and carers as much as possible:

Do not talk about us without us.

Treat us as allies.

Involve us in decisions.

Work with people to support the gaining or regaining of personal or political power.

Confidentiality

Respect confidential information:

They listen and respect confidences so that I feel comfortable enough to tell the truth.

You should always ask permission before you discuss confidential information with anyone else and explain why you want to discuss it. You should only pass on confidential information without permission if someone is in danger, or if the law requires it.

If it is not too big a deal they should keep secrets, but if it is that bad, they should tell someone else.

Skills

These are the skills we expect care workers to have, and what we said about them:

Communication

This is one of the main skill areas emphasised by both service users and carers:

They help you and listen to you.

Staff listen to you when things are really bad.

They are good communicators who listen and do not try to follow their own agenda.

The best ones impart information clearly and simply with no jargon.

They explain things to you in a good way.

They help us to share relevant information effectively.

We also ask that care workers:

- are aware of a variety of communication methods
- check back that the worker's understanding is correct
- do not talk down to people
- provide precise, clear and accurate communication.

Other skills

Care workers should:

- have good practical skills

    They should be fit for everyday tasks.
    If you cut yourself they will give you first aid.
    They must be able to do the things I am unable to do myself.

- place service users and carers at the centre of the assessment and care planning process

Meetings should be at a time convenient to us.

They should keep focused on the needs of who they are trying to help.

Service users should be given the opportunity to be involved actively in assessment as they wish.

- pay particular attention to the ending of a relationship
- be clear-headed in an emergency

They give help and support at times of personal crisis.
They should be calm in any situation.

❑ enable people to live as independently as possible and, if necessary, advocate on their behalf

A good care worker cuts through red tape and just gets on with it.
They should be able to speak for me.

Knowledge

This is the knowledge we thought care workers should have.
Care workers should:

❑ have knowledge of services and legislation relevant to users' and carers' needs
❑ know about the benefit system and sources of funding, or whom to refer to if they do not
❑ know about health and social services organisations
❑ know when and whom to ask for extra help
❑ know about the people for whom they are caring
❑ know about the roles of other people in relation to meeting service user and carer need
❑ understand their limitations
❑ know how to identify the frustrations of the service user
❑ have up-to-date knowledge.

We would like to be sure that workers really understand human development and caring at every stage of life.

A care worker must do everything they can to find out the information the person may need.

Implications for managers

We think that it is very important that managers also understand and promote the inclusion of service users and carers.

Managers should:

❑ ensure the availability of information, e.g. on other services, on ways of meeting needs of people for information

ACTIVITY 3.2

When you have read the 'Statement of Expectations', list five things that you can do to ensure that you are meeting these expectations. Make a plan about how and when you will put them into practice.

❏ provide good supervision so that workers know that they can seek additional advice and support when they do not have the knowledge and skills to respond to individuals and key people.
❏ Provide training for workers, e.g. in anti-discriminatory practice.

They should be there most of the time to see how things are going and see if the people are being listened to; reading up on everything, doing money stuff and organising trips.

GOOD PRACTICE IN INCLUDING SERVICE USERS

The Social Care Institute for Excellence (SCIE) 2004 outlined 15 factors to consider when planning and implementing service user participation for service enhancement and change.

❏ Be clear about the aims and scope of participation before starting the process.
❏ Identify and engage any existing local or regional user initiatives.
❏ Clearly communicate the aims and scope to potential participants from the outset in appropriate, accessible ways.
❏ Before participation begins, ensure there is political will and organisational commitment to change, and sufficient resources actively to address service user priorities.
❏ Ensure that user participation is responsive to the perspective, priorities, needs and aims of local service users. These may not match traditional service categories or managerial service priorities.
❏ Be aware of the power relationships, relations between service users and professionals throughout the process.
❏ Consider ways to prevent or manage creatively any conflict together with the participants, and remain aware of the need to share information and decision-making power.
❏ Value the knowledge and expertise of people who use services, and ensure that this may be communicated in ways with which they are comfortable.

❏ Work towards creating diverse flexible continuous participation strategies that are integral to the decision-making structures of an organisation. These should be appropriate to and planned with service users, so be prepared to think of those structures to accommodate new ways of working and communicating.

❏ Make sure that adequate time and resources are available to support effective, inclusive participation.

❏ Plan a framework to monitor and evaluate the impact of participation with the involved service users, as well as the experience of the process itself.

❏ During participation, plan with participants how feedback will be communicated to them and how to respond further if required.

❏ Address any issues of representation with service users.

❏ Think creatively and consult on different ways to involve people who may otherwise be marginalised from the process. Ensure that all staff involved (including frontline workers) understand the principles and the practice of service user participation, and are empowered by organisational structures, processes and management strategies to make it a success.

Meetings with service users and carers

The literature about person-centred planning provides some useful questions to ask in relation to any meetings that involve service user and/or carer participation. These questions include:

❏ How can the meeting be run to ensure that it is as meaningful and respectful as possible?

This may mean, for example, having communication that is as accessible as possible. In relation to consultation for the 2001 Valuing People white paper there was evidence that information was not presented in ways that made it accessible to people with learning difficulties. Although 9 out of 10 boards in our study were reported as providing information in large print, only 30 per cent used pictures or symbols to supplement the text and only the same proportion provided minutes, agendas or reports on tape for those unable to read.

('Valuing People fails to halt Prejudice', *Community Care*, 25 November 2004. Published by permission of the editor of *Community Care*)

❑ How do we ensure that people retain as much control as is possible?

If there are people who are unable to express their own views, this may require the use of advocates who can speak on behalf of others as if they were expressing the other person's views and not their own. It could also involve training in self-advocacy skills so that individuals are enabled to speak up for themselves.

❑ Where would the most comfortable place for a meeting be?

Try to choose a place for meetings where the participants feel comfortable. This is not usually a formal office at Council Headquarters. One group I attended met in a rather small room at a local, inexpensive hotel but really enjoyed going there because they felt that it was cosy and the staff were so welcoming. When a suggestion was made to move the meeting to a 'better' location, members resisted change so strongly that no move was made.

❑ Do we need one meeting or many short ones?

It is very rare that everything can be achieved in one meeting. It is important at the beginning to decide together how many meetings may be needed so that people can know when they will be meeting and what the time commitment is likely to be.

❑ How do we record and communicate in the meeting itself?

This should be decided by the participants themselves, according to their communication needs. Use may be made of pictures, large print, audio tapes, facilitators, signers and translators.

❑ What have people's experiences been of bad meetings and why were they bad – so that we know what to avoid?

Again, in relation to the 2001 Valuing People consultation, there was considerable variation in the organisation of the meetings, with some struggling with even the basics. Service users at one meeting complained about the lack of wheelchair access, and in several places meetings were so large that service users could not hear what was being said. In other areas, however, simple measures had been introduced to combat these problems and empower service users. One particularly successful practice was splitting meetings into sub-groups to discuss particular topics, thus making both comprehension and active participation easier for service users.

(*Community Care*, 25 November 2004. Published by permission of the editor of *Community Care*)

❏   Who should be there and who should not be there?

Care should be taken to ensure that consultations are as representative as possible and that service users and carers are not dominated or outnumbered by vocal officials who do not have any training in the methods and importance of service user/carer inclusion and participation.

❏   How do people want to handle areas that may be difficult?

In one consultation with children and young people, Joe, who had volunteered to take part, could only stand discussion for very short periods of time and hated any reference to parents. It was agreed that he would leave the room with his support worker if at any time the meeting became stressful for him. Other members of the group accepted this as one of the ground rules of the meeting. He was totally accepted even though he spent a high proportion of the time with his head and face completely buried in the very large hood of his jacket. Afterwards he was very proud of the fact that he had participated and that some of his comments were included in the final project report.

SOME EXAMPLES OF GOOD PRACTICE

It is impossible to talk about all of the good practice that is taking place in the UK in relation to service user and carer participation. Here is a small and rather random selection of examples to give an idea of work being undertaken. There is a lot of very, very good work that we do not have room to include.

1. Shaping Our Lives

This is an independent national user-controlled organisation, which works with and comprises a range of adult health and social care service users. It was established in 1996 and has worked nationally and locally to try to improve service users' involvement in and influence on health and social care, and to improve the quality of support and services they receive.

In *Community Care* magazine (4 November 2004), Fran Branfield and Peter Beresford wrote the article below which is included here with their permission and published by permission of the editor of *Community Care*.

Shape up and listen

Stephen Ladyman's 'new vision for social care' is lacking one important element: service user feedback. With the government now answering critics by extending its consultation to service users, the social care minister could do worse than heed the recommendations of user group Shaping Our Lives.

This group, which has a database of hundreds of service users and the organisations that represent them, has already submitted initial evidence to the government to express its user-centred vision for adult social care.

Its values and principles include the importance of a vision based on social models of social care. The sector needs to acknowledge and challenge the broader constraints, barriers and discriminations that service users face, and recognise their right to help shape their own wellbeing.

Shaping Our Lives also emphasises that social care needs to take as its starting point a clear rights-based philosophy that:

- ❏ sees social care as having a central role in supporting and safeguarding people's human and civil rights
- ❏ is based on an idea of independent living, which means providing the support that service users need to live on as equal terms as possible as non-service users
- ❏ builds on a holistic understanding of the individual within their community and society and seeks to support their involvement and inclusion.

Shaping Our Lives draws attention to the evidence that shows service users value social care practitioners with the right human qualities as well as the necessary skills. This means workers who are open, honest, warm, empathetic and respectful, and treat clients with equality. They recognise and address diversity, are non-judgemental and anti-discriminatory.

The relationship service users have with service workers is a key determinant of good practice. This means ensuring minimal inappropriate turnover of social care workers, and continuity and choice in whom service users have working with them.

Shaping Our Lives argues for practice which values the direct experience of staff that have used social care services and which supports and encourages the recruitment of such people. The group challenges discrimination and encourages staff development and promotion based on the contribution of service users in professional education and training.

Shaping Our Lives wants social care to prioritise equal access to support and acknowledge that clients want services that:

- ❏ address diversity, whether relating to age, race, gender, sexuality, culture, class or disability
- ❏ recognise that although different groups have shared rights, they may have different needs; and which support a range of provision to meet these different needs on equal terms
- ❏ are based on systematic and comprehensive access policy and practice. This recognises that access is about more than physical access, although this is important. It means ensuring that all groups can contribute on equal terms, have equal access to appropriate services and support, and have equal opportunities to become involved. This particularly means ensuring physical, cultural and communication access for all.

Shaping Our Lives makes the case for service users to have choice in the support they receive. This may be support provided on the basis of direct payments, which put service users in direct control of their personal care package. It may mean mainstream services, which seek to replicate the choice and control which have so far been offered to a few service users by direct payment schemes. And it may mean access to user-controlled services and support arrangements (which research shows service users particularly value) through greater government funding.

Shaping our Lives has called for social care which:

- ❏ treats people as adults, rather than putting or keeping them in independent and unequal relationships
- ❏ acknowledges its responsibilities to offer support and safeguard people's rights, as well as restrict some people's rights in order to safeguard those of others

- ❏   offers people real alternatives to residential services
- ❏   is evidence-based and includes service users' research and service users' knowledge as equal elements of its evidence base
- ❏   involves service users effectively and on equal terms, where such involvement leads to palpable change and improvement in the lives and prospects of service users.

To achieve such user-centred social care for the future, Shaping Our Lives emphasises the needs for monitoring and review, based on user-defined quality and outcome measures as well as those of professionals and policy makers.

Most of all, it re-emphasises the importance of government adequately funding an infrastructure of independent, user-controlled organisations. This provides the starting point for effective and diverse involvement and provides a framework for expanding user-led services and the extension of direct payments to more service users. This is Shaping Our Lives' vision. It is hoped it will influence the government's.

2. Carers UK

This body provides a voice for carers and is a carer-led organisation working for all carers. It is the leading campaigning, policy and information organisation for carers. Work involves:

- ❏   **Campaigning** for a better deal for carers
- ❏   **Informing** carers of their rights and what help is available
- ❏   **Training and advising professionals** who work with carers
- ❏   **A devolved approach**, with Carers Scotland, Carers Wales and Carers Northern Ireland determining priorities in their respective areas.

Imelda Redmond, Chief Executive of Carers UK, has said:

> Every day we receive calls from carers here in the UK who are at the end of their tether. Caring can be hugely demanding, particularly if you are on call 24 hours a day, seven days a week without support . . ..
> Carers often do not know where to turn to help them deal with the confusing maze of benefits and rights. Many families have also been turned away from support on the basis of poor advice. At Carers UK we help carers to solve this by giving them advice and information. However, this is only part of what they need . . ..

Carers UK will be running a Carer's Rights Day . . . to ensure that more carers are aware of their rights and entitlements. The organisation will also be launching new research on carers' health which will highlight the extent to which caring takes its toll on carers' health and wellbeing.

(Source: www.carersuk.org; 12 November 2004)

3. The Who Cares? Trust

This organisation works to improve care for around 60,000 children and young people separated from their families and living in residential care. It promotes their interests and has a website for carers and young people called 'right here, right now'. Part of the site, called O.i., is specifically for children and young people and covers such issues as finding a career, rights, bullying, after care and study skills. Who Cares? provides support to young people who need to talk to someone outside the care system. They also promote the rights of children and young people under the UN Convention on the Rights of the Child, including the right of children to express their views and opinions and have them taken into account.

Who Cares? Scotland published the results of a major consultation with children and young people entitled 'Let's Face it! Care 2003 – Young People Tell Us How It Is'. This resulted from two events and a series of individual interviews. It is full of quotes from young people about the areas that they identified as important: safety and protection; relationships with care staff; trust and quality of care; family; friendships and support. Here are some of the things they said about safety and protection:

They knew something was wrong with me and eventually I told them what was happening and they sorted it out. It was all the staff working together . . ..

I think most young people are safe in care but I do not know. I'd probably say it was 50–50. Some feel safe and some do not. I still do not trust a lot of people, because as I say I do not know them, they are not my family, so why should I trust them? They are there to look after me, but you do get some bad ones.

4. People First

This is a self-advocacy organisation run by people with learning difficulties, with local groups all over the UK. The idea of People First is that people with learning difficulties should be seen as **people** first and not seen only as their learning difficulty. Here is what they do, in their words:

1. Help local People First groups to get off the ground.
2. Train professionals about what we need.
3. Talk to government, councils, health boards and services.
4. Run conferences and workshops.
5. Write booklets and make videos so people can learn about what we want.
6. Produce a newsletter and other publicity.
7. Support each other to speak up and speak out.
8. Take part in the wider People First movement.

5. The SAY Project

This body has been established in Fife to promote inclusive services and opportunities to empower and actively to involve people with a learning disability and their families in the development and design of services. It provides them with an opportunity to contribute their views and ideas on policies and procedures, and to speak with confidence at meetings and conferences. A page of one of their leaflets is reproduced below to illustrate the aims of the project.

Figure 3.1 The SAY project - 'It's your say'

6. Heart-Felt work

This is a Welsh organisation which specialises in organising service user consultations. During the review of the National Occupational Standards in Health and Social Care, they held five meetings to consult on the standards with:

1. Ceredigion Access Group (people with physical impairments) in Aberystwyth.
2. Voices from Care (young people) in Cardiff.
3. Cardiff People First, Caerphilly People First, Bridgend People First, All Wales People First (people with learning difficulties) in Cardiff.
4. Brighter Futures in Wrexham (people with mental health problems).
5. Two teleconferences with people who are blind or visually impaired in south and west Wales.

This is an example of one organisation using the expertise that has been built up by other organisations that represent service users. All of the meetings were held in accessible venues, with dietary needs being catered for. People were offered expenses in cash on the day. The teleconference had the material to be considered available on tape, in large print and Braille as required. This was produced by Wales Council for the Blind.

7. The Map Squad

This organisation has grown from very small beginnings. In 1999, four people with learning difficulties in Tower Hamlets, bored with their day centre routine, decided to find out was happening for other people in their area and learn how to speak up for themselves. They produced a newsletter, read by a group from another day centre who joined forces with them. They are now an experienced and vocal group about local issues, with 25 members, an office which is open five days a week. They have become a leading voice in the area on services that people with learning difficulties can access, including, wherever possible, main-stream services used by everyone else. Francis Cosgrove, a group member says:

> We are a speaking-up group and we are all about people's rights and changing things for the better.

Some of the lessons learned by the Map Squad have been:

❑   Make the right impression early on. At one meeting about the Council's Community Care Plan a member stood up and said: 'Sorry, we don't know what you're talking about!' The Council took note from then on.

❏ The group uses creative ways to find out what people want, including the use of drama and painting as well as just talking.

❏ Keep things simple so everyone can understand. During housing roadshows it became clear that people needed more time and accessible information in the form of pictures to illustrate housing choices.

('Uncharted Territory', *Community Care*, 22 July 2004. Published by permission of the editor of *Community Care*)

The North West Carers Centre Respite Sitter Service

This body (NWCC) provides 60 hours a week of short-term respite breaks for carers by people who are or have been carers, usually up to three hours at any one time. The Service helps to relieve isolation and helps promote social inclusion for older people and their carers living in the North West District of Edinburgh.

It provides a free, flexible, responsive service, which aims to cover regular planned support, occasional support, or an emergency break during weekdays, weekends or evenings. A variety of assistance is given, including support, sitter service or befriending, which complements existing services.

The project aims to encourage older people where possible to participate in local activities which include lifelong learning and health promotion, and to give access to information and services so that they can make a positive contribution to their local community. The projected number of older people and their family members helped every year is between 65 and 70 people.

The client group served by the project is older people and their carers ranging from 50+ to 85+. In this area of deprivation, we would define an older person as 50+, as statistics have shown that people age through poverty and ill health.

The project offers employment and training opportunities for people who are recruited locally in line with North West Carers Centre Employment policy, building on the skills of local carers as support workers. They are recruited from the local area and it is a requirement that they are or have been carers.

The support workers are carefully matched with both the carer and the cared-for person to meet their particular circumstances. There is continuity of both service and named support worker.

The support staff are encouraged to take up further training through the North West Carers Centre, European-funded Carers Upskilling Programme (CUP). This programme provides an upskilling provision for workers and others to update and extend their skills and qualification levels in order to meet the growing demands/needs within the care sector. Examples of NWCC respite sitter service use:

Carer of sister with acquired head injury

Carer uses the time to visit her local library and calls in on her daughter for a coffee while the support worker stays at home with her sister.

Carer of wife with dementia

Carer attends evening art class, which he had wanted to attend for some time, and also enjoys bowling and meeting with friends, while the support worker stays at home with his wife.

Carer of elderly aunt

Carer attends North West Carers Centre support groups while the support worker stays at home with aunt.

Carer of elderly mother

Carer has social time while the support worker stays at home with his elderly visually impaired mother who also has dementia.

This support worker is a local carer who supports her daughter and other family members with disabilities.

She has successfully completed our Carers Upskilling Programme (CUP) and has gained six accredited units from Telford College. Having completed this programme, she is planning to pursue further education opportunities.

Quotes from carers using the service:

Knowing you were there for us was a tremendous help.

Thank you for taking such an interest in me.

Quotes from professionals:

> You are doing a great job.
> You are making a very valuable contribution.

Referrals continue to be received from the NHS, social workers, occupational therapists, other agencies, relatives, friends and carers themselves.

A carer's life

I have been a carer for 35 years, although I only became aware of this fact some 16 years ago.

My son was born disabled but it was not until he was eleven months old that I was told he was disabled. It was probably fortunate that I did not know what the future held, or what having a disabled child would mean to both me and my son. I was unaware that I would not be able to follow my career or indeed have any form of employment, which means that come retirement age I would not have a full pension. I was also oblivious to the health problems which years of lifting and sleepless nights would have. It would also have been somewhat thought-provoking to realise that I would still be changing nappies 35 years on, or that I would have to fight for almost all the support that Stephen needs.

My life as a carer is certainly not what I had envisaged while I was at college. I undertook three years full-time and one year part-time training as a manager. I was unable to make use of the qualifications I acquired, as Stephen was born 18 months after I completed the course. Although I had intended to return to work, it was impossible and so set the pattern for the next 30 years. I could not even become self-employed because I could not guarantee that I could do a job: Stephen comes first and because of his epilepsy I had to be available at the drop of a hat. Even when Stephen is admitted to hospital I go in with him, otherwise the nurses cannot cope.

There are no respite facilities where I live that can cope with Stephen's needs, and I have to arrange my own respite with people I can trust.

As a carer I want the same as everyone else, to lead an ordinary life, to be able to do things on the spur of the moment, to go out and not worry about getting home on time. I would like to be like the majority of 50+ people and live my own life.

The chapter ends with the account above from a carer, Ursula, the mother of Stephen who appeared in Chapter 1. From this account, try to identify ways in which you think the situation could have been and could still be improved for her.

ACTIVITY 3.3

Find three examples of practice in your area in relation to service user/carer participation. Identify how they are helpful to service provision.

Figure 3.2

SUMMARY

It is vital to optimise the inclusion of service users and carers in decisions that concern them. The importance of inclusion and participation is outlined in many documents, including the UK Health and Social Care national occupational standards and the UN Convention on the Rights of the Child. Service users and carers have said that their ideal workers 'go out of their way for you, try to understand what it is like for the service user and carer'. The Social Care Institute for Excellence (SCIE) and SHS (Scottish Human Services) have outlined helpful factors in consulting with service users. Examples of good practice illustrate how inclusion of service users and carers has been successful. Ursula's account at the end of the chapter indicates that there is still a long way to go before carers and service users receive the support that they would like and need.

FIVE KEY POINTS

1. Participation and involvement of service users and carers in decisions that concern them is vital in meeting their needs.
2. Service users and carers should be included because it is their right, it is empowering, practical and very important.
3. Service users and carers have said that their ideal worker is 'someone who listens to you . . . and puts what you have said into practice'.
4. Service users and carers would like managers to ensure the availability of information and provide good supervision to workers.
5. Good practice in including service users and carers means being clear about the aims and scope of participation before starting the process.

THREE QUESTIONS

1. In a service that you know, what are three ways in which service users and/or carers could be involved in decision-making?
2. What five factors do you think are important in setting up a consultation with service users and/or carers?
3. Are there things that you would do differently in consulting with carers from consulting with service users?

RECOMMENDED READING

RITCHIE, P. *et al.* (2003) *People, Plans and Practicalities.* Edinburgh: SHS Ltd. A book full of examples and good practice in relation to involving service users.

SANDERSON, H. *et al.* (1997) *People, Plans and Possibilities.* Edinburgh: SHS Ltd. A substantial and philosophical look at person-centred planning, which involves optimising service user participation.

Social Care Institute for Excellence (SCIE) (2004) *Position Paper 3: Has service user participation made a difference to social care's services?* London: SCIE (www.scie.org.uk). This paper is about how social care services can be improved by the people who use them.

CHAPTER 4

INTERPERSONAL SKILLS AND COMMUNICATION

Ellen Lancaster

A warm, mutually satisfying relationship with clients is built on the foundation of good listening and talking.

(Jenny Rogers, 1990)

By the end of this chapter you should be able to:

- ❑ revisit and apply the values and principles outlined in Chapter 2, since these are needed to communicate effectively
- ❑ understand and practise the skills required in effective communication and be able to identify some of the difficulties associated with communication
- ❑ know about and practise recording, receiving, transmitting and organizing information.

The content of this chapter provides you with underpinning content and context for all care qualifications. It relates especially to the following units:

NVQ and SVQ Level 2 Core Unit HSC21: Communicate with and complete records for individuals

NVQ and SVQ Level 3 Core Unit HSC31: Promote effective communication for and about individuals; HSC369: Support individuals with specific communication needs; HSC371: Support individuals to communicate using interpreting and translation services

HNC Social Care Unit: Social care theory for practice.

INTRODUCTION

This chapter is divided into three sections:

1. Promoting effective communication and forming meaningful relationships.
2. Barriers and dilemmas which may affect effective communication.
3. The importance and implications of recording, receiving, transmitting and organising information.

Interpersonal skills

Interpersonal is defined as 'of or relating to relationships or communication between people'; skill is defined as 'the ability to do something well; expertise; difficult work' (Oxford English Dictionary). Interpersonal skills are the heart and soul of good care practice. The skills rest upon:

- ❑ working from the care value base
- ❑ empowering individuals through positive working relationships
- ❑ using your essential qualities and attributes
- ❑ communicating effectively
- ❑ using theory and knowledge.

This is important for you to understand and practise if you are to assist in improving the quality of people's lives. It is the intention in this chapter to look at the constituent parts of interpersonal skills through emphasising the importance of the underpinning value base for care, looking at communication, its importance and the necessary components of good communication and that little bit more, 'the oomph factor'. The chapter also examines barriers and difficulties in relation to communication and the importance of updating and maintaining records and reports.

A commitment to the values and principles of care is the foundation of good practice. This underpins communication and interpersonal skills, the heart of care

Good practice	Poor practice
Happy	Unhappy
Optimistic	No hope
High self-esteem	Very low self-esteem
Choice	No choice, given orders
Privacy	Exposure of their lives
Important	Lonely
Comfortable with self, others	Awkward and no confidence
Not threatened	Intimidated and bullied
Safe	Scared, in danger

Figure 4.1 Individual receiving care

practice, as well as every other aspect of care. Reference will therefore be made to this value base as communication and interpersonal skills are discussed.

The difference for the individual between good practice based upon care values and principles, and poor practice which is not, is illustrated above (Figure 4.1).

ACTIVITY 4.1

Before reading the section on communication look at the case study on the next page. Identify the links between the value base and communication.

Maureen and Mr Iqbal

Maureen has worked with Trust Housing Association for several years. Recently an Asian man, Mr Iqbal, came to live in the complex. Maureen explains in her words:

Mr Iqbal, who is 97 years of age and wears a hearing aid, was offered a flat at our complex as he was living in a high rise flat and was isolated due to lifts never working. He is our first Asian tenant. Knowing that my colleagues and myself had little experience of Mr Iqbal's culture and language, I contacted the area manager to see if we could have training in this area. The company has a liaison officer who came to give us training and information which would enable us to communicate effectively with our new tenant. Rahinni, the liaison officer, brought along literature, a video and also a list of useful agencies and telephone numbers we could use if we needed further assistance. We watched the video and discussed all the information, which I found invaluable in understanding Mr Iqbal and his culture.

Before Mr Iqbal moved in he came in initially to view his flat and the complex, and also to sign the tenancy agreement if he decided to move in. If any prospective tenant has difficulty in understanding the agreement then they are offered the services of advocate and interpreter, who will enable individuals to express views and concerns, access information and services, defend and promote rights and responsibilities and explore choices and options. As Mr Iqbal's grandson, Shaheen (his grandfather's main carer), was with him, he said that with his grandfather's consent he could interpret and assist Mr Iqbal. Shaheen informed us that English is his grandfather's second language.

When Mr Iqbal moved in, I noticed that sometimes he was having problems understanding me. I was not sure if this was because of a language barrier or his hearing problem. At this time I did not pursue this as I realised that he might be a little distressed at moving into his new home. When I had to explain our company fire procedures to Mr Iqbal, I arranged a time with him that I knew would suit him. I sat close to him so that he could see my face and I began by speaking very slowly, using hand and body gestures, and using non-jargon explanations. I also used pictures and signs, as it was important that Mr Iqbal understood what to do in the event of a fire. Shaheen later informed the staff that his grandfather had told him that I had explained the procedures well to him. Shaheen has built up a good relationship with all the staff, and he keeps us informed of when his grandfather will be going out and what he needs. Shaheen has also invited staff and tenants to his mosque at any time.

The links between the value base and communication that you may have identified are:

- ❏ Maureen demonstrated respect for the worth and dignity of Mr Iqbal.
- ❏ She promoted Mr Iqbal's rights and welfare.
- ❏ She offered choices.
- ❏ She demonstrated an approach based upon equality.
- ❏ She was professional in her approach, and developed her practice to meet Mr Iqbal's needs.

PROMOTING EFFECTIVE COMMUNICATION AND FORMING MEANINGFUL RELATIONSHIPS

Effective communication

Communication is defined as:

the imparting, conveying or exchange of ideas, knowledge etc. (whether by speech, writing or signs); interchange of speech.

Effective is defined as:

producing a desired result; impressive; operative.

(both definitions from Oxford English Dictionary)

From these two definitions, it is apparent that communication is more complex than just 'speaking' or 'listening' to a person. Speaking is effective only if an individual can hear, and listening is effective only if an individual can talk. Therefore workers have to be skilled and knowledgeable in many ways to communicate effectively. The ways in which care workers communicate convey to the individual how they value that person.

Think of someone in your life, perhaps a friend or a relative whom you admire and find it easy to speak to. Your reasons probably include the facts that you know that person well, they know you well, they accept you for you, they are warm, understanding, they listen to you and they do not criticise or judge you.

ACTIVITY 4.2

In the light of the values and principles of care and the above definitions of effective communication, consider the quotes below:

He has lived in an institution all his life. How would he know what he wants, never mind be able to tell us?

What is the point of speaking to her if she has dementia? She has no idea what I am saying to her.

The manager has told me to explain the fire drill to Mr Iqbal, but he does not speak English very well.

I have given up trying to speak to her as she never replies to me.

What am I supposed to say or do when she tells me she is going to self-abuse herself again?

I do not have the time to puzzle out what he is saying, so I just guess.

How often have you heard such statements made? What have you thought, or have you just accepted them?

Write down for each quote how you would overcome the lack of communication. All will be revealed when you read examples of good practice throughout the chapter.

Recall the statement 'The manager has told me to explain the fire drill to Mr Iqbal but he does not speak English very well'.

In the example of Maureen at the beginning of the chapter, she was well prepared before Mr Iqbal moved in by making arrangements for herself and other staff to find out about his culture, and meeting his main carer. She took a genuine interest in getting to know Mr Iqbal and his grandson, which assisted her in communicating effectively with Mr Iqbal. This is an example of effective use of interpersonal skills, where the worker not only demonstrated application of the value base, but also good communication, taking into account feelings, culture, language and beliefs.

Effective communication involves many skills, which include:

- ❏ caring, valuable relationship
- ❏ listening skills
- ❏ non-verbal communication
- ❏ using appropriate language
- ❏ using the right pace and tone
- ❏ exploring new and other ways to communicate.

Caring, valuable relationship

Forming and sustaining a caring, valuable relationship is the main essence of effective communication between an individual and a care worker. Without a good relationship, there will be no mutual respect. This is likely to result in failure to meet the needs of an individual. The ingredients necessary to form relationships are the practice of all of the values and principles, knowledge of human behaviour, a knowledge of the person and also that bit extra – the oomph factor (Figure 4.2)

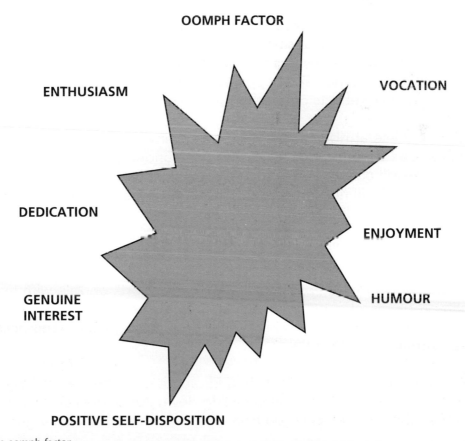

OOMPH FACTOR

ENTHUSIASM

VOCATION

DEDICATION

ENJOYMENT

GENUINE
INTEREST

HUMOUR

POSITIVE SELF-DISPOSITION

Figure 4.2 The oomph factor

The oomph factor

An explanation of the ingredients which bind together the oomph factor is as follows:

- ❏ **Enthusiasm**: ardent interest, eagerness, encouraging and having great faith in others. You need to be energetic, possess inspiration in what you are practising, and have the stamina to keep going 'that extra mile'.
- ❏ **Dedication**: consistent support and commitment to the wellbeing of an individual. Be prepared to put in that bit extra when no one else will, because you know that it will benefit an individual. Dedication is not just for those who need assistance but also for fellow workers.
- ❏ **Vocation**: emphasises the professionalism of care work and that it is not 'just a job'.
- ❏ **Genuine interest**: includes being interested in all people, knowing people's likes and dislikes, frustrations, expectations and also being truthful.
- ❏ **Enjoyment and humour**: involve you in showing and feeling genuine pleasure in what you are doing, and sharing successes or even failures however great or small.
- ❏ **Positive self-disposition**: emphasises that you should be confident and happy with yourself in what you are doing, and striving to share this confidence and happiness with the individual. This positive practice reflects onto others, enabling them to feel more positive.

In addition to these attributes, it is necessary to involve further qualities, identified by Carl Rogers (1902–87) as **warmth**, **understanding** and **sincerity**. These qualities will ensure a rich, secure and valuable relationship, and without them an individual will not feel valued. These, together with listening, are the basis of counselling skills.

> ### Example
>
> Margaret works with an organisation which supports people with mental health problems who live in their own homes. There is an office for the workers and at least one worker is there from 8pm to 8am. This account is in her own words.
>
> One night when I was on night shift, Elizabeth came to see me. She often does this, especially when she is feeling down. Over the last six months since Elizabeth was discharged from hospital, I have built up a good

relationship with her. On several occasions when Elizabeth has visited me in the office, she has cut her arms. When she first moved to her new home, my line manager ensured that the staff had immediate training in working with people who self-harm. I felt that this training made me and my colleagues much more understanding of Elizabeth's needs. Also, we liaise very closely with the community psychiatric nurse, the hospital social worker and Elizabeth's family. She threatened that she was going back to her home and that she was going to cut herself. I remained calm and listened to her in a manner that she knew meant that I was interested in her and felt that she should not abuse herself. By giving her the space and attention, we eventually moved on to talking about other things. In confidence she recalled her youth and that she had been abused by a relative. Her mother had refused to believe her and Elizabeth felt her mother did not want to as she would be unable to 'handle' this dilemma. I truly empathised with Elizabeth and always listened with sincerity, genuine concern and never judging her. As a result of this, I felt that we formed a very close and valuable relationship which helped her to ventilate pent-up feelings and on occasions saved her from cutting herself. As well as the genuine friendship that we have, which helps Elizabeth in that she will not abuse herself, she can convey to me what her present needs are and these can be addressed in her personal care plan.

ACTIVITY 4.3

Consider the statement 'What am I supposed to do when she tells me that she is going to self-abuse herself again?' and write down the interpersonal and communication skills that Margaret practised which helped Elizabeth.

In the above example and Activity 4.3, you may have suggested the following skills that Margaret used:

- ❏ She participated in training on self-abuse.
- ❏ She showed warmth, understanding and empathy.
- ❏ She collaborated with other professionals.
- ❏ She used good listening skills.
- ❏ She remained calm, patient and positive.
- ❏ She gave Elizabeth space and time.
- ❏ Margaret was non-judgemental and sincere.

❏ Margaret and Elizabeth were able to identify Elizabeth's needs together.

Conveying warmth

The worker who conveys warmth will be seen as a warm and accepting person. This acceptance will ensure that an individual who may be feeling helpless, threatened or embarrassed will then feel valued and worthy.

The worker may reflect warmth by non-verbal or verbal communication.

Non-verbal communication

- ❏ a warm smile (facial expression)
- ❏ open welcoming gestures
- ❏ friendly tone of voice
- ❏ confident manner – this reassures the service user that they can be helped
- ❏ offering physical help – e.g. a guiding arm to an elderly or distraught person
- ❏ general appearance of the care worker
- ❏ calm gestures and movements.

Verbal communication

- ❏ use of friendly words that show respect
- ❏ expression of a wish to help
- ❏ clear explanation of what the care worker is trying to do
- ❏ reassurance about confidentiality
- ❏ clear understanding of what has been achieved and what can be achieved.

In developing the skill of showing warmth it is important to be oneself, to be natural and genuine. If the care worker *pretends* to be interested, warm or understanding, then the individual will sense this and it will jeopardise the whole relationship.

Conveying understanding

Understanding has to be shown through **empathy, acceptance** and **being non-judgemental**. It means learning about the individual's identity and beliefs. Carl Rogers (1991) saw the idea of understanding or empathy as 'the ability to experience another person's world as if it was your own world'. Service users may have completely different life experiences from you, so it is important to try genuinely to understand the individual's thoughts and feelings. Many people who are given the opportunity of talking freely often experience great relief at being able to tell their innermost feelings without getting a negative reaction. This process is sometimes referred to as 'ventilation'. It can lower anxiety and can, if you provide warmth and acceptance, be sufficient in itself to let the person see their own solution to their problem.

Also, when individuals feel comfortable with you, they will be more likely to talk about themselves, which will enable you to learn more about them and understand their views. Understanding can grow from a conversation which conveys value for the individual. Understanding is also conveyed when you are competent in showing knowledge of a particular physical, intellectual, emotional or social need of a person.

Example

David, who works in a care home, recalls when Mr Makin came to the home:

Mr Makin, 61 years old, had lived for 50 years in a large institution. For several days he never spoke to anyone, he never asked for anything and did not venture anywhere alone in the home. I was concerned about him and when I spoke with my line manager about this, I remembered what I had learned while on my social care course about the effects that institutional life has on people. 'Patients' were never given any choice, they were told what to do, they were not allowed to wear what they wanted, and worst of all, they were never treated as an individual.

I realised then how difficult it would be for Mr Makin to change, but with continual acceptance, understanding, warmth, encouragement and genuine interest in Mr Makin, he gradually became more confident with me. We became really good friends. We discovered that we both liked football, and I said that I would try and arrange for him and me to go to a match. We arranged this and went together. Mr Makin is now a much happier person who speaks to everyone and enjoys letting us all know what he wants.

Remember the statement 'He has lived in an institution all his life. How would he know what he wants, never mind be able to tell us?'.

The above example shows the difference which 'good' practice makes to a person. Because of David's dedication to his work, showing warmth, acceptance and genuine interest in Mr Makin proved this statement to be wrong.

Conveying sincerity

Being sincere is paramount. It means that you have to be honest, open and yourself, and give to others. There is no room for acting or using language that confuses the individual. This only gives the impression that you are superior to others. When a person talks to a friend or relative, there are no barriers because each is relaxed, natural and genuinely interested. When you talk to the service user, it should be just the same. It is essential that you convey a little of what kind of person you are, and share information which may help the person feel relaxed and comfortable. In some situations this could encourage the individual to be more forthcoming with information about themselves.

Like any other skills, forming a supportive relationship with an individual improves with practice, and you should continually evaluate yourself. It is necessary for you to accept feedback from colleagues, supervisors and most importantly the service users themselves. It is possible to tell if communication is effective by the response of people. They will show trust, be honest with you and show that they enjoy your company.

Without these kind, humane ingredients, the relationship will be doomed and very difficult to redeem.

Listening skills

> 'If you are going to work with me, you have to listen to me. And you can't just listen with your ears because it will go to your head too fast. If you listen slow, with your whole body, some of what I say will enter your heart.'

> (Christine Meyer, 2004)

Listening is as important as verbally communicating. Listening should not be passive but active. This involves more than just hearing, but also concentrating on what the person is saying, responding to what has been said and then acting on it. Being a good listener involves practising all the values, principles and attributes in caring as well as the following attributes.

Being attentive

This means actively listening and concentrating on what is being said, and being aware of what is *not* being said by sensing that the individual is perhaps shy, feeling awkward, feeling embarrassed or unable to express how they feel. They may show signs of these feelings by silence, eye movements, and nervous movements like wringing their hands or turning a ring on their finger. Facial expressions, posture and other forms of body language all give clues to a person's feelings. You should try to understand these signs and allow the individual time to relax and feel confident to talk.

Using prompts

People who may be shy, nervous or hesitant about talking for various reasons may need your encouragement. This can be done, for example, by nodding at appropriate times which shows acceptance and understanding, by eye contact which shows attention is being given, and by using words and sounds like 'oh', 'really', 'mmm', showing that you know what they are saying and are happy to listen further.

Using appropriate questions

Questions may be asked to clarify what people have said and to establish more information. To encourage them to talk, it is better to use 'open' questions which invite answers that are longer and more involved. They usually start with words like 'how', 'why', 'what', 'when', 'where'. For example, rather than asking a young person, 'Do you like your new school?' which would likely be answered with a 'Yes' or 'No', it would be better to ask, 'What do you think of your new school?' You are then more likely to learn more information about how the young person feels about the school.

Using appropriate language

Each person is an individual with their own social background, culture, character and abilities. For these reasons it is necessary for you to adapt and tailor your language to suit each individual person. The choice of words, the length of what is said and the content are all important. Too often care workers, without thought, use jargon, e.g. 'goal setting', 'empowerment', 'interaction', which will only confuse people.

The age of the individual has to be considered. When speaking to an older person, for example, they should never be spoken to as if they are a child by using childish words. This is patronising and shows no respect to the person. Would you like to be spoken to in this manner? Similarly, when speaking to a child, language should be kept simple in order that the child can understand. It is useful to check, in an appropriate way, that what is being said is understood.

When working with people who have a **hearing** impairment, it is best to be familiar with sign language for individuals who use this, and know the different meanings which they attach to signs. Alternatively, an interpreter could be present. Also, when working with those who have a **visual** impairment, it is advisable to describe objects and situations. It would be ineffective and insensitive for you to show a visually impaired person something and ask 'Do you want this just now?'

Recall the statement 'I do not have the time to puzzle out what he is saying, so I just guess'. In the example below, the student who was disappointed in herself that she could not communicate with Jake was determined to learn by observing

Example

A student, on her first day in a day centre for young adults with hearing impairments, was asked to assist a young man, Jake. Jake is deaf and has very little speech. The student, inexperienced, found she had great difficulties communicating with Jake. At the end of the day she felt despondent and unsure that she would be able to continue in her placement. However, she decided that she would try harder the next day and she would find ways of communicating with Jake.

Initially she observed Jake's care worker. She learned that the care worker, through using signing, touch, giving encouragement and time, had built up a trusting relationship with Jake. She realised that it would take time and perseverance. She was given the opportunity of training in signing which she readily accepted. She learned that Jake could lip-read, so she made sure when she was talking to him that he could see her face and she spoke slowly, making sure that she formed words with her lips. She showed signs of expression on her face to suit what she was saying and also used her hands to express herself.

At first, Jake was amused by the student's efforts, but it helped to 'break the ice'. Jake responded well. Within a few weeks, she was a good friend to Jake and was able to communicate with him. She had gained confidence and Jake felt comfortable with her. The student has now formed a trusting and valuable relationship with Jake.

Example

A student who recently took up part-time employment as a care worker in a local authority home for elderly people, noticed that Madhu, an Indian woman who was in the home for a period of assessment and respite, seemed very unhappy and isolated. When she asked another care worker about Madhu, she was told that English was her second language. It had been assumed by the staff that there was no point speaking to her as she would not understand. It was the opinion of the staff that she was in the home for a short time, and that they did not have the time to communicate with her. They had attended to her physical needs, washing, dressing, giving her meals, but they had not attempted to communicate with her. When they did have to speak to her they had used inappropriate language such as 'You sit up', 'Me feed you'.

The student approached Madhu with a smile and introduced herself. She found that Madhu understood what she was saying and continued to tell her name and a little about herself. The student realised that the other members of staff had assumed that because English was Madhu's second language, she would not understand what they were saying. By not speaking quickly or shouting and by being patient and repeating some words, the student was able to communicate with Madhu. If there were words that were not understood, the student used facial expression and hand gestures. Some of the other staff noticed the attempt made by the student and they too made more effort to speak to Madhu. The student was pleased to find that after a few days Madhu seemed happier and she had made friends with other residents.

an experienced worker and also by attempting to learn sign language (real vocation). With grit and willingness she succeeded not only in enabling herself to communicate with Jake, but in forming a good and worthwhile relationship with him.

You may work with people who speak in a **different language**. This should not cause a barrier in communication, nor should the service user be made to feel inferior because they do not speak English. In this situation, an interpreter may be required. Ideally you could make an effort to learn the person's language, or at least a few words of it.

The example of Madhu above shows that the student was determined to help her in the hope that she would feel more welcome, happier and accepted. This example also relates to another of the statements: 'I have given up trying to speak to her as she never replies to me'.

Individuals who have a **learning disability** need you to be patient and capable of using words that they will understand. The length of what is being said should take into account the person's ability to understand. It may be advisable to repeat what has been said so that the individual understands. Adults should not be spoken to as if they are children, and time should be given for the person to express themselves. To aid communication, facial expressions, gestures and appropriate touch are useful.

Using the right pace and tone

The pace of the communication, like the language used, should take into account the age, the ability/disability and culture of the individual. It would be of no avail to talk on and on very quickly when in fact the person is still trying to understand what was first said. The tone of voice that you use should again be appropriate to whom is being spoken to. You should not 'talk down' to people, and there is no room for abruptness. The tone should be friendly and warm, irrespective of who is on the receiving end. Remember that 'Civility costs nothing and goes a long way'. For example, 'What do you want?' with the emphasis on *what*, could easily be replaced with 'What would you like?' said in a warm and friendly tone. The first tone and question would make the person feel that it was a bother for you, whereas the other reflects that you are genuinely interested in those you are talking to. There are times when the tone of voice has to be different, e.g. when the service user has received disturbing news, and then the tone should be comforting. You have to be sensitive to what you say and how you say it, and it should stem from a good understanding and interest in the person you are working with.

Non-verbal communication

Non-verbal communication comprises appearance, gestures and movements. There are four main ways in which non-verbal communication is used:

1. **Eye contact** – this is very useful to show that the worker is paying attention to the person when they are speaking. It also conveys sincerity and genuineness. However, it would not be appropriate to stare continually at someone; it is best to be natural.
2. **Posture** – when two people are talking, they generally feel more comfortable if they are at the same level. If you were to tower over an individual they may feel intimidated, frightened or that they

cannot move away. You should be relaxed, not so relaxed that you put your feet up, but sufficiently relaxed to be friendly and calm. Positioning of seating is important and it is better to be facing the person and leaning forward slightly, showing willingness to listen. Such mannerisms as hands in pockets, playing with hands, running hands through hair, should be avoided as these would be distracting to the person.

3. **Facial expressions** – the expression on a person's face can often convey how that person is feeling and can be used effectively to communicate feelings. Therefore it is essential that you show warmth and friendliness. It is difficult to communicate with someone who shows no emotion in their face, and it can be very unsettling. Of course, the expressions that you show should be appropriate and not signs of laughing, sneering or superiority.

4. **Physical contact/touch** – when a person is distressed, very upset or frightened then you might show understanding and empathy by giving a child a cuddle or perhaps an older person a reassuring arm around their shoulder. However, you have to take care that your concern is not misinterpreted. Knowing when physical contact is not appropriate can be difficult. Generally, when a good helping relationship has been formed with an individual, you will know whether physical contact is appropriate or not. It should be remembered that this is a controversial subject and it helps to discuss appropriate physical contact at team meetings and to come to some agreements within the team on this subject.

Communicating with children

Children are people first, and all of the communication skills discussed in this chapter are relevant when communicating with children. There are also some special considerations to take into account:

❑ Adapt to their developmental level; beware of 'talking down' to children or talking over their heads.
❑ Try to be clear, specific and straightforward.
❑ Show interest in things that interest them. This does not mean pretending to be interested in the same things, but showing that you are genuinely interested in what they are doing and saying.
❑ Listen patiently and with care. The Children's Society produced a very meaningful poster which said: 'What I need is a good listening to'.

❏ Take time doing ordinary things, without making a 'big thing' of communicating.

❏ Do not expect an instant relationship; children and young people will choose when they want to communicate with you, if you have taken the trouble to build a relationship with them.

❏ Develop sensitivity to incidental remarks or opening and closing remarks that may have great significance but which can be easily missed.

❏ Respect confidentiality while helping children to understand that not everything they may communicate to you can be kept secret; enable children to know what may happen to information they give to you and why this happens.

❏ Communicate what you mean and mean what you communicate.

❏ Remember the importance of physical comforting gestures, while being careful that these are appropriate to the child and the situation, and are within the agreed guidelines of your agency.

Exploring new and other ways to communicate

You should never say that you 'cannot communicate' with someone. Recall the oomph factor and the ingredients which make the 'impossible' work. A positive attitude will encourage you to say 'I will work out a way to communicate', just like the student in the example of Jake above. Sheer determination inspired her to explore, observe and learn skills.

Suggestions:

❏ Speak to and learn from experienced workers.

❏ Find out about training in sign language and/or other forms of communication.

❏ Know how to contact an interpreter.

❏ Learn at least some of the person's language.

❏ Never assume that the person cannot hear you or understand you.

❏ Ask the person's relatives or friends for help.

❏ Continue your personal development by embarking on further training.

❏ Remember, speaking is not the only way of communicating.

BARRIERS AND DIFFICULTIES WHICH MAY AFFECT COMMUNICATION

It is important to understand that there are situations where there are possible barriers which may impede communication. Some of these have been

ACTIVITY 4.4

You are unable to speak, write or walk following a stroke. You are able to understand what people say to you. You will need a partner for this activity.

1. Tell your partner that you are hungry.
2. Tell your partner you need to go to the toilet.
3. Tell your partner you want to go out.
4. Explain to your partner that you are uncomfortable and want to be moved.

What were your feelings during this exercise?

What did your partner do that was most helpful?

What could he or she have done that they did not do?

How did your partner feel?

Can you suggest a method of communication that would be useful in this situation?

ACTIVITY 4.5

You are unable to speak or write following a stroke. You are able to understand what people are saying to you. You cannot use your hands. You will need a partner for this activity.

1. Tell your partner that you are thirsty.
2. Tell your partner you would like the television on.
3. Tell your partner you want a friend to come and visit you.
4. Explain to your partner you are concerned about how hard they are working to look after you.
5. Tell your partner that you are worried about the future.

What were your feelings during this exercise?

What did your partner do that was most helpful?

What could he or she have done that they did not do?

How did your partner feel?

mentioned earlier in the chapter; Mr Makin who had been discharged from a long-term hospital, Jake who is deaf, Madhu who seemed unhappy and spoke only limited English. It is useful at this stage to do Activities 4.4 and 4.5, which may give you some idea about how it feels when you are unable to communicate using speech and gesture.

You need to be aware of personal and physical obstacles which impede communication and which may deter a person from expressing their feelings. Failure to understand and detect these obstacles will affect communication and make it impossible for you to understand and respond to the needs of the individual. Below is a list of possible barriers:

Personal barriers

A person who:

- is very nervous
- is distressed
- feels uncomfortable with any care worker
- feels their problems are too personal to discuss with you
- feels embarrassed
- is angry
- fears being ridiculed
- fears being abused
- fears being misunderstood
- fears being neglected
- has no self-esteem
- is wary of confidentiality
- has a different mother tongue
- feels inferior and prejudiced
- is unable to express their feelings
- is uncomfortable with age difference.

Impairment, disability and illness

A person who:

- has a hearing impairment
- has a speech impairment
- has a visual impairment
- suffers from a mental illness
- suffers from dementia

- ❏ is very depressed
- ❏ has a physical disfigurement
- ❏ has a learning disability.

It is advisable to consider the **environment** where communication is taking place.

An ideal meeting place

- ❏ is the choice of the service user
- ❏ is safe and comfortable
- ❏ is private and quiet
- ❏ is free of any interruptions
- ❏ is appropriate, with suitable lighting (especially for those with visual impairments)
- ❏ positions the seating in a friendly way
- ❏ has the care worker sitting in full view (especially for those with hearing impairment)

The care worker who is sensitive and responds to these aspects will be competent in achieving effective communication with those for whom they are caring.

ACTIVITY 4.6

Read the case studies below and write down how you could optimise communication with each person. For example, what methods are you going to use; what should you avoid doing; what might help? Think about what or who might be of assistance to you.

Case Study 1: Miss Miller

Miss Miller has recently moved to sheltered housing because she has dementia and she cannot manage on her own. There are times when she seems very confused and cannot remember where she is or those who know her.

Case Study 2: Mr Jenkins

Mr Jenkins has a hearing impairment and wears a hearing aid. On many occasions he will not use his hearing aid, especially when he attends a social club run by his church.

Case Study 3: Ms Taylor

Ms Taylor, who is staying in a care home for a short period, becomes very frustrated when she has difficulty communicating, due to a stroke which has affected her speech.

Case Study 4: Mr O'Donnell

Due to an accident while working as a lorry driver, Mr O'Donnel has lost his sight in one eye and is partially sighted in the other. He is finding it hard to adjust to his new way of life, and has reluctantly agreed to attend a resource centre twice a week.

Case Study 5: Mr Kederinski

Mr Kederinski has learning difficulties and has been discharged recently from a long-stay hospital where he had spent 20 years. He is now living in the community.

Case Study 6: Mrs Hussein

Mrs Hussein is an elderly lady who has lived in Britain for ten years. She lives in her own home with the help of home support workers. She has little command of English and has difficulty speaking to her carers.

Case Study 7: Andrew Patel

Andrew, aged ten, has epilepsy and an autistic spectrum disorder. He frequently becomes frustrated and angry when his needs are not met immediately.

Case Study 8: Julie Donaldson

Julie is 14 years old and is looked after in a care home for children and young people. Her parents, both drug abusers, were unable to cope with her increasingly disruptive behaviour and often left her alone at weekends.

Improving communication

Case Study 1: Miss Miller

- Use short, simple sentences; speak slowly.
- Talk about one thing at a time.
- Find similar ways of saying things, or repeat if necessary.
- Use facial expressions and gestures.

- Objects and pictures can help the service user who is confused.
- Consult relatives or friends
- Do not shout or contradict the service user.
- Be patient and understanding.
- Show the person what you are talking about.

Case Study 2: Mr Jenkins

- Try not to surprise the service user, be sure you can be seen approaching.
- Make sure you have the service user's attention.
- Sit close to the service user.
- Sit where the light is on your face; this way the service user can see your facial expressions.
- Do not cover your mouth; speak normally in sentences.
- Have patience, do not rush, and use different words if necessary.
- Make sure the hearing aid is working properly.
- Use a writing pad or sign language if necessary.
- Use gestures, facial expressions.

Case Study 3: Ms Taylor

- Do not shout; speak slowly and clearly.
- Do not say too much at once; give the service user time to respond.
- Do not speak to the service user in childish language.
- Use a writing pad and pen.
- Use facial expression and gestures.
- Be patient and calm.

Case Study 4: Mr O'Donnell

- Tell the service user who you are.
- Do not surprise the service user; approach gently.
- You could use touch to let the service user know that you are there.
- Do not shout; speak clearly.
- Let the service user speak.
- Describe objects and events.
- Explain when you are leaving or someone else is approaching.
- Make sure that lighting is not too bright.

Case Study 5: Mr Kederinski

- ❑ Support the service user in expressing himself.
- ❑ Let the service user take his time; do not rush.
- ❑ Support your verbal communication with gestures and touch.
- ❑ Work at showing the service user that he is valued.
- ❑ Do not hurry to do things; give the service user the opportunity to say what he wants.
- ❑ Do not speak in a childish way.

Case Study 6: Mrs Hussein

- ❑ Speak slowly.
- ❑ Speak clearly without raising your voice.
- ❑ If you have not been understood, repeat what you have said using the same words.
- ❑ Keep sentences simple.
- ❑ Do not use expressions only used in English such as 'it's raining cats and dogs'.
- ❑ Do not use broken English such as 'you happy'.
- ❑ Make sure the service user understands what you have said before moving on to something else.
- ❑ Try using pictures or objects.
- ❑ Make an effort to learn a few words of the service user's language.

Case Study 7: Andrew Patel

- ❑ Communicate clearly and calmly.
- ❑ Be specific and straightforward.
- ❑ Listen attentively to what Andrew is saying, and respond so that he knows that you have heard him.
- ❑ Spend time getting to know him so that you know what works when he is frustrated or angry.

Case Study 8: Julie Donaldson

- ❑ Find out about Julie's likes and dislikes and show a genuine interest in things that interest her.
- ❑ Do not avoid difficult subjects, but make sure you have enough time to listen if Julie wants to talk to you about these.
- ❑ Do not be afraid to suggest more specialist help for Julie if you feel that you cannot help her enough.
- ❑ Use non-verbal as well as verbal communication.

❏ Communicate with Julie as part of doing other things, e.g. preparing a meal or doing an enjoyable activity.
❏ Do not treat Julie as if she was a small child; do not talk down to her.

THE IMPORTANCE AND IMPLICATIONS OF RECORDING, RECEIVING, TRANSMITTING AND ORGANISING INFORMATION

> **It may seem a chore, but clear and concise report writing is vital for maintaining good standards of residential care.**
>
> (Clough, R 2004)

Care providers are akin to any other business. In business, administration is at the centre of success and if records, reports, accounts and updates on the choices of customers are not kept, the company will go bankrupt. The difference between commercial business and care business is that instead of dealing with products and losing goods and money, in care we are providing a service to meet the needs of people, human beings. Is it not then more important that we keep records, update reports on the needs of people, share information with colleagues and be particular in storing paperwork and adhering to confidentiality?

Recording is important because it:

❏ helps in the planning and organisation of health and social care
❏ helps in the continuation of good practice
❏ meets the values and principles of care such as promoting individuals' rights, choices and preferences
❏ can avoid discrimination
❏ updates the needs in a person's care plan
❏ ensures that all workers are informed of any changes.

If recording, receiving, transmitting and organising information is not being practised:

❏ National minimum standards and national care standards may not be met.
❏ The workplace may fail the criteria of the Care Commission.
❏ Legislation such as the Data Protection Act 1998 may not be adhered to.
❏ The quality of life and future of an individual may be adversely affected.

Example

When checking financial records, the manager of a voluntary organisation that supports people with learning difficulties realised that a young man, John, had in the last six months spent an excessive amount of money on clothes. She double-checked the shop receipts given to her by John's support worker which recorded men's clothes and cost. She then spoke with John's support worker, and said that she was concerned at the amount of money spent and that she would need to check with John. She made an appointment with John to visit him in his own home with his support worker. She asked John if she could look in his wardrobe, to which he agreed, only to find that not many of the clothes that had been bought were there. The manager then visited the shop where the clothes had been bought and was able to look at the actual items bought. She discovered that half the clothes bought were not in John's size. On return to the workplace, the manager questioned the support worker on what she had found out, and then the support worker admitted that she had bought clothes for her own son with John's money.

This abuse might never have come to light had there not been procedures in place for recording John's finances and also the manager checking the accounts. Also, when the support worker attended an inquiry, the records were there to prove the case.

Example

When Mary started her shift, her colleague Lillian was finishing her shift. As she was in a hurry, she rushed out without saying much to Mary. The first thing Mary did was to look at the diary to learn that Mrs Smith's son had visited her earlier in the day. He had been very drunk when he came into the home, and he had caused a great deal of disruption which had really upset Mrs Smith and others. Mrs Smith had said later to Lillian and other workers that she did not want to see her son again as this was not the first time that he had upset her. Lillian had recorded this information. Later that night, when Mrs Smith was sleeping, her son called at the home. Mary went to the door but refused him entry and told him to go away, that his mother was sleeping and she could not see him. Fortunately, even though he was still under the influence of alcohol, he went away. Mary recorded in the diary exactly what had happened. As a result of Lillian recording in the diary the incident of Mrs Smith's son, Mary was alerted to the possible danger of him entering the home, and also that Mrs Smith did not want to see him.

Receiving information

Information can be received in different forms.

Figure 4.3 Forms of information

Telephone

- ❏ Answer pleasantly.
- ❏ Speak clearly and politely.
- ❏ Say who you are.
- ❏ Ask whom the caller wishes to speak to.

- Clarify exactly what the caller is saying.
- If the caller is not sure, help him by suggesting whom he might need to speak to.
- Take any message.
- Repeat to the caller to make sure the message is accurate.
- **Never** disclose any personal or confidential information.
- **Always** write down the message and either give it to the appropriate person immediately if it is urgent (if you are not sure then ask your line manager) or put in the appropriate place for messages.
- **Never** leave messages carelessly lying anywhere, in case they are mislaid or read by someone who is not privy to the information.

Fax

- If this is part of your role, then check the front page of the fax to determine whom it is for; on this page it will tell how many pages there should be, so check and then pass on to the appropriate person.
- If it is addressed to you, then deal with it immediately.

Computers and emails

Beware of receiving or retrieving information from the computer, as it is governed by the Data Protection Act 1998 (see below). Be sure that you do have the right to be using it in the first place. Be sure that the information is genuinely to provide care for someone and not to satisfy your own curiosity; *never* tell anyone, relatives, friends, any information about another individual; *never* print out anyone's details unless it is necessary and you have permission from your line manager.

There will be procedures within a workplace for the receiving of emails, such as printing them out and giving to the appropriate person, or sending a message to whomever the email concerns.

Never leave confidential computer files open. If for whatever reason you are called away, *always* close the file and return to the home page. Confidentiality has to be adhered to at all times.

Verbal information

Information may come from the service user, their relatives or friends, colleagues, or other professionals such as social worker, doctor, community psychiatric nurse. When this information is received, it should be recorded immediately and accurately. When discussing any information with the above people, ensure that it is in private and that no one else can hear what is being said. Be sensitive to what an individual may tell you, because what you think is trivial may not be to them. Never judge, jest or laugh. Listen, reassure and then decide if you need to consult with another colleague or your line manager. Record accurately, legibly and sufficiently.

Mail

- ❏ Check that you are allowed to open mail.
- ❏ Do not open if it is marked private and personal.
- ❏ Give it to the addressee immediately.
- ❏ Never open mail that is for a service user unless you have their permission.
- ❏ Mail must be opened immediately.
- ❏ Record on the letter when it was received.
- ❏ Attend to it if required and then file appropriately.
- ❏ Never leave correspondence lying about.

Recording information

Recording involves:

- ❏ writing reports, minutes of meetings
- ❏ writing down messages
- ❏ writing in the daily diary
- ❏ updating care plans
- ❏ sending a fax
- ❏ recording incidents such as accidents, complaints, unacceptable behaviour
- ❏ writing risk assessments.
- ❏ writing on behalf of service users such as birthday cards, letters.

The essential components of record-keeping involve:

- ❏ being accurate, clear and legible
- ❏ keeping to the point and ensuring relevance
- ❏ recording dates, times and names of writer and other key people
- ❏ whenever possible and appropriate, sharing recording with service users and enabling them to contribute to and understand records and reports concerning them

- ❏ writing in a way which can be understood, without using jargon or 'buzz' words
- ❏ attending to spelling and grammar
- ❏ distinguishing opinions from facts and avoiding unnecessary labels and judgements
- ❏ recording and reporting any signs and symptoms that indicate a change in the condition and care needs of the individual
- ❏ maintaining confidentiality by keeping records in a safe, secure place
- ❏ passing on information appropriately, while respecting confidentiality
- ❏ filing correctly
- ❏ ensuring that you know and follow legal and organisational procedures in relation to recording.

Storing information

It is of utmost importance that information is stored and filed efficiently, correctly and in a fashion that makes the information easy to retrieve. Should an emergency arise and information be required immediately, it is important that it can be retrieved as quickly as possible. If the records have been written inaccurately or illegibly, this could cause serious mistakes to be made.

Information has to be stored in a safe and secure place, and it should be made clear who has the authority to retrieve the information.

- ❏ Always put away all records as soon as possible when they have been completed.
- ❏ Appreciate the importance of records and their contents.
- ❏ Do not leave files lying about.
- ❏ Mark files confidential.
- ❏ Ensure that records have been completed, are accurate, dated and signed.
- ❏ Know how to access files and who should have access to them.
- ❏ Realise the implications if files go missing.

Transmitting information

Transmitting information can be done by telephone, fax, emails or letter, and it is essential that the information is sent at an agreed time, on time and is accurate. Attention has to be paid to what is actually sent, details given and who has to receive the information.

Detail to be remembered:

❑ Ensure that the person who is receiving the information is entitled to the information.
❑ Always mark it confidential.
❑ Check that the information goes to the correct person.
❑ Never pass on information that the individual has not agreed to.
❑ Type or wordprocess letters.
❑ Be accurate, precise, date and sign.
❑ Keep a copy of what you have sent.
❑ File copy immediately.

Retrieving information

If receiving, recording and storing have been carried out correctly with accuracy, retrieving information should be very easy. If you should have difficulty in retrieving information, especially if it causes any problems, then speak to your line manager and ask that this is addressed. 'Prevention is better than cure' and may well save a real emergency.

You may not like having to write up records, and may never have thought when going into your job that you would need to. However it is now expected and important that you learn. With practice it will become easier and you might even enjoy it!

Legislation relating to receiving, recording and organising information

Data Protection Act 1998

The Data Protection Act (DPA) gives people the right to see personal information held about them. This includes computerised records held by private companies, employers and public sector organisations such as hospitals and doctors, housing departments and social services departments. People can also see housing, education, social services/social work and health records which are kept on manual files. There are exemptions and these are to third-party information where the author has refused consent to access (e.g. letters from relatives held in social services files) and where there may be a serious risk of harm.

If someone wants to see their record, they should apply in writing to the relevant organisation. The Act means that if you work in care settings, people may seek access to their records. You are under a clear obligation to ensure that what you write is accurate and that any opinions can be justified. Dalrymple and Burke (1995) note:

> One of the steps towards empowerment of users is the sharing of information. A concrete way of sharing information is through access to one's records. Sharing of records equalises the relationship between users and the provider of a service and enhances participation . . .. Sharing information in an open and honest way demonstrates respect.

Freedom of Information Act 2001/Freedom of Information (Scotland) Act 2002

The Freedom of Information Acts(FOI) are:

> challenged with the task of reversing the working premise that everything is secret, unless otherwise stated, to a position where everything is public unless it falls into specified excepted cases.

(Lord Chancellor, 2001)

The Data Protection Act already gives people the right to access information about themselves. Freedom of information legislation extends this right of access, as far as public authorities are concerned, to allow access to all the types of information held, whether personal or non-personal. This may include information about third parties, although the public authority will have to take account of the Data Protection Act 1998 before releasing any personal information.

The FOI Act gives two related rights:

1. The right to be told whether the information exists.
2. The right to receive the information, but taking account of the Data Protection Act.

The right to access the information held by public authorities can be exercised by anyone, worldwide. The Act is also retrospective. The right to access information came into effect on 1 January 2005.

This practice described in the Example opposite reflects the necessity of monitoring, recording and passing on information in order to keep Alan's care plan up to date and concise, and so that everyone working with him is aware of his needs. It also highlights the positive communication and practice of Kathleen with Alan.

ACTIVITY 4.7

1. Write down a message which you have received and ask a colleague to read it and confirm she understands exactly what the message means.
2. Ask what the policies and procedures are in your workplace about storing and filing information.
3. Record information that a person has given and judge if it will help to improve delivery of care to them.
4. Write a summary of the Acts (legislation) that are relevant to recording information and what this means for how you keep records.

Example

Kathleen works in a residential unit for people who have cerebral palsy, and the following actual practice is an example of the importance, necessity and benefits of recording.

Alan has physical disabilities which affect his body from functioning correctly. His bowels do not work properly without the aid of prescribed medication. Alan's doctor stated that he requires an enema once a week. Alan accepted this and let me know with his Bliss board (a board that has symbols, words and pictures which help Alan communicate), by showing me the 'smiley' face. I communicated with Alan with this board. However, I have been with Alan so long that I understand a lot of what he is saying to me by his facial and body gestures. I explained to Alan that we would start keeping a chart as part of our monitoring system and Alan agreed to this. I assured Alan that this chart would be kept in the medication folder so that the senior staff have easy access to this sheet.

The purpose of this chart is so that when one of the workers is administering Alan's medication, they can see instantly which day and date he requires to have his enema administered. Any issues regarding continence or incontinence are always discussed with Alan in the privacy of his own room in a manner and at a level which demonstrate sensitivity towards him. All changes which were discussed and made with Alan by the doctor are recorded in his care plan for future reference.

The dietician, Sue, is also involved in supporting Alan as Alan's doctor contacted her when his medication changed. Sue advised Alan on his dietary needs to help Alan and staff deal with his constipation. Alan, Sue and myself arranged a meeting to review Alan's food and drink intake, because Alan's doctor recommended that Alan should stop taking his iron tablets, and he is only receiving his enema once a week now instead of twice a week.

Sue made suggestions to Alan on what foods he should try and incorporate into his diet so that his iron levels would remain at an appropriate level which will be monitored by his doctor. Sue asked Alan what kind of foods he liked, and she noted this and drew up a suggested menu plan that Alan should try. Alan agreed and gestured to Sue and myself that he was happy with this. Sue explained to Alan that by eating these foods it would also help his bowels to move, and that the colour of the bowel movements would change because he would not be taking the iron tablets. Sue informed Alan and me that she would monitor Alan's progress with the changes made to his medication and diet.

Two weeks later when I arrived at the workplace, I noticed that Alan appeared to be in discomfort. I asked him if he was all right and he indicated to me by moving his head 'no'. I asked him if he wanted to go to his bedroom and he gestured 'yes'. When we arrived at his bedroom he indicated to me that his tummy was sore. I asked him if he would like to lie on top of his bed, to which he indicated 'yes'. As I used the hoist to move Alan out of his wheelchair onto his bed, he appeared very agitated. When I noticed that Alan was soiled and it was through his clothes, Alan gestured to me that he was sorry and I replied to him not to worry that it would not take us long to change his clothes. Alan indicated to me that it had happened twice already that day.

I explained to Alan that I would need to let the senior staff member know about what had happened and he agreed. The senior spoke to Alan and explained that further monitoring would continue for a short time, and if there were any further changes then we should notify Alan's doctor and in the meantime contact Sue for advice. Alan agreed to this and everything that happened was recorded in Alan's care plan.

ACTIVITY 4.8

Describe at least two ways in which recording information was important in Alan's care.

And finally . . .

- ❑ Always be tidy and organised.
- ❑ Never leave recording until later – do it there and then.
- ❑ Write down messages yourself. Do not leave it to someone else.
- ❑ Ensure that you have used the correct names. This may seem obvious, but it is so necessary.
- ❑ Return files immediately and correctly.
- ❑ Seek training in using the computer, which saves time and can be much more efficient.
- ❑ Do not forget to share this part of your practice with service users, and involve them as much as possible.
- ❑ **Enjoy this part of your work**, as it also reflects your respect for the people with whom you work.

SUMMARY

Interpersonal skills, including communication, are the foundation of caring, valuable relationships with service users, and your main tools as a care worker. They determine to a large extent the success or failure of all other work. Effective communication rests upon a sound value base and may be verbal or non-verbal. Listening skills are vital and so is that bit extra: oomph. There are some special points to bear in mind where there may be barriers to communication and when communicating with children and young people.

The all-important acts of recording, storing, transmitting and retrieving information are vital skills to develop, and demonstrate your respect for service users. Recording should be done whenever possible in partnership with them. The philosophy of person-centred planning in Chapter 8 emphasises the individual's participation in their own care plans. Competently using interpersonal skills in practice optimises this possibility.

FIVE KEY POINTS

1. Interpersonal skills rest upon a sound value base, effective communication and qualities such as warmth, understanding and sincerity.
2. If you go beyond what is necessary, give that bit of extra oomph and actively listen to what is communicated, it is likely that you will be more effective in helping people.
3. Practice is enhanced through making the effort to overcome barriers to communication, giving consideration to the particular needs of individuals, including children and young people.
4. Accurate, timely and shared recording is an aid to good practice and demonstrates respect and concern for the individual.
5. The Data Protection Act 1998, the Freedom of Information Act 2001 and the Freedom of Information (Scotland) Act 2002 relate to the rights of individuals in relation to information held.

THREE QUESTIONS

1. What are appropriate ways (including from the individual) to obtain information about a person's communication abilities? How may these vary in different settings and for different individuals?
2. How would you confirm that the information that you have gained about an individual is correct?
3. How might you alter or modify your communication with someone who:

    ❑   has had a stroke
    ❑   is deaf
    ❑   has dementia
    ❑   has a mental health problem
    ❑   has learning difficulties
    ❑   does not want to speak to you

RECOMMENDED READING

BIESTEK, F.P. (1961) *The Casework Relationship*. London: George Allen and Unwin. A classic work which looks at the importance of relationships and the principles upon which these are based.

ROGERS, J. (1990) *Caring for People, Help at the Frontline*. Milton Keynes: Open University. A warmly written, practical and relatively short introduction to care practice.

TOSSELL, D. and WEBB, R. (1994) *Inside the Caring Services*, 2nd edn. London: Edward Arnold. Provides an 'insider's view' of the caring services with helpful guidance about communication, among other things.

NELSON-JONES, R. (1988) *Practical Counselling and Helping Skills*. London: Cassell. An excellent book to read more about the qualities and skills required to build meaningful helping relationships.

Figure 4.4

CHAPTER 5

HEALTH AND SAFETY

Doris Graham

By the end of this chapter you should be able to:

- ❑ monitor and maintain the safety and security of the working environment
- ❑ promote health and safety in the working environment
- ❑ minimise risks arising from emergencies.

The content of this chapter provides underpinning content and context for all care qualifications. It relates especially to the following: NVQ and SVQ level 2, 3, and 4 Core units HSC22: Support the health and safety of yourself and individuals; HSC32: Promote, monitor and maintain health, safety and security in the working environment; HSC42: Contribute to the development and maintenance of healthy and safe practices in the working environment.

INTRODUCTION

Most students approach this subject with a feeling of gloom – 'Not health and safety again; that is all you ever hear. It is all just policies, procedures and legislation'. And yes, to an extent you would be right, but only to an extent. There are numerous pieces of legislation and lots of practices to be observed – but boring? I don't think so. Let me put it this way. Before I started writing this chapter, I probably had similar feelings to yours about the subject, and then a thought came to me about just how important this subject really is for people working in both health and social care. Interestingly, the thought came to me, not when I was studying health and safety but when I was teaching psychology to a group of care workers. We were looking at Maslow's Hierarchy of Needs (Maslow, A 1954). I must have taught this class on many occasions, when suddenly it jumped out at me that the first two levels of basic needs, which all individuals strive to achieve, are **health and safety**. That is when I realised that I would be writing one of the most important chapters in the entire book.

Health and safety are often regarded as just common sense. But they are clearly much more than that. Years ago, they were considered important only in so-called 'dangerous' industries such as coal mining, steel making and construction, where injuries and fatalities were more commonplace than today. Health and safety were then a much more simplistic affair. I can recall only too clearly a well known government public safety campaign which appeared on television. Find someone over the age of 40 and tell them the first line of this anonymous poem. You will be amazed how many of them are able to remember it!

> Sir Isaac Newton told us why
> An apple falls down from the sky,
> And from this fact it's very plain
> All other objects do the same.
> A bolt, a brick, a bar, a cup
> Invariably fall down not up,
> And every common working tool
> Is governed by the self same rule:
> If, at work, you drop a spanner
> It travels in a downward manner.
> So when you handle tools up there
> Let your watchword be 'take care'.

Today, health and safety feature not only at work but in every aspect of your life: on transport, when you go shopping, go on holiday, where you study, in the places you worship, or even in your own home. However, it is in the workplace that you, as workers, share the responsibility with your employers to ensure that the working environment is a safe place for everyone who uses that environment. This includes individuals, workers, key people and others.

Responsibilities of employers	Responsibilities of employees
Employers must, as far as is reasonably practicable, safeguard the health, safety and welfare of employees.	Employees must take reasonable care of their own health and safety and those of others who may be affected by their acts or omissions.
Employers must prepare, and revise as necessary, a written statement of safety policy.	Employees must also cooperate with their employer so far as is necessary to enable the employer to comply with his/her duties.
Employers must consult with employees on health and safety matters.	It is an offence for anyone intentionally or recklessly to interfere with or misuse anything provided in the interests of hygiene.

Figure 5.1 The Health and Safety Act 1974

The main piece of legislation covering the workplace is the Health and Safety Act 1974. This is a comprehensive piece of legislation which spawned many later, related laws about health and safety. The Act outlines the responsibilities of both employers and employees in the workplace. They are outlined in Figure 5.1.

Although it may appear at first glance that employers and employees have different responsibilities, it is clear that both are charged with the safety of the environment in which they work and the safety of all individuals who are in that environment. That working environment now covers a variety of care settings in which you, as a worker, could find yourself working.

ACTIVITY 5.1

Can you list all the possible working environments that provide care for individuals?

Care of individuals comes in many forms. Here are some of the environments I thought of:

- ❏ residential care
- ❏ hospital ward

❏ supported accommodation
❏ hostel
❏ individual's own home
❏ GP's surgery
❏ small group home
❏ day care centre
❏ sheltered housing
❏ clinic
❏ hospice.

This list is not exhaustive and you have probably thought of many more that are not on my list. What the list does show is that there is a variety of working environments in which you could find yourself working and, in each one of these, health and safety are of paramount importance.

MONITORING AND MAINTAINING THE SAFETY AND SECURITY OF THE WORKING ENVIRONMENT

Health and safety are an integral part of the work you do to provide care for individuals. As with all aspects of care, your practice must be underpinned by legal and organisational requirements on equality, diversity, discrimination and rights. You must also provide active support which promotes the individual's rights, choices, and wellbeing. That is fine, I hear you say – but can it be that simple? Well, as in all care work, we may face issues that cause dilemmas.

ACTIVITY 5.2

Look at the case study below and then answer the question: Do you think Joseph behaved in a safe manner?

Joseph is a nightshift worker in a nursing home for 20 residents. Joseph is a smoker. One other member of staff sleeps on the premises.

Emma, a woman in her 90s, is also a smoker. At home, she always had a cigarette in bed before she went to sleep. When she came into the home, she pleaded with Joseph to let her smoke in bed. Joseph knew that there was a strict policy about smoking in the bedrooms, but he knew that it settled Emma down for the night and stopped her wandering during the night looking for cigarettes. He made a point of sitting with her while she had a cigarette and in fact he had one as well, and they had a pleasant time chatting together before she went off to sleep. Joseph made sure that both cigarettes were safely disposed of.

You might think on first reading that Joseph was indeed behaving in a safe and caring manner. He was promoting an individual's choice (to have a cigarette) and acting safely by sitting with her and making sure that she had finished her cigarette.

Now look at it from a health and safety point of view.

- ❏ What if Joseph is suddenly called away on an emergency, leaving Emma with a lighted cigarette?
- ❏ What if Emma starts to smoke when Joseph is not there?
- ❏ There is a strict policy on smoking that must be followed by everyone using the building.

Fire remains one of the greatest threats to safety in care establishments. In February 2004, a fire in the Rose Park Care Home in Lanarkshire, Scotland, caused the deaths of 14 residents. In retrospect, Joseph was not acting in a safe manner. He should report the matter to his line manager and discuss some way of working through the problem, e.g. by encouraging Emma to have her last cigarette in the smoke room.

Working with and resolving conflicts over the individual's right to choose and the impact on their own health and safety will no doubt arise in your work with service users. Individuals may choose to smoke, drink too much alcohol, use illegal drugs, use prescribed medication in excess, eat food which damages their health (especially those who have diabetes), and eat foods which make them overweight. Individuals do, of course, have the right to express their needs and preferences, but in situations where there is a danger to themselves or others, you, as a care worker, should assist them to understand and take responsibility for promoting their own health and care, and support them to assess and manage risks to their health and wellbeing. Offering support, providing advice, and seeking support from outside agencies such as drug or alcohol groups, are some ways in which you can support people to promote their own health and care. Working with the care team and the individual to provide a care package to meet the needs of the individual is the most effective means of resolving these conflicts and dilemmas.

We will now look more closely at how we can achieve a safe working environment and continue to keep it safe. To do this, we will look at five main areas:

1. right of entry
2. keeping property and valuables secure

3. hazards – hazardous equipment and materials, spillages, body fluids, clinical waste, disposal of waste, laundry, drugs and medicine
4. aggressive and violent people
5. reporting and recording health and safety issues.

Right of entry

All individuals have the right to feel safe in the place where they live, whether this is a residential home, hospital or their own home. To ensure that feeing of safety, you have to check people's right to enter, be in or around the premises in which you are working and take appropriate actions to deal with people who do not have that right. Organisations should have procedures which apply to these, and workers should be aware of these and always follow any guidelines.

In large organisations such as hospitals, employees normally wear some form of easily identifiable uniforms and identity badges. The badges may also have a photograph and built-in 'swipe' system, which allows access to secure areas. Employees may also be given entry codes to secure doors, and many hospitals now have CCTV equipment and buzzer entry systems on some wards, e.g. baby and children's wards.

In care homes and day centres, workers normally do not wear uniforms but may wear badges as proof of identity. Some work environments may have a reception area to which all visitors should report and where they may be given a visitor's badge. If there is no formal practice, you should be aware of visitors on the premises and be vigilant. A member of senior staff should make staff aware if there is to be a visit from the utility companies such as gas, electricity or water, and workers from these agencies should all carry identification. All visitors who represent outside agencies, such as health, social work, Care Commission inspectors, plumbers or electricians, should, unless known to staff be required to produce evidence of identity.

ACTIVITY 5.3

Describe what guidelines you would put in place to ensure that only designated people were allowed the right of entry to the following:

- ❏ a hospital ward
- ❏ a residential home
- ❏ a day centre.

What is the appropriate action to take if you encounter someone who does not have the right to be in or around the premises? Again, organisations should provide staff with guidelines. You should familiarise yourself with frequent visitors from external agencies. If you do not recognise a visitor, you should always be polite and ask if you can help them. If they are from an outside agency, ask for proof of identity and escort them to a senior member of staff or to the reception area. Do not direct them to an area of the building, always take them. You are advised never to tackle an intruder whom you encounter on the premises. Call for assistance from other staff or the police if required.

If a visitor asks to see someone, always check with the individual first to find out if they wish to receive the visitor. This is very important, as people have the right to choose whether or not to receive a visitor. If the person does refuse to see someone, then the worker should inform the visitor in an assertive manner that the person does not wish to see them, rather than falling into the trap of telling white lies such as 'they are sleeping'. You should be aware that this might be upsetting for the visitor. However, you should advise the visitor that if the individual changes their mind, you will contact them. You might take a contact telephone number for the visitor but you should not take any messages from them, as this may upset the person in your care.

This may be a very difficult area for you to deal with, especially if relatives are insistent. You should seek advice from a senior member of staff, especially if the individual is very vulnerable, e.g. has dementia, learning difficulties, communication difficulties, is very ill, or is a child. There should be some mention of acceptable visitors in an individual's care plan in these circumstances.

Care in the community now means that more individuals live in their own home, and this situation demands special consideration of who has right of entry. Many people who live on their own are vulnerable and may need additional support from workers. The police provide information on how to deal with bogus callers or telephone calls. You are advised to provide individuals with the relevant information about this, as well as provide short bullet-pointed lists at the front door and at the phone to remind them. Several local authorities now have 'Safe as Houses' and 'Care and Repair' schemes, which provide protection for vulnerable people who live alone. The Homewatch (known as Neighbourhood Watch in Britain) Scheme, first introduced from the USA to Millington, Cheshire in 1982, is now becoming popular in many areas, and has a special remit in 'keeping an eye out' for vulnerable people who live alone. It may in some instances be prudent to inform the local police that a vulnerable person is living alone in their area.

People who live alone may be vulnerable to unwanted visitors, either relatives or friends. Of course, people do have the choice and the right to admit anyone they wish into their own home, and these rights have to be respected. However, you should be aware that some visitors may prey on vulnerable people and workers should be vigilant. As you cannot be with the individual on a 24-hour basis, it is critical that you report immediately any signs of abuse of which you may become aware. This may take many forms including physical, emotional, sexual or financial.

Keeping property and valuables safe

Most individuals have personal possessions which are precious to them, whether these items are valuable or not. To ensure that these items are kept safely for individuals, organisations should have some policies for recording and storing them, and you should be aware of these.

Most organisations have some system whereby all items are recorded on admission or as required. This will normally be some type of book that should be signed by the individual (if possible) or relative and at least one member of staff. More valuable items may be recorded separately and may require the signature of a senior member of staff. Valuables should be kept in a locked area and only designated staff should have access. It is not advisable to keep items of great value or large sums of money on the premises. Individuals should be given advice about how to deposit such valuables in a bank or other secure area.

Dealing with hazards

- ❏ A hazard is something with the potential to cause harm.
- ❏ A risk is the chance, high or low, that someone will be harmed by that hazard.

As you will no doubt anticipate, the number of potential hazards in the working environment is numerous.

As a worker, you have responsibilities in relation to hazards:

1. You need to be aware of potential hazards.
2. You need to deal with hazards, if appropriate, by taking individual action.
3. You need to report hazards that you are unable to deal with to your manager, so that they then become an organisational responsibility.

Hazards come in many shapes and forms. We will examine three main sources of hazards:

1. Equipment.
2. Hazardous materials – chemicals, body fluids, laundry, drugs.
3. Aggressive and violent people.

Equipment

Equipment comes in all shapes and sizes, from the simplest to the most complex. This may range from hi-tech hospital machines, to lifting and moving equipment, to a vacuum cleaner, kettle or washing bowl. All equipment is designed to assist the user to carry out a job in a safe manner, both to themselves and to the people they are assisting.

Three general rules apply to the use of equipment:

1. Safe use of equipment.
2. Care of equipment.
3. Reporting of unsafe equipment.

Employers have a duty, in law, to provide safe equipment. You, as a worker, have a duty in law to use that equipment safely. You should receive training in the use of all specialist equipment, and you should always follow the guidelines given to you. If you have any doubts about the safety of any equipment you are asked to use, even if you are unsure, you should stop using the equipment immediately, and report it to the appropriate person. Often workers, especially those who are new or unqualified, feel uncertain about reporting unsafe equipment to their superiors in case they are labelled as 'fussy' or 'troublemakers'. You will remember the quote at the beginning of the chapter – 'health and safety are everyone's business'. I cannot emphasise strongly enough that even if you are unsure, you should always err on the side of caution and report anything, no matter how small, to a superior. After all, your own or others' safety could be put at risk.

ACTIVITY 5.4

Take a minute to jot down all the equipment you use in your workplace. You may be surprised at the number. Remember, if you use a kitchen, to include all the items you would use there.

Example

Nothabo was recently employed as a care assistant in a nursing home for older adults, many of whom require assistance with washing. In her first week, she was asked to clean the plastic bowls used for bed-bathing individuals. No one had shown her how to carry out this task. The only instructions given were 'to make sure she made a thorough job of it'.

Keen to make a good impression, Nothabo took all the bowls into the designated washing area. She washed them in hot soapy water and disinfectant, and to give them an extra good clean, scrubbed them with abrasive pads she found in a box in the cupboard under the sink.

Satisfied she had done a good job, she dried them with paper towels and stacked them neatly on top of each other and put them away in the cupboard. No one had provided Nothabo with the proper training, and so she was unable to carry out the task in a manner that took care of the washing bowls.

The correct way to clean these bowls was to wash them with hot soapy water and disinfectant but *not* to use any abrasive material on them, as this roughens the surface and provides a perfect place for micro-organisms (germs) to stick to and multiply.

Also, the bowls needed to be thoroughly dried with disposable towels, and *not* stacked inside each other but stored upside down in a pyramid to allow air to circulate through them.

Taking care of equipment is also a vital part of health and safety. People can be careless with equipment, sometimes deliberately or sometimes because they have not been given the correct instruction on the proper care procedures.

Hazardous materials

The Control of Substances Hazardous to Health Regulations 1999, usually referred to as COSHH, require employers to prevent or control exposure to hazardous substances such as chemicals, dust, fumes and micro-organisms. Employers are required to protect everyone who is present in the working environment.

In a care environment, hazardous substances fall into two main categories:

1. Cleaning materials and related products.
2. Clinical waste.

All workers should receive training in the risks and precautions to be taken when working with hazardous substances. There should be a COSHH file which clearly outlines the type of substances kept in the workplace, where and how they are stored, the type of labels on the containers, the effects of the substances and how to deal with an emergency involving any of the substances.

In care settings, the most common types of materials are cleaning materials, disinfectants, bleaches and pesticides. None of these substances should be used without workers receiving clear guidelines for their use. For example, some commonly used household products which may be relatively harmless when used on their own can become extremely dangerous when mixed or even used together. A good example of this is that some types of toilet cleaner and bleach mixed together may give off chlorine gas!

All types of cleaning materials and related products should be stored in the correct manner, in a safe place, in safe containers which have safety lids and caps, and should be correctly labelled. It is important that products are always kept in their own containers and labels are not changed. If you are supporting an individual in their own home, it is important that you help them to store their cleaning materials safely. Always check that cleaners etc. have not been decanted into other containers such as lemonade bottles or cartons, as in the past there have been deaths caused by people mistaking cleaning fluids or bleach for a drink.

Dealing with spillages

Spillages fall into two main categories:

1. Chemical-based products.
2. Body fluids.

All workers should receive training in how to deal with spillages of chemical-based products. These products may come in many forms – liquid, powder, cream, aerosol, spray. Each container should be clearly marked with a yellow triangle hazard symbol which will have a picture of the potential hazard and words to describe the hazard. The most common ones are listed below:

- ❑ Danger Highly flammable material
- ❑ Dangerous Chemicals
- ❑ Danger Poison
- ❑ Danger Caustic
- ❑ Danger Corrosive Substance.

Any spillages of these products, which have a hazard symbol, should be treated with care. You should check with the COSHH file, or a senior member of staff if you need assistance, to find out what precautions you should take to deal with a spillage, and you should follow any guidelines given. This may involve the use of protective clothing and gloves, apron or even goggles. If you are in any doubt, always ask for assistance, and if you have any concerns about the storage methods, use, or types of materials kept in your working environment, then you should report this immediately to your line manager who will then assume responsibility for dealing with the problem.

Body fluids

Care must be taken when cleaning up body fluids. These fluids include blood, semen, vaginal secretions, sputum, fluids from lung, brain and other areas, tissue, organs, and saliva in dental procedures. It also includes any other body fluid such as urine, faeces, nasal secretions and vomit.

Some general rules apply to the cleaning up of body fluids:

1. Restrict access to the area.
2. Wear gloves to protect your hands. Avoid tearing your gloves on equipment or sharp objects. Torn gloves should be replaced immediately.
3. Use additional personal protection as needed (e.g. leakproof apron and/or eye protection).
4. Use disposable towels to soak up most of the fluid.
5. Clean with an appropriate disinfectant solution, such as ten parts water to one part bleach. Bleach will kill both HIV and hepatitis B virus. After cleaning, promptly disinfect mops and other cleaning equipment, otherwise you might spread the viruses to other areas.
6. Put all contaminated towels and waste in appropriate, sealed, labelled, leakproof containers (see Figure 5.2 below).

Clinical waste

All waste generated in a care setting and that has been in contact with blood or other body fluids is classed as clinical waste and has the potential to harm.

Here is a very useful list I came across in the booklet 'Health and Safety in Care Homes 2001', produced by the Health and Safety Executive.

While you might think that this type of list would be more appropriate to health care workers such as nurses, it might surprise you how many care workers in any care setting now have to deal with many of the items on the list.

Waste groups	Type of clinical waste
Group A	Identifiable human tissue, blood, soiled surgical dressings, swabs and other similar soiled waste. Other waste materials, e.g. from infection disease cases, excluding any in groups B–E.
Group B	Discarded syringe needles, cartridges, broken glass or other contaminated disposable sharp instruments or items.
Group C	Microbiological cultures and potentially infected waste from pathology departments and other clinical or research laboratories.
Group D	Drugs or other pharmaceutical products.
Group E	Items used to dispose of urine, faeces, and other bodily secretions or excretions that do not fall within group A. This includes the use of disposable bedpans or bedpan liners, incontinence pads, sanitary towels, tampons, stoma bags, urine containers and laundry.

Note: Group E only constitutes clinical waste as outlined in Group A if a risk of infection has been identified.

Figure 5.2 Clinical waste

ACTIVITY 5.5

List the types of clinical waste you may have to deal with as a care worker.

Disposal of waste

The disposal of waste is a crucial part of the care process as it is the most direct means by which infection can be passed on to individuals and workers. Infections are dangerous to everyone, but in particular to those individuals who are in poor health, are old or young and therefore more vulnerable to infection. You are probably aware of the term MRSA (methicillin-resistant staphylococcus aureus) that has been in the news recently. MRSA is the best-known form of a range of infections which are resistant to treatment. Individuals and workers have become extremely ill from this, and in some cases have died. Reducing the spread of infection requires the use of *universal precautions*, which will be described later in the chapter.

All staff should receive the appropriate training in the disposal of waste, and be clear about what is classified as clinical waste and what constitutes domestic waste. There is a widely used system of colour-coding to aid the process of waste segregation.

Laundry

Laundry, often referred to as linen, has also to be given careful consideration in relation to its disposal. When working with any type of linen, it is advisable to wear gloves and aprons.

Type of container	Type of waste
Yellow plastic sack	Group A Clinical waste for incineration.
Yellow plastic sack with black stripes	Non-infectious waste, e.g. Group E and sanpro (sanitary towels, tampons, nappies, stoma bags, incontinence pads); waste suitable for landfill or other means of disposal.
Black plastic bags	Non-clinical waste; general waste that poses no threat to others.
Yellow sharps bin (a special rigid, puncture-resistant and leakproof bin)	Needles, scalpels or lancets.

Figure 5.3 Waste segregation

Used linen refers to the bulk of linen, which is used on a daily basis but is not soiled. This would include sheets, pillowcases, towels and items of clothing.

Soiled linen is linen that has been contaminated with blood or other body fluids, e.g. urine, semen, sputum or faeces. Your organisation should have clear guidelines about how this type of linen should be dealt with. Normally there will be specific types of clearly marked plastic bags for this, and these bags will be dealt with separately in the laundry.

Infected linen is linen which has been in contact with infectious conditions such as hepatitis, MRSA, HIV, pulmonary tuberculosis etc. Again, this linen must be dealt with carefully. Guidelines should be clearly given to workers who have to deal with this. Glove and aprons are essential and linen should be placed in special clearly marked bags (usually red or with red markings), which are specially designed to dissolve when washed at high temperature washes of 95° centigrade or above.

Drugs and medicine

Drugs and medicine require particular attention, as they are dangerous if misused. All drugs should be stored in a safe place, clearly labelled, and only authorised workers who have been fully trained should have access to them and be allowed to administer them to individuals. Some drugs will require specific storage, e.g. in specific temperatures, and a small number of drugs, such as some creams and powders, may require particular methods of handling.

In cases where workers are supporting individuals in their own homes, due caution to ensure safe storage should be adhered to and strict adherence to the prescription directions should be followed. Again, only qualified, trained staff should administer drugs to individuals in their own homes. Advice should always be sought from medical professionals, e.g. GPs or pharmacists, if there is any doubt.

All drugs and medicine are classed as clinical waste (see above) and as such are governed by rules of disposal. Never flush unused drugs or medicines down the toilet or place them in the refuse bin. Workplaces which use large amounts of drugs, such as hospitals, clinics and care homes, should have guidelines for these procedures and these should be strictly adhered to. If working in an individual's home, it is advisable that all unused medicines should be returned to the nearest pharmacist.

Aggressive and violent people

Violence towards workers is today an all too common occurrence. The Public Accounts Committee recently reported that in 2002, over 95,000 incidents of violence were reported against NHS staff (www.bbc.co.uk, 2003). It is now recognised that aggression and violence to workers are a source of injury and distress. Violent incidents may include verbal abuse, threatening behaviour or assault.

What must be considered is that not only workers but also service users, key people and others may also be at risk. It is therefore vital that the care environment is made as safe as possible for everyone who uses the setting, and that there should not be a tacit acceptance that aggression and violence are unavoidable occupational hazards. Protection of staff and service users falls under the remit of both the Health and Safety at Work Act 1974 and the Management of Health and Safety at Work Regulations 1999. Organisations should have a policy relating to aggression and violence. As with all hazards in the workplace, a risk assessment should be carried out by the organisation (see next section) to establish if there is a problem with aggression and violence. Methods of reducing these risks should be sought, clear guidelines given for areas of responsibilities, and a procedure for supporting people who have been assaulted or who have experienced verbal abuse should be in place. All workers should receive training and information about potentially violent situations within the organisation, and be kept up to date with relevant information about individuals.

Lone workers should be alert to potential violence or aggression. If there is any concern about the likelihood of this arising, you should not work alone but should always have a partner with you on visits, or extra staff on night duty in a care establishment. You should not be put at risk from violent individuals, and it may be that alternative or additional support should be provided by the managers of the care team.

Violence or the threat of violence may have serious repercussions on the stress levels of workers, service users, key people and others. If you feel that you or others have been affected in this way, it is important that you report the incident and its effects to your line manager.

RECORDING AND REPORTING HEALTH AND SAFETY ISSUES

It is essential that all health and safety issues are both reported and recorded. It is your duty to report anything in the workplace which you think is a potential hazard to yourself or to others, no matter how trivial the hazard might seem. As you will see in the last section of the chapter, there are particular procedures for reporting incidents and accidents.

ACTIVITY 5.6

Reporting health and safety issues may present the worker with dilemmas regarding confidentiality. What would you do in the following situation?

You are a health promotion worker who is visiting a care unit for young people to provide information on sexual health. One of the young people, Varinda, takes you aside and tells you that he has been diagnosed with HIV and Hepatitis B. He asks you not to tell anyone. What would you do?

In Activity 5.6, the most important consideration is that Varinda should not be treated any differently from others in the unit. In the next section, we will consider the use of universal precautions that should be used in all care environments to protect both individuals and workers alike. Varinda, however, does present a health risk to workers and others in the unit, and you would have to inform him of this. And further, that his information would have to be passed to an appropriate senior member of staff (e.g. Varinda's key worker), but with the reassurance that the information would not be passed on to all staff members or others living in the unit.

Reporting of health and safety issues should always be taken seriously and organisations should have procedures for this. Normally, you should report your findings to an appropriate member of senior staff. It is simply not enough to complain to a fellow worker that you are fed up because the hoist to assist individuals into the bath is not working. Issues such as these should be brought to the attention of an appropriate member of the senior staff, who should record in writing all such issues. If issues are not dealt with to your satisfaction, you should report the issue again, and if necessary take the matter to a more senior member of staff or to your union representative.

Recording of health and safety information is governed by the same legislation and organisational policies that apply to all information. Chapter 4 has examined this in more detail, covering aspects of confidentiality, storage of information and the requirements of legislation, including the Data Protection Act.

PROMOTING HEALTH AND SAFETY IN THE WORKING ENVIRONMENT

Promoting health and safety in your working environment is all about *your* approach to health and safety and how *you* demonstrate your commitment to it. You can do this in a variety of ways:

- ❑ how you, as a worker, always consider the importance of health and safety
- ❑ how you try to keep yourself and others safe by minimising and managing risks and hazards
- ❑ how you follow health and safety guidelines and act as a role model to others
- ❑ how you work with others to support them to follow these guidelines.

Minimising and managing risk

As an integral part of your everyday work, you should always be vigilant to potential hazards in the workplace, and act appropriately to minimise any risks both to yourself and to others. As a care worker, health and safety should always be uppermost in your mind as part of your role in supporting others. One of the main ways you can do this is by minimising and managing risks, and you would do this by the procedure of **risk management**. This term originated from industries such as engineering and construction, but has now become firmly embedded in all areas in the workplace.

The Management of Health and Safety at Work Regulations 1999 require that all workplaces with five employees or more must carry out risks assessments to both workers and any other persons using the workplace. They must provide training and information for employees, who in turn have a duty to follow any training and instructions given to them and to report any situations which they believe to be unsafe.

ACTIVITY 5.7

Take a walk around your place of work. It may be useful to do this task with someone you work with or with a service user. Take a clipboard and pen and write down all the possible risks that you can see.

The aim of any risk assessment is threefold:

1. to investigate what might cause harm to individuals
2. to determine whether you have done enough to prevent harm
3. to determine whether more action needs to be taken.

The Health and Safety Executive (2001) in *Health and Safety in Care Homes* has outlined five steps in risk assessment:

Step 1 – Identify the significant hazards

These can be concerned with the physical environment, the actual jobs which workers have to do or the behaviour of people in that workplace.

Step 2 – Decide who might be harmed

In deciding this, you should consider *everyone* who might use the work environment. This should include not only all workers and individuals, but also visitors, workers from other care agencies, utilities personnel and outside contractors.

Step 3 – Evaluate the risks and decide whether existing precautions are adequate

Risks should be categorised as high, medium or low. You may not be able to determine on your own whether a risk is high, medium or low. You should always seek advice on anything about which you are unsure. Some risk assessment may be quite simple. A bag left on the floor, for example, in a residential home for older adults who have mobility problems may pose quite a high risk. High risks should always be approached as a priority and in a way that aims to get rid of the hazard altogether. In this case, it is a simple matter of removing the bag and placing it in a safe place.

What about hazards that cannot be easily removed: a toilet that does not flush; an outside step that has become worn and uneven; a radiator that is overheating?

ACTIVITY 5.8

Using the three examples above, describe ways in which you could reduce the risk.

In cases such as these, it is necessary to control the risk by taking additional precautions until such time as the hazard has been removed. Preventing access to the risk is one way of doing this.

You could lock the toilet and place a notice outside the door advising everyone that the toilet is out of use, and directing them to another toilet. A plumber should be contacted to fix the problem as quickly as possible. You could place a notice above the step advising people of the hazard, ensure that all staff are aware of the problem, and assist anyone who needs help to go up or down the step. A builder should be contacted as soon as possible. While waiting for the central heating engineer to arrive, a blanket or other covering should be placed over the radiator. A notice may also be placed near the radiator and, if necessary, individuals could be prevented from using the room.

Step 4 – Record your findings

Organisations with more than five employees must have a system for recording the significant findings (hazards and conclusions) of the risk assessments reported by workers or individuals using the environment. There should be a mechanism for informing the staff about this, e.g. instructions issued to staff not to use one of the toilets.

Step 5 – Review your assessment and revise it if necessary

It is useful to keep records to demonstrate that you have considered all the necessary aspects. These records are useful as a reference point for when the assessments need to be reviewed (whenever circumstances change, or periodically to ensure that they remain current).

HOW TO FOLLOW HEALTH AND SAFETY GUIDELINES

In this section we will look at why you should follow approved methods and procedures when you carry out potentially hazardous work activities. We will look at the importance of how *you* should follow health and safety guidelines, and how *you* should support others to do the same. There are many situations in which you are required to follow guidelines. We will examine five:

- ❑ moving and handling
- ❑ cross infection
- ❑ food preparation
- ❑ lone working
- ❑ water temperatures.

Moving and handling

Each year an estimated 428,000 people in Great Britain suffer from back problems, which they attribute to manual handling activities at work. Disorders affecting the back may cost Britain £3 billion per year. In the social and health care sector, almost 50 per cent of accidents reported each year involve manual handling, in particular assisting people with mobility (HSE, 2001).

It is not possible to provide complete instructions in this chapter for the safe moving and handling of individuals and heavy objects in care settings. However, the subject deserves close attention due to the potential risk it poses both to workers and those for whom they care. Employers now have a duty to train all staff required to undertake these duties. You should not attempt to lift heavy objects or individuals unless you have been fully trained. Back injury among nursing and care workers is one of the most common reasons for time off work. Individuals who do not receive proper care when they need assistance to move can be seriously affected in relation to their recovery, rehabilitation or general health and wellbeing.

The Manual Handling Operations Regulations were introduced in 1992 and outlined clear practices that had to be put in place. Responsibilities were designated as in Figure 5.4.

Put simply, employers have the responsibility to provide relevant and up-to-date equipment and training to help workers lift people and objects. Workers have a duty to attend the training and use any lifting aids as directed. Employers have a further duty under the Lifting Operations and Lifting Equipment Regulations 1998 to ensure that lifting equipment for people is thoroughly examined every six months unless a scheme of thorough examination is devised by a competent

Responsibilities of employers	Responsibilities of employees
Employers have a duty to ensure the safety of all employees involved in manual handling and moving.	Employees have the responsibility to obey reasonable and lawful instructions in relation to moving and handling, and to act with reasonable care and skill.
Employers have a responsibility to make a thorough assessment and implement measures to avoid risk, or minimise it to the greatest possible degree.	

Figure 5.4 Manual Handling Operations Regulations 1992

ACTIVITY 5.9

Consider the following scenario and then answer the following questions: What would you do if you were Hassan? In what ways is this poor practice?

Hassan and Richard work in a residential home for older adults, most of whom have dementia. Some have incontinence problems and it is not uncommon for some of them to soil themselves. There is a hoist to assist people into the bath, but when the ward manager is not about, Hassan and Richard lift people into the bath rather than use the hoist. Hassan is quite a new worker and has on occasion said to Richard that they should be using the hoist. Richard, who has been working in the house for nearly ten years, tells Hassan that using the hoist 'takes too much time' and in any case most of them 'are as light as a feather'. 'If we save time bathing, it will leave us more time to do other jobs around the home.'

person, usually an insurance engineer. As a worker, it is therefore your duty to use equipment in the manner you have been shown, and to report any fault in equipment you have been asked to use.

In Activity 5.9, Hassan should encourage Richard to use the hoist. If this fails, then he should insist, and if Richard continues to refuse to use the hoist, then Hassan should report the matter to his ward manager. It is poor practice because there is a real risk, not only to Hassan and Richard but also to those they are lifting.

Using moving and handling equipment when it is required is an essential part of providing a safe environment. You should always use equipment as you have been instructed. You should encourage everyone you work with to do likewise, and report any poor practice you witness. If the equipment you are asked to use is broken or faulty, you must report this immediately.

Cross infection

The subject of cross infection, especially in relation MRSA, has been discussed earlier in the chapter. In many care settings, vulnerable children, adults and older adults are cared for, and the risk of infection to them may have serious consequences. Procedures to minimise the risk of cross infection are often referred to as 'universal precautions' with the word 'universal' meaning that they are used when dealing with *all* individuals at *all* times. This in effect protects all individuals and all staff from cross infection from each other.

Remember Varinda who had HIV and Hepatitis B and who did not want everyone to know; we did say that the worker would have to inform her line manager but not other staff, as they should be using universal precautions when dealing with *all* the individuals they support and not just the ones that they know or suspect of having an infectious disease. This not only protects everyone on a health basis, but also protects the confidentiality of the individual and prevents workers from being discriminatory towards certain individuals.

So what are these universal precautions?

They come in three basic forms:

1.   Hand washing.
2.   Gloves.
3.   Protective clothing.

Hand washing

The Government, the British Medical Association and the Royal College of Nursing have all highlighted hand washing as a major factor in the battle against cross infection. Not only do they give advice to nurses, doctors and ancillary staff about *how* to wash hands, but also *when* to do it.

Try listing *when* you should wash your hands. Here is my list (remember that this applies even when you are wearing gloves!):

- ❑   At the beginning and end of every shift.
- ❑   Before and after all contact with individuals when undertaking personal care (washing) or medical procedures, e.g. giving an injection, changing dressings.
- ❑   After handling body fluids.
- ❑   After handling soiled linen, incontinence pads, sanitary products etc.
- ❑   Before giving medication.
- ❑   Before and after assisting an individual to go to the toilet.
- ❑   Before and after serving meals.
- ❑   After using the toilet.
- ❑   After you cough, sneeze, or blow your nose.
- ❑   Before and after removing gloves, aprons.
- ❑   **If in any doubt.**

You must wash your hands thoroughly. The picture below (Figure 5.5) shows the areas of the hands that are most frequently missed when you wash your hands.

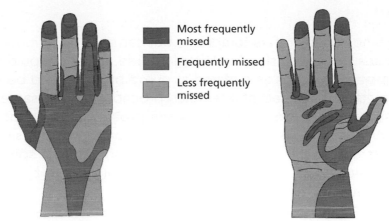

Most frequently missed

Frequently missed

Less frequently missed

Figure 5.5 Wash your hands thoroughly

Any cuts or abrasions should be covered with the appropriate plasters or dressings. Some hospitals now have a hand gel beside each patient's bed that all staff are asked to use before assisting a new patient. It is also recommended that staff should have short, clean nails, and that rings should be removed, as they harbour germs.

Gloves

Wearing gloves is a crucial factor in minimising the risk of cross infection, but it must be remembered that the use of gloves does not reduce the need to wash your hands. Small puncture holes may not be noticed and the warm, moist atmosphere created by the gloves provides a perfect environment in which germs can grow and multiply. Gloves should be damage-free, seamless, single use and made from latex or vinyl, and importantly should be the correct size.

Gloves should always be worn whenever you have contact with any body fluid (faeces, urine, sperm, blood, mucus, sputum (spit) sweat or vomit); or when you are in contact with any area of the skin which has a rash or is broken or bleeding. When removing gloves, do not touch your wrists or hands with the dirty gloves. Using a gloved hand, pinch up the cuff of the other hand, and pull the glove off inside out. Keep hold of this glove in the remaining gloved hand. Using the ungloved hand, insert it behind the other cuff, and pull the glove off, turning it inside out. Both gloves should be folded together inside out and should be discarded immediately into the clinical waste bag. Remember to wash your hands. If there are no gloves in the dispenser, you must never carry out procedures without them. It only takes a few minutes to get a new box!

Protective clothing

Protective clothing usually refers to aprons, but can also mean gowns and protective glasses or face masks. As a simple guide, aprons should be worn when you are wearing gloves as outlined above. Aprons should be made of plastic and should be disposed of after each procedure in the same way as gloves. They should never be used to carry out procedures with more than one individual. When removing an apron, pull the neckband and the side, thus breaking the ties and fold the apron in on itself to prevent the spread of germs. Discard it in a clinical waste bag. And again, wash your hands before going to assist another individual.

Food preparation

Increasingly, care workers find themselves assisting individuals to prepare food. Following guidelines regarding food preparation and encouraging others to do the same are crucial in minimising the risk of food poisoning. The Food Safety (General) Regulations (Department of Health, 1995) document forms the basis of good practice in any catering establishment, and this includes residential homes and hospitals. If you are involved in the preparation of food, you should receive appropriate training from your employer. This training should include topics such as food handling, preparation and storage.

General rules for all food preparation are as follows:

- ❏ Wash hands before touching or preparing food.
- ❏ Cover cuts with brightly coloured waterproof plasters which can be easily identified if they fall into the food.
- ❏ Do not cough or sneeze over food.
- ❏ Do not pick your nose, touch your hair, lips or mouth when working with food, unless you wash your hands immediately afterwards.
- ❏ Keep equipment and utensils clean.
- ❏ Keep food clean and covered, and handle it as little as possible.
- ❏ Keep lids on waste sacks and dustbins.

Lone working

Lone working has now become a much more common method of providing care. The rise in the number of individuals receiving care in their own homes has escalated in the past ten years. This has resulted in a vast army of workers in both health and social care now working alone to visit individuals in their own homes. This includes night visits to provide medical care, meals and 'tuck in' services.

Figure 5.6 New Health and Safety Regulations, Brenda

Organisations should have clear procedures to minimise the risks to lone workers. Usually this involves providing workers with a mobile phone or paying for any work-related calls, providing a 24-hour contact number and instructing workers to contact this number on a regular basis, e.g. when they have finished a visit or dropped someone off. Workers may also be issued with an alarm. You should always follow the procedures outlined by the organisation and report any issues or worries connected with your visits to your line manager.

Water temperatures

Despite guidelines from the Department of Health as long ago as 1998, which specified 'safe' hot water temperatures to be used in showers and baths, several cases of death and serious injury from scalding in care and nursing homes continue to be highlighted in the press. Some individuals have been fatally scalded after being lowered into a bath that had not been tested and was too hot. Appropriate thermostatic mixing valves (type 3) should be fitted to prevent water being hotter than 44° Centigrade in baths and 41° Centigrade in showers. Workers should be trained to carry out the following procedures:

- ❏ Check the temperature with a thermometer before the individual gets into a bath or shower.
- ❏ Periodically check the temperatures of the water flow (weekly).
- ❏ If more hot water is required, add slowly and check the temperature with a thermometer.
- ❏ Carry out risk assessments on individuals to ascertain the vulnerability and capabilities of individuals to determine the level of support they require while bathing or showering.

If you follow the guidelines given to you when carrying out potentially harmful procedures, you will act as a role model to your fellow workers. Remember, good practice can be copied, as well as bad. Explaining to others why you are carrying out the procedure in a particular way may also encourage them. Explaining the repercussions of poor practice may help them to change the way they do things. Persistent dangerous practice should be reported to prevent lives being put in danger.

MINIMISE RISKS FROM INCIDENTS AND EMERGENCIES

Despite all our efforts to ensure that the environment surrounding the people for whom we care and ourselves is safe, there will always be occasions when emergencies and incidents happen.

An **emergency** means that there is an immediate and threatening danger to individuals and others, and comes in two main forms – health and environmental. An **incident** is an occurrence that requires immediate action to avoid possible danger and harm to people, goods and/or the environment, and again comes in two main forms – health and environmental. An **accident** is an unforeseen major or minor incident in which an individual is injured.

- ❏ **Health emergencies** occur when there is a threat to someone's life. This could be in the case of a heart attack, stroke or when the person has a life-threatening accident, e.g. a road accident.
- ❏ **Incidents relating to health** can be categorised as minor or major accidents. While some accidents may cause only a slight cut or bruise, others may result in more serious injuries.

ACTIVITY 5.10

In the space below, list as many types of emergencies and incidents as you can.

	Health	Environmental
Emergency		
Incident		

- ❏ **Environmental emergencies** are serious events. In Activity 5.10, you may have suggested fire, gas leak/explosion, or flood.
- ❏ **Environmental incidents** might include intruders, a lost key or purse, a person being locked out or missing, not being able to gain entry to an individual's home, finding out that someone has no heating or lighting or discovering infestations such as fleas, bees, ants, rodents, wasps etc. Also in this category is the occurrence of a bomb scare. Since the events of 9/11 (the terrorist attacks in New York in 2001), many organisations now have procedures in place in the event of a bomb scare.

It is not possible here to detail all the required procedures for the whole range of health emergencies which you may encounter at work. Your employer should ensure that you have the appropriate training required for your role in the workplace. You should at least be trained in first aid measures to deal with the following:

- ❏ cardiac/respiratory arrest
- ❏ chest pains
- ❏ loss of consciousness
- ❏ choking/hanging
- ❏ electrocution
- ❏ severe external bleeding
- ❏ haemorrhage

❏   burns and scalds
❏   epileptic seizures
❏   shock
❏   suspected fracture
❏   poisoning.

The extent of your training will depend on the type of job and the level of responsibility which you have.

In the event of any emergency or incident, you should be fully aware of what you should do, what correct safety procedures you should follow and how you should support others to follow these procedures. All workers should have the appropriate training to deal with emergencies and incidents that might happen. At all times it is crucial that you follow the procedures in which you have been instructed, as they are designed to save lives or prevent further injury or danger. You should deal with them within your own range of training and competence.

You might be very clear about some of the above situations because you have received clear training, but for others you might feel quite apprehensive. Take this list to your line manager and ask him/her to give clear instructions about organisational procedures that deal with these situations. You need to be clear about your own level of competence. For example, if you think someone has had a heart attack and you have had no first aid training, what should you do? Your employer should have instructed you about what to do in the case of a health emergency.

ACTIVITY 5.11

What would you do in the following situations?

❏   The fire alarm sounds.
❏   Someone you are with collapses in the street.
❏   You think someone has just had a heart attack.
❏   You answer the phone and someone says there is a bomb in the building.
❏   Someone is locked out.
❏   You discover a fire in the toilet.
❏   Someone falls and cannot get up.
❏   You detect a strong smell of gas.
❏   Someone goes missing.

Depending on the location of the health emergency, you might be instructed to do different things. For example, in a hospital you would call for the assistance of a medically qualified colleague; in a care home or hostel you would call for the member of staff trained in first aid. If you were in the individual's own home, you would call for an ambulance.

Of course, you will be able to assist at the situation once the qualified person has arrived by following closely any instructions given to you. You might be asked to phone for an ambulance, fetch some blankets, or remove any source of further danger such as spillages or obstacles such as broken furniture or broken glass. You could also be asked to remove any onlookers, not only for their own safety but also to protect the privacy of the individual who has had the accident. Others who have witnessed the accident may be in need of support. This may apply to both workers and others and you might find yourself undertaking this role. You should do so in a sensitive and professional manner and report to your line manager if you feel that anyone may need additional support such as medical or psychological care.

Reporting of incidents

The Reporting of Injuries, Diseases and Dangerous Occurrences Regulations 1995, often referred to as RIDDOR, require employers and others to report certain types of injury, illness and dangerous occurrences that are caused by the work environment. All employers should have some type of recording system for this purpose, which should ensure that all the appropriate details are recorded. Records should be kept for a period of three years. The following should be reported if they arise 'out of or in connection with work':

❑ Accidents that result in an employee or a self-employed person dying, suffering a major injury, or being absent from work, or unable to do their normal duties for more than three days.
❑ Accidents that result in a person not at work (e.g. a service user or visitor) suffering an injury and being taken to hospital.
❑ An employee or self-employed person suffering one of the specified work-related diseases. (The range of diseases which have to be reported is comprehensive and includes tuberculosis, dysentery, typhoid and food poisoning. See Schedule 3 of the Act for a full list.)
❑ One of the specified 'dangerous occurrences' – these do not necessarily result in injury but have the potential to cause significant harm.

(HSE, Health and Safety in Care Homes 2001)

Important legislation	Year
Health and Safety at Work Act	1974
The Manual Handling Operations Regulations	1992
The Reporting of Injuries, Diseases and Dangerous Occurrences Regulations (RIDDOR)	1995
The Food Safety (General) Regulations (Department of Health 1995)	1995
The Control of Substances Hazardous to Health Regulations (COSHH)	1999
The Management of Health And Safety at Work Regulations	1999

Figure 5.7 Health and Safety legislation

If you have been a witness to an incident, you should complete the appropriate forms required by the legislation. You should do so in an accurate and legible manner. Ask for assistance if you have difficulty in completing any form or do not understand any of the wording. Try to remember the important aspects of the incident, especially in relation to what actually happened and which actions you took.

SUMMARY

Health and safety are a very important part of care work. Organisations have a responsibility to provide a safe working environment. Workers also have a responsibility to cooperate with their employer. Working together, employers and employees should monitor and maintain the safety and security of the working environment, promote health and safety in the working environment and minimise risks arising from emergencies.

FIVE KEY POINTS

1. You and your employer have a duty to keep the working environment safe.
2. You have a duty to report any issues which threaten safety.
3. You should minimise risks.
4. You must follow health and safety guidelines.
5. You should know what to do in an emergency.

THREE QUESTIONS

1. How do you make your workplace safe? Give at least six examples.
2. How do you promote health and safety in your workplace? Give at least four examples.
3. Describe three emergencies and say how you would deal with them.

RECOMMENDED READING

The literature on health and safety in the workplace is abundant. You should find a good source of information at your place of work, either from your line manager or union representative. I have suggested the following:

UKHCA (1998) *The Home Care Worker's Handbook: The essential guide to care in the Home*. A basic guide for those working in the individual's home

Health and Safety Executive (2001) *Health and Safety in Care Homes*. HSG220 A straightforward account of various areas of health and safety in care homes

KENWORTHY, N., SNOWLEY, G., GILLING, C. (eds) (2002) *Common Foundation Studies in Nursing*, 3rd edn, London: Churchill Livingstone. A more detailed insight into clinical practice for nurses.

Health and Safety Executive (2001) *Handling Home Care*.

RECOMMENDED WEBSITES

www.hse.gov.uk A comprehensive website which covers all aspects of health and safety, including legislation and lists of publications.

www.bbc.co.uk An excellent website for finding out about news items relating to health and safety.

www.healthandsafetytips.co.uk An excellent site which provides links to a wide range of related sites, providing detailed information about all aspects of health and safety.

www.unison.org.uk/safety/index.asp A good site that provides a union perspective on health and safety.

CHAPTER 6

PROTECTION FROM ABUSE

Janet Miller

> **Abuse is a terrifying and humiliating experience. It is always wrong and can threaten people's identity. It can cause a lack of trust in other people, loss of self-esteem and self-confidence and feelings of worthlessness.**
>
> (SH, student)

By the end of this chapter you should be able to:

- ❏ examine your own thoughts and feelings in relation to abuse
- ❏ understand the meanings of different kinds of abuse
- ❏ be able to recognise different kinds of abuse
- ❏ know about things you should and should not do if abuse is disclosed
- ❏ understand lessons from inquiries into abuse.

The content of this chapter provides underpinning content and context for all care qualifications. It relates especially to the following units:

HSC24: Ensure your own actions support the care, protection and wellbeing of individuals

HSC34: Promote the wellbeing and protection of children and young people

HSC35: Promote choice, wellbeing and the protection of all individuals

HSC325: Contribute to the protection of children and young people from danger, harm and abuse

HSC335: Contribute to the protection of individuals from danger, harm and abuse

HNC Unit: Protection of individuals from possible harm and abuse.

INTRODUCTION

Abuse has never been easy to discuss in a reasonable way. It is a very emotional, complex and painful subject. Those who are abused need support, but often those who abuse need it too. Some of those who read these pages may have been abused, or may have abused themselves or others. Jacki Pritchard points to the reality of this and mirrors my own experience of providing training on abuse:

> I usually train two or three days each working week. During the past year I have kept a record of how many course participants disclose to me about abuse – it is exactly one-third – this includes men and women. Some have been abused in childhood or earlier adulthood, some are still involved in abusive or violent relationships.

> (Pritchard, J. 'Forewarned is forearmed', 9 August 2001. Published by permission of the editor of *Community Care*)

People who have been abused often do not think that what has happened to them really counts as abuse. They have no physical scars or, quite mistakenly, perhaps they feel that what happened to them was deserved in some way. But, as you will see from the accounts below, abuse comes in many forms and is never deserved. At its core is a misuse of power.

Abuse is hardly a new phenomenon, though there are no reliable historical statistics to tell us how prevalent or serious the problem was in the past. There are biblical references to abuse, and Charles Dickens writes of the most terrible child abuse in such novels as 'Oliver Twist' and 'Nicholas Nickleby'.

ACTIVITY 6.1

An exercise in self-awareness: identify three feelings that you have about abuse; discuss your feelings with at least one other person in a supportive environment.

Society and communities have often colluded to condone abuse, and although our awareness of abuse today is probably greater than it has ever been, its incidence may not be.

Why care workers need to know about abuse

Part of the social care task is to protect people from abuse. Another task is to support those who have been abused or who abuse. In order to perform these tasks, you need to know what abuse is, which forms it takes, how to identify it and the most appropriate processes for dealing with it.

Rather than discuss different client groups separately, abuse is initially discussed in general. Examples are used to discuss issues in relation to particular groups, such as children and young people and vulnerable adults.

What is abuse?

There is no one single definition of abuse, but the one provided below gives a basis from which to discuss its many manifestations:

> The violation or neglect of those unable to protect themselves, to prevent harm from happening, or to remove themselves from harm or potential harm by others.

> (City of Glasgow Multi Agency Procedures, 2001)

FORMS OF ABUSE

Abuse can take many forms, and has various consequences for those who are abused. Often one form of abuse goes alongside another or others, and the dividing lines are not always clear-cut. The following list of forms of abuse is followed by a brief discussion of the signs and consequences of abuse for each one, with the use of some examples. Abuse can be:

- ❑   physical
- ❑   emotional

- ❏ neglect
- ❏ sexual
- ❏ financial
- ❏ inexplicable failure to thrive.

Physical abuse

Some of the signs of physical abuse include:

- ❏ bruising, from being slapped, shaken, squeezed or punched
- ❏ cuts, scratches, bite marks, torn frenulum (the web of skin inside the upper lip)
- ❏ burns and scalds
- ❏ fractures
- ❏ poisoning
- ❏ head injury.

The occurrence of these signs does not, of course, necessarily indicate abuse, and great care needs to be taken to ascertain whether or not abuse has taken place. Inevitably there are sometimes errors of judgement in this minefield. Some illnesses such as brittle bone disease and ringworm can be mistaken for abuse, and some abuse can be overlooked because it resembles illness and injury from other causes such as scabies and genuine accidents.

The tragic case of Victoria Climbie illustrates this very well.

> Victoria died in February 2000 with 128 separate injuries to her tiny body, after enduring months of agony at the hands of her aunt Marie Therese Kouao, 44, and her boyfriend, Carl Manning, 28, of Tottenham, North London . . .. Giving evidence to the inquiry in London . . . Dr Schwartz said that her [earlier] diagnosis of scabies was 'not 100 per cent', and that she thought other marks on Victoria's body could have resulted from insect bites or 'knocks' from playing.

> (*Daily Express*, 13 October 2001)

Emotional abuse

Emotional abuse is one of the most difficult forms of abuse to detect and confirm. Unless it is combined with physical abuse, there are no physical marks and its consequences could often have other causes. Often people who are emotionally abused know that they feel distressed by what another or others do or say to them, but often do not feel that what they are experiencing actually constitutes abuse. They may go for years or even their whole lives thinking that they must be inadequate in some way, and that what they are experiencing is deserved. Among the actions that can be considered to be emotionally abusive are the following:

- humiliation
- intimidation
- ridicule
- causing fear, mental anguish and/or anxiety
- threats/threatening behaviour
- bullying
- verbal abuse, e.g. shouting, swearing
- harassment
- denial of basic rights, e.g. choice, opinion, privacy
- being over-protected – not allowed to do things, kept back
- deprivation of the company of others and isolation from friends, family and own community and culture. This is sometimes defined separately as **social abuse**, but since it results in extreme isolation and the same consequences as other forms of emotional abuse, it is included here.

The signs that someone has been emotionally abused may include:

- withdrawal
- inability to participate in everyday life or have fun
- telling lies
- speech disorders, e.g. stammering
- low self-esteem
- lack of self-confidence
- attention-seeking behaviour
- temper tantrums inappropriate to normal development.

I went recently to see the play 'Adult Child/Dead Child' by Claire Dowie. It was a harrowing experience illustrating the psychological consequences of emotional abuse. Many people who have experienced such abuse felt that it gave a very vivid and accurate account of what they had gone through, and I quote from it here to illustrate some of the points made above.

> I wasn't abused
> I was never what you'd call an abused child
> not abused
> not by any stretch of the imagination

but there was the cupboard, the
cupboard under the stairs
dark, silent, claustrophobic . . . .
sitting in the cupboard 'til I learn to
behave myself and show some respect
in the cupboard under the stairs . . . . .

You want to hit out because of this lack
of love that you can't explain
so you hit out because of this lack of love
you hit out at the people around you
hit out at the people, the adults around you . . .

You build a wall of anger and mistrust and hatred
and you build a wall because they wouldn't help you
and you hate these adults because they
made you build a wall . . . . . .

Further and further away, no
understanding, no communication . . .

(Claire Dowie, *Adult Child/Dead Child* (1987))

Neglect

The dividing line between physical or emotional abuse and neglect is a fine and blurred one. Indeed, neglect is a form of abuse. The main distinguishing factor is that abuse is doing something and neglect is not doing something. They often go hand in hand. Physical neglect occurs when a lack of attention to physical needs results in negative physical (and usually other) consequences. The vulnerable person may be frequently left alone and unattended, and may not have adequate food, sleep, clothing, a clean environment, warmth, supervision, stimulation or medical care. Emotional neglect may include a lack of love and/or acknowledgement including completely ignoring someone. Physical neglect is almost inevitably accompanied by emotional neglect, and most forms of physical neglect are also emotionally abusive. Similarly, emotional neglect is often, though by no means always, accompanied by physical neglect. The signs of neglect include:

- ❑ below average weight and sometimes a failure to thrive
- ❑ clothing may be inappropriate, smelly and or dirty
- ❑ frequent illness, pallor, poor skin tone, matted hair, rashes (including nappy rash in very young children), cold sores etc.

- ❏ constant hunger, tiredness and listlessness
- ❏ frequent injury from accidents
- ❏ delayed development; in children, failure to reach developmental milestones
- ❏ behavioural difficulties, low self-esteem, inability to form relationships
- ❏ there may be an air of 'frozen watchfulness', an inability to smile or have fun.

Sexual abuse

Sexual abuse may be defined as any sexual contact between an adult and a sexually immature child or vulnerable person, for the purposes of the adult's sexual gratification; or any sexual contact made by the use of force, threat, or deceit; or sexual contact to which the individual is incapable of consenting by virtue of age or power differentials and/or the nature of the relationship. Sexual maturity is socially as well as physiologically defined. (Finkelhor and Korbin, 1988). In addition to sexual contact, which may or may not involve vaginal or anal penetration, sexual abuse may involve looking at pornographic material (e.g. films or magazines), vulnerable people being encouraged in sexually explicit behaviour or oral sex, masturbation or the handling of sexual body parts. Approximately 10 per cent of sexual abusers are women, and both males and females may be abused.

The physical signs of sexual abuse include:

- ❏ bruises or scratches inconsistent with accidental injury
- ❏ difficulty in sitting or walking
- ❏ sleep disturbances and bed-wetting
- ❏ pain or itching in the genital area; discharges from the vagina or penis
- ❏ bloodstained or torn underwear
- ❏ loss of appetite.

There may also be behavioural and psychological indicators that include:

- ❏ lack of self-confidence
- ❏ poor self-esteem
- ❏ flirtation as if to please adults
- ❏ withdrawal
- ❏ fascination with sexual behaviour
- ❏ use of explicit sexual language

- ❑ unusual amount of knowledge about sexual behaviour shown through work, play, drawings etc.
- ❑ poor sleep patterns.

The sexual abuse of Colm O'Gorman is used here as an example. He was five the first time he was raped.

> His abuser was a male babysitter, a friend of his father. At the age of nine, he was raped once a week for about a year by a neighbour who gave him violin lessons.
> 'By this time I knew how I was expected to perform. I was much more compliant,' he says.
> When he was 14, he became involved in church youth activities. Here he met Father Sean Fortune who sexually abused him for the next two years.
>
> (*Community Care*, 'Prisoner of the Past', 19–25 April 2001. Published by permission of the editor of *Community Care*)

Colm O'Gorman has in later life set up an organisation 'One in four' to support adults who were abused as children. It is called 'One in four' after research by the University of London found that approximately one in four children will experience some form of sexual abuse by the age of 18. The consequences of this abuse may include

- ❑ low self-esteem
- ❑ difficulty in forming and maintaining relationships
- ❑ problems with being a parent
- ❑ sexual problems
- ❑ suicidal thoughts, or attempted or actual suicide
- ❑ psychiatric illness, e.g. depression
- ❑ self-harm
- ❑ eating disorders
- ❑ drug and alcohol misuse
- ❑ sexual abuse of others.

Financial abuse

Financial abuse can take many forms and can include stealing money, taking an individual's pension book or cashing someone's pension but only giving them some of the money. It could also be saying that something cost more than it did and pocketing the difference; saying that bills or rent have been paid when this is not the case; withholding money so that the person never has enough, or forcing someone to transfer money or other assets to someone else. Where people have made others responsible for their financial affairs, as in the case of appointeeship (through the Department of Social Security) or granting power of attorney (through the courts), abuse can occur when money is unreasonably withheld. Finally, relatives who expect to inherit from a vulnerable, often elderly, person may refuse to allow that person to go into residential care or to receive services because they wish to maximise their inheritance.

Sometimes a vulnerable person can be aware that financial abuse is occurring but decide not to do anything about it. The following quotation illustrates this:

> I can think of an older woman. She was being financially exploited by her carer who was her only relative and who had moved in with her. She didn't want the relationship to end. There can be interdependent relationships – the old person needed the care, the carer needed shelter and money.

(Cherry Rowlings in Pritchard, J 1999)

ACTIVITY 6.2

What action would you take, if any, to protect the older adult in the above situation?

Inexplicable failure to thrive

Failure to thrive occurs when someone, usually a child or young person, fails to reach physical and developmental milestones expected for someone of their age and/or stage of development. Sometimes there is no apparent physical explanation for failure to thrive. This is included under forms of abuse mainly to safeguard children who, while there is insufficient evidence of actual abuse, are not thriving and could be in need of help and protection.

Even before the first signs of the physical abuse of Jasmine Beckford (Brent, 1985) were identified when she was 20 months old, there were indicators of inexplicable failure to thrive. At birth, Jasmine weighed 5lb 11oz. By the age of four months, she had reached an average weight for a child of her age and it could be expected that she would continue to develop and gain weight within normal parameters. However, after 10 months Jasmine's weight was below the third centile, i.e. she was among the three per cent of most poorly developed children. At 15 months, with a weight of 18lb 6oz, she was even further down the third centile. There were sufficient indicators here to ring alarm bells.

James (not his real name) had a similar history but was later diagnosed with a rare endocrine disorder. Prior to diagnosis, his GP had alerted the health visitor to his weight loss and she had subsequently alerted the Social Services Department since she suspected that James was being neglected. James's parents were adamant that they were providing good care for James, but agreed to a period of voluntary supervision by a social worker. It was during the period of supervision that James's condition was diagnosed. The social worker was able to give valuable support to the family, but no compulsory measures were needed because the failure to thrive was eventually found to have an organic basis, and the care of James was sufficient and loving.

FACTORS IN ABUSE

The forms of abuse can occur among all age groups and all kinds of person, but it is usually the most powerless people who are also the most vulnerable. In this section, some factors that may lead to abuse are examined. These factors fall mainly into the categories of:

- ❏ stress and stressful environments
- ❏ psychological or emotional disturbance
- ❏ lack of love and attachment
- ❏ learned behaviour
- ❏ communication between family members and significant others
- ❏ the use of drugs and alcohol
- ❏ poor support, even when stress and/or possible abuse have been identified.

These factors do not necessarily cause abuse, but one (or often more than one) of these factors is usually present when abuse occurs. The most useful approaches to abuse take a very broad approach, seeing that factors not only in the individual perpetrators but also in the environments and cultures in which it occurs may predispose some people in the direction of abuse, making it more likely that abuse may occur. This does not mean that people who experience one or a combination of these factors will abuse. Indeed, most of them do not. Seeing abuse in this multi-dimensional way, however, enables care workers to seek to support people on an individual, family, social and environmental basis.

Stress and stressful environments

One of the first theorists to put forward ideas about predisposing factors in abuse was Professor Cyril Greenland (in Jay and Doganis, 1987). He set out a high-risk family checklist, in which many of the factors listed were stress factors. He saw that the greatest value of this checklist was to raise warning signals and to indicate where child abuse may occur and where stress could be relieved. Among the features of the high-risk family are:

- parents under the age of 24
- parents who were themselves abused in childhood
- parents of low intelligence and inadequate education
- parents who are socially isolated with no immediate family or supportive friends
- parents who abuse alcohol and drugs
- mother who is pregnant or has recently given birth
- parents with a previous record of abuse or neglect of their children
- parents with poor housing or who move frequently from one place to another
- parents with several children under the age of four
- parents where the male partner is not the biological father of all the children
- parents who are unemployed or in poor economic circumstances.

A combination of these factors is likely to give rise to stress and increase the possibility that abuse will occur. Although the list relates specifically to child abuse, many of the factors can be seen as factors in any kind of abuse.

Sometimes carers experience enormous stress and become abusive because of the constant demands placed upon them. John Bayley (1998) in his book 'Iris', a memoir of the author Iris Murdoch, gives an account of 'that day I went suddenly berserk'.

> The rage was instant and total, seeming to come out of nowhere. 'I told you not to! **I told you not to!**' In those moments of savagery neither of us has the slightest idea to what I am referring. But the person who is speaking soon becomes more coherent. Cold too, and deadly. 'You're mad. You're dotty. You don't know anything, remember anything, care about anything.' This accompanied by furious gestures. Iris trembling violently.

Here, the stress of looking after his wife with Alzheimer's disease tipped someone usually reasonable, rational and loving, over the edge. He was abusive.

The relationship between stress and abuse, however, is not always a straightforward one. Alison Marriott (1997), in examining elder abuse, points out that it is often the way in which stress is perceived and reacted to that is more important than the stress itself. This leads to an examination of numerous other factors such as individual psychological and emotional differences, pre-abuse relationship between the abuser and the abused and, where the abuser is a main carer, the different expectations of the outcome of caring.

Psychological and emotional disturbance

One form of psychological disturbance that can be a factor in abuse is mental illness. Mental illness, though, does not necessarily predispose people to abuse, and where it is present as a factor, it is often in combination with others such as stress and a lack of love and attachment. In a study of men who are violent to women, for example, Morran and Wilson (1997) concluded that there is no major support for theories that suggest that in general men are violent to their partners as a consequence of mental illness. Although some men's violence is related to mental illness or instability, this appears to be so in a small minority of cases.

Psychological and emotional disturbance may take many forms. Gretchen Percey (1995) describes the case of Karen (not her real name). She first came to the attention of Gretchen when William, a four-year-old child whom Karen was looking after as a babysitter, was admitted to hospital with an overdose. A story gradually emerged of Karen purposely inducing medical symptoms in her own children through sodium overdose, ingestion of mouse poison and overdose of imiprimine. She sought medical attention for them, thus gaining a great deal of attention. Once the pieces of a very complicated jigsaw were put together, her children were removed from her care. Karen had experienced a childhood of sexual abuse by her own father. This was probably the source of her pathology, though does not wholly explain her subsequent behaviour.

Lack of love and attachment

Various studies (e.g. Crittenden and Ainsworth, 1989) have indicated that a lack of love and attachment is a factor that can be associated with people who abuse. Corby (2000) states that:

> Currently, poor attachment experiences are seen to be both a cause
> and a consequence of . . . abuse . . .. This process is not considered
> inevitable because the effects of poor early attachment experiences are

thought to be remediable by attachment to a surrogate figure or by successful counselling . . ... Studies (Gray *et al.*, 1977; Browne and Saqi, 1988) have produced evidence to support this connection between parental non-responsiveness and later abuse and neglect.

Although there is evidence for this connection, the majority of parents who have lacked love and attachment and/or experienced abuse themselves do not go on to abuse their own children. Other factors need to be considered, such as the way in which family members relate to one another, and stresses such as poverty and unemployment.

Learned behaviour

Many abusers were themselves abused as children and thus learned the possibility of abusive behaviour from an early age. It was part of their socialisation to expect ill treatment at the hands of those more powerful than themselves. For example, Morris Beckford, found guilty in 1985 of causing the death of his step-daughter, Jasmine Beckford, was at the age of 13 severely beaten by both parents and forced to sleep in an outhouse with no bed and one blanket shared with his sister. Both he and his sister were subsequently received into care. Although the abusive behaviour can be seen as partly learned, it probably also had its origins in the emotional disturbance caused by that abuse. Disentangling causes from one another is impossible.

Communication between family members and significant others

Communication and relationships are often another contributory factor in abuse situations. There are usually other contributory causes but their significance has been discussed by various studies, e.g. Corby (2000) and Decalmer *et al.* (1997). One of the ways in which abuse arises through relationship and communication difficulties is where one family member is subjected to abuse as a way of getting at another family member. This is sometimes a relevant factor in child abuse situations where there is friction between parents, especially where one of them is a step-parent. A family member may be a scapegoat for the ills of the whole family, and that member may be singled out for abuse. The abused person may sometimes also be abusive. This sometimes occurs where there is dementia, and the abuser has been subjected to considerable stress and inability to communicate adequately with the person cared for. Paveza *et al.* (1992) found that in various studies dementia sufferers are aggressive three to five times more frequently towards their carers than the carers are aggressive towards the dementia sufferer. Although cause and effect are difficult to disentangle in family and other relationship situations, family therapy, with its emphasis upon working with the family group as a whole, is often seen as a way of breaking or changing entrenched patterns of communication and behaviour.

The use of drugs and alcohol

Alcohol and drug abuse raise many concerns in connection with abuse, because of the effect they have on the ability of one person to care for another, or to act rationally and reasonably when under stress. Although there is conflicting evidence about the links between drug and alcohol misuse and abuse of others, several studies have convincingly demonstrated an association. A study of elder abuse reported by Decalmer *et al.* (1997) found that in 63 per cent of cases of physical abuse, the abuser was suffering from alcohol and/or drug abuse and severe stress. Corby (2000) reports several American studies showing a strong link between alcohol and drug use and child neglect, but also indicates the need for more research in Britain. An automatic linkage between drug or alcohol use cannot be assumed, especially in the absence of thorough research.

A related concern is the impact of drug and alcohol misuse on the unborn child. This can result in subsequent learning difficulty, stillbirth or health problems for the child. The excessive use of drugs and alcohol is often indicative of and may mask other causal features in abuse, such as psychological distress and stress.

Poor support, even when stress or possible abuse have been identified

Sometimes there is a failure by the services responsible for the prevention of abuse to provide adequate support, even when stress or possible abuse have been identified. Child and adult protection procedures are in place in all local authorities, but these are not foolproof in protecting vulnerable people. In the case of Victoria Climbie, the counsel to the inquiry, Neil Graham QC, outlined 12 missed opportunities to save Victoria. These included admissions to hospital with suspected non-accidental injury on 14 July 1999, and a further admission with scalds to the head and face on 24 July 1999, when Victoria remained in hospital for two weeks. With hindsight, it seems incredible that little significant support was offered to her family and that no child protection measures were taken. Victoria experienced bruising, burns and scalds as well as showing signs of physical and emotional neglect. There were also allegations of sexual abuse.

> . . . she was known to 70 health, social and child care professionals. Yet somehow she suffered alone.

> (*Community Care*, 'Behind the Headlines', 4–10 October 2001. Published by permission of the editor of *Community Care*)

The abuse of people in residential settings is a further example of poor support, or rather the opposite of support, abuse, where people have already been identified as vulnerable and in need of protection. The report 'Lost in Care' published in February 2000 as a result of the inquiry led by Sir Ronald Waterhouse into the abuse of children in homes in North Wales, uncovered 'deeds of appalling mistreatment and wickedness, of sexual, physical, and emotional abuse, and of the total abuse of trust'. Although the report concerned abuse between 1974 and 1990, more recent cases of abuse in residential settings indicate that there is still considerable progress to be made in the protection of those who have already been identified as in need of support. The development of UK-wide codes of practice, procedures for 'whistle-blowing', improvements in training, and the registration of the workforce will begin to provide additional safeguards.

RESPONDING TO ABUSE

You may have many mixed feelings about abuse and its perpetrators. It is necessary to be open about these, to establish your sources of support and to work through your feelings and any problems you may have about working in this area. This will enhance your ability to help others. Abusers and abused people often need skilled and long-term help, but there are some things that a care worker is able to do.

In relation to what you can do for others, there are some things you must do, especially in relation to the abuse of children and young people, some things that are helpful and some things you definitely should not do.

Things you must do

Anyone who tells you about abuse needs to be believed, and needs protection from further abuse. You must ensure that you stay calm, listen and do not show disbelief. The person telling you about the abuse needs to realise that in all probability you will have to share this information with your manager. In the case of the abuse of children and young people, you *must share* this information with your manager, and feel assured that adequate steps are taken in relation to meeting the needs and protecting the individual. All care workers should be familiar with their agency policy on abuse. If you find that there is not an agency policy, there should be. You may need not only to ask about when this is likely to be produced, but indicate the requirement for such a policy as a condition of agency registration or re-registration, and in order to meet the care service standards. Such a policy is also required to fulfil the code of practice for employers.

Things that are helpful

All of the communication skills discussed in Chapter 4 are important in your work with people who have been abused. Reassurance is vital, and encouraging the person to talk through the use of open-ended questions is much better than an interrogation. Often people need to tell but do not wish to accuse. The use of too many questions can close rather than open doors.

Do discuss not only the abuse situation but also how you feel with your line manager/supervisor. Working with an abuse situation can be extremely stressful, and can create all kinds of mixed feelings. All of this needs to be dealt with. You may need support in order to maximise the help that you are able to provide. Seek that support if it is not offered, and make sure that you take care of yourself. Additional training can be beneficial both to service users and to your own confidence and ability in coping with service users who have experienced abuse.

Writing things down

Accurate, timely recording of conversations and disclosures, of the person's manner and any indicators of abuse (physical or psychological) may be vital in ensuring that any abuser is not only questioned but is also prevented from gaining opportunities to abuse again. You should record events leading to abuse and disclosure, and the disclosures made, while also taking account of the individual's rights in relation to confidentiality and your responsibilities to protect individuals. You should also gather together any information that you already have that could be of relevance to police and social workers. Record dates and times, and ensure accuracy of information. Ensure that agency policies in relation to recording are followed.

Some things you definitely should not do

There is often a temptation to try to resolve a situation where this is not within your ability or remit. Unless you are trained to work in this area, it is much better to refer on the specialised therapeutic aspects of dealing with abuse, while you provide the listening, support and empathy that are a part of your responsibility and role. If you have additional training that you can use, then this is a different matter.

In relation to the disclosure of abuse, a women's support project suggests trying to avoid saying:

- ❑ Why? How? When? Where? Who?
- ❑ Are you sure?

- ❏ Why didn't you say so before?
- ❏ I can't believe it.
- ❏ This is really serious; Don't tell anyone; I am shocked.
- ❏ Ideas or statements of 'bad'.
- ❏ False promises.

Helpful things to say

The same project suggests the following helpful things to say:

- ❏ I believe you.
- ❏ I am glad that you told me.
- ❏ I am sorry that it happened.
- ❏ It is not your fault.
- ❏ I care, and I will help.
- ❏ You were right to tell, and it is okay to tell.
- ❏ You were brave to tell.
- ❏ The abuser was wrong (it is better not to say 'bad').
- ❏ You are not to blame.

To finish

Tell the person again that you believe them. Let him/her know what you are going to do, and, as far as possible, what is going to happen next. Do what you said you were going to do. Praise the person for telling you, and for surviving the abuse. Try always to finish on a positive but realistic and honest note.

Prevention is better than cure

All of the above assumes that abuse has already taken place. The care worker does, however, also have a part to play in preventing abuse from happening. It could be assumed that since factors associated with abuse can be identified, those possessing some or all of these predisposing factors could be identified and offered additional support. What is wrong with this approach? Nothing and everything. There is nothing wrong with supporting people who present or are referred as stressed and/or in need of help, especially if they have caring responsibilities and abuse is thought by them or others to be a possibility. But to identify a specific section of society as potential abusers has other and different implications and dimensions.

The main disadvantage of this approach is a moral one. People who have done nothing at all except to possess some factors that some researchers have found may be associated with people who abuse, are to be singled out for special treatment because they may abuse. There are not only human rights issues here (the label of potential abuser – isn't that all of us?) but also practical ones. Although most predictive studies are between 60–80 per cent accurate in identifying people who go on to abuse (Corby 2000, p188) they also identify a much, much greater number of people who are considered to be at risk but who never abuse. A study by Parton (1985) in Bradford predicted that 17 of 28 children who ended up on the child protection register would be registered, but in their research they wrongly predicted that 483 others would end up on the register who did not, a very high false positive rate. Although there is not a complete correlation between registration and abuse, the correlation is high and means that preventive work would have supported, and possibly labelled as potential abusers, 500 people or families of whom only 17 ended up as abusers. Eleven more people or families would have fallen through the net. This does not denounce prevention or support, but suggests that identifying people as potential abusers is probably not the way forward. What is?

An approach that does not label but shares the process of assessment and assistance is likely to be just as beneficial. Where there has been a referral, or a care or other support worker identifies concerns, or a person identifies issues with which they would like help, assessment and support are offered. This approach relies upon respect for the people concerned, a collaborative approach and shared assessment, planning and implementation. Help provided is based upon a thorough shared assessment of need. Care workers respond according to their role in implementing the care plan and as members of a care team. Any of the helping approaches presented in this book, ranging from activity work to crisis intervention to the use of counselling skills, on their own or in combination, may be identified as the most helpful way forward. These utilise generic skills. Working in the field of abuse is not completely different or separate from any other area of work, though there are issues of protection of vulnerable people that also need to be taken into account.

It is a different matter where previous abuse has taken place, or where there are serious concerns, or where people identify themselves as at risk of abusing or being abused. Here assessment based upon need, including degree of vulnerability and need for protection, is vital, especially in the case of children. Sometimes measures of protection must be taken that do not involve choice or collaboration with family members because of the degree of risk involved. Even in these situations, though, a supportive approach that shows respect for the worth and dignity of individuals and works towards a shared understanding and solution is likely to have the most positive and lasting long-term effects.

LESSONS FROM THE CLIMBIE INQUIRY (2003) AND 'IT'S EVERYONE'S JOB TO MAKE SURE I'M ALRIGHT' (2002)

> I have suffered too much grief in setting down these heartrending memories. If I try to describe him, it is to make sure that I shall not forget him.
>
> (Quoted at the beginning of the Climbie Inquiry Report from 'The Little Prince' by Antoine de Saint-Exupéry)

Two recent reports have highlighted the need to improve practice drastically in relation to child abuse. The first was the 'Report of the Victoria Climbie Inquiry' by Lord Laming. This report set out:

> to find out why this once happy, smiling, enthusiastic little girl – brought to this country by a relative for 'a better life' – ended her days the victim of almost unimaginable cruelty.

The second is the report entitled 'It's everyone's job to make sure I'm alright' – a report of the Child Protection Audit and Review for Scotland, published in November 2002. This report emphasises everyone's responsibility in ensuring that children and young people are protected from abuse and harm. It was commissioned by Jack McConnell following the May 2000 report by Dr Helen Howard into the death of Kennedy McFarlane, at the hands of her step-father, Thomas Duncan.

The most notable shortcomings in practice described in both reports relate to a lack of communication among agencies and between professional disciplines, the lack of expertise of those with frontline responsibilities, and the poverty of supervision and responsibility by those in managerial and supervisory positions. There is nothing here that should not apply to any service user group.

Unlike the Climbie Inquiry, which was confined to the examination of the abuse of one child, the 'It's everyone's job to make sure I'm alright' report found that there were many examples of good contributions to child protection in the past 20 years.

The implications of these reports for social care are:

1. Communicate, communicate, communicate – communicate with vulnerable people, their families, carers and friends; with other workers including your own team, supervisor, social workers and relevant members of your own and other disciplines. Communication includes accurate recording.

ACTIVITY 6.3

There have been many other reports that relate to the abuse of vulnerable people. Find out about one of these and list five lessons that can be learned from it.

2. Improve your knowledge about abuse, its recognition, your agency policy and ways of helping people who are abused, fear abuse or themselves abuse or may abuse.
3. Use supervision to discuss your own practice, thinking, knowledge and feelings about abuse.
4. Take responsibility compatible with your role in relation to the prevention, recognition and support for those involved in abusive situations.

SUMMARY

This chapter has examined the difficult subject of protection from abuse and potential abuse. It may have implications for you, both in relation to your own life and the lives of those you work with. An understanding of the meaning and forms of abuse, and factors associated with abuse, is a prerequisite to being able to help people who have been or may be abused. Some ways of working with people are suggested, and lessons learned from reports about failure to protect people have been outlined.

FIVE KEY POINTS

1. Care workers have a role to play in identifying abuse when it occurs and in protecting people from abuse.
2. There are several forms of abuse that overlap with one another. These are physical, sexual, emotional, neglect, financial and inexplicable failure to thrive.
3. There are many physical, behavioural and psychological indications that abuse may have occurred. These include bruising, sleep disturbance, bed-wetting and fascination with sexual behaviour.

4. Factors often associated with abuse include stress, lack of love and attachment and learned behaviour.
5. Care workers can provide support through listening and responding, empathy and attention to agency policy.

THREE QUESTIONS

1. What are five indications that may raise concerns that someone has been abused?
2. What are three factors that are often associated with abuse?
3. How do you view your role in relation to protecting people from abuse?

RECOMMENDED READING

Child Protection Audit and Review (2002) *It's everyone's job to make sure I'm alright*. Edinburgh: Scottish Executive. A wide-ranging inquiry into child protection in Scotland, full of examples of practice and very useful recommendations.

CORBY, B. (2000) *Child Abuse, towards a knowledge base*, 2nd edn. Buckingham: Open University Press. This is a comprehensive and informative book that places child abuse in a historical, social and political context. The causes and consequences of abuse are discussed and a wide range of research is examined.

HARRIS, J. and CRAFT, A. (1994) *People with Learning Disabilities at risk of Physical or Sexual Abuse*. London: Bild. A thought-provoking and thorough examination of issues in relation to the abuse of people with learning disability.

LAMING, LORD (2003) *The Victoria Climbie Inquiry*. Norwich: HMSO. A moving and damning account of just about everyone's poor practice in relation to Victoria Climbie, and one of the saddest documents I have ever read.

CHAPTER 7

INTRODUCING PSYCHOLOGY AND SOCIOLOGY

Susan Gibb

> **There is a history in all men's lives.**
> (William Shakespeare, *Henry IV, Part II* in Staunton, H 1996)

By the end of this chapter, you should be able to:

- ❑ explain some key ideas from psychology
- ❑ explain some key ideas from sociology
- ❑ understand how they might be relevant in care work
- ❑ access up-to-date sources of information on sociology and psychology.

The content of this chapter provides underpinning content and context for all care qualifications. It relates especially to the following HNC units:

Psychology for social care practice

Sociology for social care practice.

INTRODUCTION

Why do people act the way they do? Why is society organised the way it is – and why do they organise things differently in other countries? Who decides on

Perspective	A particular way of looking at something. An area of thought based on assumptions, within which there can be a number of more specific theories.
Theory	A system of ideas which explains the relationship between events. It provides a framework for understanding the complexity of something. A theory allows us to explain rather than just describe something, and to see beyond the particular facts to the general picture, because it is based on research. A theory also helps us look beyond the obvious to the hidden aspects of something.

Figure 7.1 Key concepts in psychology and sociology

which laws we will have? Psychologists and sociologists try to explain the answers to questions like these. They describe and analyse influences on behaviour, and look at patterns and trends in society. Although each person is unique, it is useful to try and understand some of the general principles and forces which shape each individual, so that we can understand more clearly how to anticipate and respond to the inevitable changes we face throughout our life.

In some subjects, such as car mechanics or anatomy, there is only one theory. People who study these subjects learn the theory about how a car or how the human body works and never need to question it. More information is maybe added as the subject is studied in more depth, but the basics remain the same and every mechanic or physiotherapist will apply the same theory in their work.

The same is not true for sociology and psychology: there are a number of perspectives about why people and society operate the way they do. The variety of psychological and sociological perspectives help to remind us that human life is diverse and complex. Each perspective has a number of writers who agree on the basic assumptions about people and society, but take a slightly different viewpoint and develop a particular theory. Each theory asks certain questions about how we develop and provides concepts to help us understand and explore the human condition.

In this chapter we will consider a few of the main perspectives and theories in sociology and psychology which have relevance for care settings. No single theory explains all human behaviour: any act we perform or thought we have can be analysed in a number of different ways. It is up to you to read about the different theories and see which ones might be useful in gaining insight to the particular situation you are in. Indeed, you may find that you will use elements from a variety of perspectives to understand any situation and consider ways of dealing with it.

Psychology and sociology both attempt to help us understand how we develop and how we behave. Psychology is more concerned with the 'inner life' of an individual (how their mind works or how their personality develops), while sociology is more interested in how individuals act with others in relationships and groups, and with the influence which society has on behaviour. Psychologists and sociologists research their ideas in many ways, such as laboratory experiments, observing people in their real life settings or asking them questions in interviews and surveys. All the writers in this chapter have carried out some form of research to establish or test their ideas.

PSYCHOLOGY

We will consider the work of writers from four different psychological perspectives. These writers explain how our thoughts and personalities grow and develop during the different stages in our life: infancy, childhood, adolescence, adulthood and older adulthood. All psychological theories recognise that a human being has a range of needs which will vary over time. These needs can be categorised into five general strands: social, physical, intellectual/cognitive, cultural and emotional, or 'SPICE'. The theories differ in the emphasis which they give to the importance of each life stage, and which of the needs seem to be most important in affecting the kind of person we become.

Psychodynamic perspective

This was the first psychological approach. It took issues which had been discussed for centuries within religion and philosophy, and sought to investigate them in more detail. It is based on the idea that people have aspects of their mind and personality which are in conflict, and so the human psyche is seen to be in a dynamic, or constantly moving, state. The psychodynamic approach focuses on the belief that people are born with certain unconscious drives (both for life and for death) that have an impact on their behaviour.

Freud and psychoanalytic theory

Sigmund Freud (1856–1939) is probably the best-known psychologist in this chapter. Although much of what he wrote has been discredited or questioned by other psychologists, many of his basic ideas are still useful and relevant today.

Perspective	Theory	Main theorist
Psychodynamic Looks at the importance of early childhood experiences and how they affect our later development	Psychoanalytic	Freud
	Lifespan	Erikson
Behavioural Looks at the observable, measurable actions which we display	Behavioural theories	Skinner, Pavlov and Thorndike
	Social learning theory	Bandura
Cognitive Looks at the way in which we build up our pictures of the world, and how our thinking and understanding develops	Developmental psychology	Piaget
	Cognitive therapy	Beck
	Rational emotive behaviour therapy	Ellis
Humanistic Looks at the whole person (thoughts, actions, experiences) and how they experience the world – from their point of view	Person-centred	Rogers
	Hierarchy of needs	Maslow

Figure 7.2 Psychological perspectives, theories and theorists

Freud believed that babies are a bundle of id. They seek pleasure (feeding, cuddles, attention) immediately and have no awareness of other people's needs. As their ego develops, they become aware that their demands do not always need to be met immediately. They realise that other people do exist and that they have needs too. They learn to repress the urges of the id until an appropriate time or situation arises. They begin to develop a sense of the real world and how they are only part of it, not the only thing. Then, as they grow older, their superego develops, and they gain a clearer awareness of what is right and wrong. External punishments from parents and others are replaced by internal rule following: a child will not steal money, even if no one else is around, because they know it is wrong. The superego uses feelings of guilt and

Parts of the personality: three conflicting internal states	
Id	The 'childlike' part of your personality; the part which demands things now; the part which seeks pleasure.
Ego	The 'adult' part of your personality; the part which knows it may have to wait for your needs to be met; the part which understands reality.
Superego	The 'parent' part of your personality; the part which knows right from wrong; the part which understands morals; the 'conscience'.
Levels of the mind: memories can move between the three levels	
Conscious	All the things you are aware of, or can recall easily.
Preconscious	Things you can recall after a bit of thought or effort.
Unconscious	Thoughts and feelings you are not aware of.
Defence mechanisms	Thoughts and behaviours which your ego uses to deal with anxiety caused by the conflicting demands of the id and superego: the way in which you cope with guilt, embarrassment, fear etc., which can help you temporarily stay in a more balanced frame of mind.

Figure 7.3 Freud's key concepts

self-reproach to enforce these rules and inhibit the person from following the demands of their id. According to Freud, this process happens in the first few years of a person's life, and their basic personality is formed by the time they reach their adolescent years.

As adults, we have all three aspects – id, ego and superego – in our personality. A psychologically healthy person has a strong ego, which can deal with the impulses and demands from both the id and superego. If you have ever said to yourself 'I am bored and depressed, I am going to have a chocolate biscuit,' you will have felt the effect of id on your behaviour. If you have been able to say 'No, I will not, I am trying to diet,' then that is your superego coming in to counterbalance the urge from the id. Your ego will consider both sides of this debate and your behaviour will be affected by its decision. For most of us, we have little debates within ourselves all day long about what we should or should not do: your ego is balancing out conflicting demands all the time. Sometimes the id wins, sometimes the superego does. A problem arises only when one aspect (id or superego) becomes dominant and your behaviour is driven by it too often. The extreme result in the above example would be either obesity (the id, pleasure principle, demanding immediate gratification, not thinking of the consequences) or anorexia (a superego which is so rigid and controlling that it is unable to allow any pleasure at all).

This example illustrates the relationship between id, ego and superego at a conscious level: I know what I am doing and I am aware of it. However, Freud was interested in this dynamic as an unconscious process. Our thoughts, actions and behaviour are affected – we are driven by urges, or constrained by internal rules – and yet we are often not consciously aware that we are being influenced. This is when our defence mechanisms come into play.

Freud suggested that there is a range of defence mechanisms which people use to reduce anxiety. Some examples are:

- ❏ **Repression:** we put it to 'the back of our mind' and do not think about it. In extreme cases this would result in **denial** where we do not even admit that something happened; e.g. I have noticed a lump in my breast when having a shower, but 'keep forgetting' to phone the doctor for a check-up.
- ❏ **Displacement:** we take our anger/anxiety out on someone or something else, because to express it directly to the person causing the emotions is too frightening or difficult; e.g. a young child breaks a toy because she is angry with her father for saying no to her demand, or someone swears and blasts his horn at a minor inconvenience on the drive back home from another long wait at the hospital clinic.
- ❏ **Sublimation:** we divert our anxious/angry energy into another activity, generally one that will tire us out; e.g. vigorously cleaning the house after an argument with your teenage daughter, playing sport after a difficult day at work.
- ❏ **Regression:** we return to a state that gives us comfort, from a time in our life when we felt safer; e.g. sucking our thumb/twiddling our hair when we are nervous, staying in bed instead of getting up to face the day when we are depressed.

Practice focus: attachment

Many people, such as his daughter Anna Freud (1896–1982), Melanie Klein (1882–1960) and John Bowlby (1907–90), have conducted further research into Freud's ideas about the importance that experiences in our early years play in the development of our personality. Unlike Freud, they have carried out significant research work with children and their families. In particular, they have researched the importance of attachment and bonding between babies and their primary carers in the first months and years of their life.

The Anna Freud Centre in London is involved in a project with mothers in prison, aimed at helping them understand their babies' emotional and developmental needs, and prepare for separation. Evidence shows that, where there is a long sentence and it is in the child's best interests, the mother and child will separate in the first six months or so. That allows the mother to begin the bonding process with her child, but then the child is able also to bond with an alternative carer who will be more involved with the child in the early years (www.annafreudcentre.org).

ACTIVITY 7.1

Provide short answers to the following questions:

1. Do you agree that it is best for a baby to spend time with its mother in prison?
2. What might the advantages or disadvantages be for the mother, and what might be the impact on the baby?
3. What psychological theories in this chapter may help in enabling you to answer the first two questions?

Erikson and the psychosocial or 'lifespan' theory

Erik Erikson (1902–94), Alfred Adler (1870–1937) and Carl Jung (1885–1961) developed Freud's ideas. Writing half a century after Freud, Erikson agreed with concepts such as the ego, but he differed from Freud because he believed that psychological development was a lifelong process which was greatly influenced by our social environment.

Stage	Age	Conflict to be resolved	Ego strength developed if the conflict is resolved
1 Oral–sensory	0–1½	Trust *versus* mistrust	Hope
2 Muscular–anal	1 1/2–3	Autonomy *versus* shame and doubt	Will
3 Locomotor	3–6	Initiative *versus* guilt	Purpose
4 Latency	6–puberty	Competency *versus* inferiority	Competence
5 Adolescence	12–18	Identity *versus* role confusion	Identity
6 Early adulthood	19–40	Intimacy *versus* isolation	Love
7 Middle age	40–65	Generativity *versus* stagnation	Care
8 Maturity	65 +	Integrity *versus* despair	Wisdom

Figure 7.4 Erikson's key concepts

Erikson believed that we develop our sense of self (our ego) as we interact with people and face challenges at each stage of our life. The newborn baby, completely dependent on other people to meet his or her needs, will learn either that the world is a safe, reliable place where he or she feels comfortable if his or her needs are met and therefore develops a sense of hope, or that the world is a hostile, unfriendly place if he or she is neglected. Equally, adolescents are faced with the task of working out who they are and where they fit into the world. Teenagers try out hairstyles, lifestyles and musical tastes, and many experiment with relationships, cigarettes and alcohol. Many of the ideas, thoughts and feelings at this stage will not remain permanently, but they are intense and bound up tightly with their sense of identity – which group they do or do not belong to, which ideas of their parents/community they agree or disagree with. By the end of this stage, an adolescent who has support from family, friends and school (but also freedom to make mistakes and change their mind) will move onto the next stage with a relatively clear idea of who they are. However, many people still remain confused, misunderstood and unhappy. They have not yet found where they fit into their community and society, and will spend more time in the future trying to resolve this conflict. For instance, many people come back to this dilemma later in life, as they look at the consequences of the decisions they made during adolescence. At this later stage, they are perhaps more able to understand and act on their 'real' identity than they were as a teenager.

So, at each stage in our life, we have a conflict (a dilemma or task) which we need to resolve (work through), so that we can develop our sense of self and develop good psychological health. If we do not manage to resolve the conflict, it means that we will 'carry it forward' to the next stage(s) where we might meet the necessary social situations to develop the ego strength. Obviously, if we have managed to build the strength at the appropriate stage, then we are psychologically more ready to meet the challenges of the next stage.

However, developing the relevant ego strength at each stage does not guarantee a stress-free life. Circumstances can change, and someone who has previously been psychologically strong and healthy can still struggle to overcome a situation such as divorce, death of loved one or redundancy.

Behavioural perspective

Within two decades of Freud publishing his psychoanalytic theory of personality, other psychologists were questioning the usefulness of his introspective approach. Behaviourists said that you could not prove or disprove most of psychoanalytical theory, e.g. if the superego existed, or if someone really was motivated by their unconscious drives; it was all subjective and could not be tested. Behaviourists claimed that psychology should concentrate on observable facts which can be measured, and not on the inaccessible inner thoughts or memories of a person.

Pavlov, Skinner, Thorndike and laboratory experiments

Behaviourists believe that everyone is born 'a blank slate' and that our personality and all our behaviour are learned through a process such as trial and error, or by observing and imitating other people. They make the assumption that human beings are like animals and that their actions are always reactions, so they can be studied using the same techniques. Therefore, a lot of the initial research into behavioural theory was carried out in laboratory experiments on

Stimulus/antecedent	A trigger (e.g. an event, smell, word) which sets a behaviour in motion.
Response/behaviour	The behaviour which is a reaction to the stimulus.
Association	The connection which a person makes between a stimulus and a response; can be conscious or unconscious.
Consequence	What happens as a result of a behaviour.
Reinforcement	The reward which makes it more likely that a behaviour will be repeated.

Figure 7.5 Key concepts of behavioural theory

animals. The work of Ivan Pavlov (1849–1910) with dogs led to conditioning theory based on the stimulus-response model; B F Skinner's (1904–90) work with rats looked at the importance of reinforcements (rewards) in maintaining behaviour, and E L Thorndike's (1874–1949) work with cats resulted in his concept of trial and error learning. Much of this work was then applied to people: e.g. in 1906. Thorndike's ideas were used by teachers in schools in America to work with their pupils in a more systematic way.

Behavioural theories are particularly useful when targeting specific behaviours which someone wants to change. They look at one or more of the three stages in the ABC process (Antecedent – Behaviour – Consequence), and develop strategies to create change. There are numerous examples of how this can work:

❑ When trying to eradicate phobias, people can be systematically exposed to more frightening triggers until they have learned to control their anxiety response by using relaxation techniques.
❑ When treating people with addictions, it can help to target times or situations which might trigger a desire for the drink/drugs, and help the person work out strategies to avoid these triggers.
❑ When looking at episodes of challenging behaviour, it can help to keep a diary to note in detail which events predate an episode, so that plans can be developed to avoid or deal with these.
❑ Offenders are helped to develop behaviour modification strategies to move away from offending behaviour; reinforcements are tied in to encourage the maintenance of these behaviours.

Albert Bandura and social learning theory

Albert Bandura (born 1925) developed the ideas of the early behaviourists, but believed that social factors play an important part in the development of human behaviour. He was particularly interested in whether our behaviour, such as violence and aggression, is influenced by watching television and films.

This theory suggests that we pick up behaviour throughout our lives, just by being in the presence of other people and 'vicariously' absorbing their behaviour. As adults we often find ourselves acting like parents, having sworn that we would never be like that with our children. Much of the practical training of care workers is based on the principles of modelling good practice and observing others who are more experienced. Health promotion is heavily based on presenting positive models of behaviour as an alternative to antisocial or self-destructive habits. Care workers, befrienders, advocates and others can be strong and positive models of behaviour to service users, and service users can be strong role models to each other. By observational learning, service users can pick up more effective ways of communicating with others. Care planning should

Observation	Looking at other people and watching how they behave.
Imitation	Deliberately copying someone else's behaviour; acting the way they do.
Model	Person that you look up to and want to emulate.
Vicarious learning	Learning new ways of acting without being aware consciously that you are learning; passively picking up behaviour without realising you have been influenced.
Intrinsic reward	Feeling of pleasure which comes from within the individual, e.g. pride or satisfaction.
Extrinsic reward	A reward from outside, e.g. money, a medal, a certificate.
Reciprocal determinism	People are influenced by intrinsic and extrinsic rewards and by vicarious rewards – the rewards they see others getting for doing something.
Self-efficacy	The belief we have in our ability to do something.

Figure 7.6 Key concepts of social learning theory

Practice focus: The impact of images on young people's behaviour

Images which young people see of people who smoke, drink or take drugs have greater impact on their behaviour than anything others might say to them, and these impressions can affect people without their being aware of it. Young people are generally not affected by what other people think, particularly when it comes to risk-taking pursuits such as smoking and drinking. If they decide to smoke, use drugs, or indeed take healthy exercise, they will probably go ahead and do so. But, in coming to that decision, they are more impressed by what others do than by what they say. The research shows that images can influence people, even though they do not believe this to be the case. (Sheeran, 2004)

ACTIVITY 7.2

Many health promotion initiatives and awareness-raising campaigns (on issues such as child poverty, zero tolerance to domestic violence or the stigma associated with mental illness) are based on influencing people's ideas and actions through the medium of advertising. Given the discussion above, do you think this is a good way of changing attitudes and behaviour on these issues? If not, what else might be more effective? You could look at the following websites for more information:

- ❏ www.seemescotland.org
- ❏ www.zerotolerance.org.uk
- ❏ www.healthpromotionagency.org.uk

take into account the range of people a service user might meet with, for maximum variety of models.

Workers can also think carefully about which behaviour they might inadvertently be reinforcing; e.g. giving someone more attention when they display challenging behaviour than when they do not, might actually encourage the person to continue being challenging in order to receive attention. Workers could concentrate on reinforcing desirable behaviour. Understanding the role of a person's often limiting belief in themselves can help workers to plan effective ways of raising a person's self-esteem.

Cognitive perspectives

Cognitive perspectives look in detail at how the mind works – how we build up the pictures in our mind, develop patterns of thinking, solve problems and make decisions. With the technological advances in computer science in the 1950s, psychologists became more interested in the way in which people developed their thoughts and the processes they used to come to decisions. They wanted to move on from the behaviourists' emphasis on the end product – behaviour – and look in more detail at the thinking processes behind the behaviour. Again, they faced the same problem as the psychodynamic writers: in the 1950s you could not actually observe the inner workings of the brain, although it is now more possible to do that with modern technology. However, they could assess and evaluate cognitive processes (the way someone thinks) from their speech or actions.

Piaget and developmental cognitive psychology

Jean Piaget (1896–1980) was one of the first people to recognise that in terms of thought processes, children were not just 'little adults'. Through his research, observing and talking to children, he saw that children developed strategies to see and understand the world as they grew older. They developed schemas, or mental structures, at various key points in their childhood which helped them conceptualise the world. These are a bit like building blocks, because once they have worked out one idea (if I reach out and grab, I can hold a spoon), they can add another dimension to it (if I move while grabbing, this will throw the contents about!). A child adapts this new knowledge into their picture of the world and organises their thinking based on their experiences. Piaget's work has been very influential in understanding how children develop their thinking, and has been used as the basis for the way in which children are taught.

Beck and cognitive therapy

Aaron Beck (born 1921) is an American psychiatrist who initially trained in the psychoanalytical approach but felt that it was limited. He saw through his contact with adult clients that the way in which the person currently 'structures the world' in their mind was what influenced their mood and therefore determined their behaviour. He believed that depression, for instance, was often caused by people's 'faulty' beliefs and expectations about themselves or the world. These thoughts led to feelings of helplessness and hopelessness about their life, in a world which they saw as being empty and uncaring. He developed techniques which helped the person look at how they saw the world, test this reality and correct their distorted beliefs. Like most cognitive approaches, this involves giving the client a lot of work between sessions,

Focus on practice: depression

Twelve per cent of men and 20 per cent of women will experience an episode of clinical depression at some time in their lives. At any one time, there are around five per cent of the population who are suffering depression of this severity. Twenty-five per cent of these episodes last less than a month; a further 50 per cent recover in less than three months. However, the depression can develop into a longer-term problem, with around one-quarter being seriously depressed one year after symptom onset, and one-fifth remaining depressed two years later. The most commonly used treatment for such depression is antidepressant medication. It is cheap, easy for GPs (who treat the majority of depressed people) to use and effective. Depression tends to return, however, and within two years of recovering from one episode, around a half of patients will have suffered another episode of depression.

However, not every patient regards medication as the appropriate treatment, and some tolerate the side effects poorly. But the main problem is that no antidepressant has yet been found that has a long-term effect in reducing the relapse after stopping taking the medication. Evidence suggests that once a person has recovered from depression following cognitive therapy, their risk of having a further episode falls to 25 per cent over the following two years. Cognitive therapy is successful because it encourages people to 'catch' whatever thought is going through their mind when their mood shifts and write it down so that it can be evaluated against evidence later. Over time, the person will gradually extend their range of activities, which restores a sense of mastery and pleasure in their daily lives. (Williams, 2004)

applying the new learning they have gained and trying out new techniques for coping with their problems.

Ellis and rational emotive therapy

Albert Ellis (born 1913) was another cognitive theorist developing his ideas in the 1960s at the same time as Beck. His focus was on the 'irrational beliefs' that people held about themselves and the world. He identified 11 standard irrational beliefs that many people hold, which influence how they interpret and respond to situations. Among these are the beliefs that: it is necessary to be thoroughly competent in everything if I am not to be seen as worthless; unhappiness is always caused by other people; things should be the way I would like them to be; it is necessary to be loved by everyone, and past history will always determine present events. People who hold these views may be unduly stressed if they are not perfect at something or unduly upset if they think someone has ignored them. They may spend the rest of the day, week or month obsessing about the event and how imperfect the world is, and this will have a knock-on effect on how they interpret other events that happen to them. He believed that if people were helped to confront and challenge these beliefs, they would be able to replace them with more rational ones which would allow them to develop a more flexible and realistic response to situations.

Cognitive/behavioural approaches

Cognitive and behavioural theories are often spoken about together because, when studying humans, the two cannot really be separated. They are both enormously useful for certain issues in care settings, because they enable people to deal with problems in a focused, step-by-step manner. Big problems can be

---

Practice focus: cognitive behavioural approaches to chronic pain

Factors which predict the development of chronic pain following an acute episode do not entirely relate to biological factors, but also to what are termed 'psychosocial variables', such as mood, stress (as noted by depression scores and anxiety levels) and the social situation in which the pain occurs. Even following routine surgical operations, the amount of pain experienced by a person does not relate simply to the operation type or the length of the incision; other factors such as past experience, age, sex, anxiety, fear and depression all have a bearing. People find themselves in a vicious circle: people who have pain, especially on movement, tend to avoid doing things that provoke their symptoms, but this only leads to stiffening and weakness, worsening the symptom which the person is trying to avoid. Inability to function leads to a loss of role and self-esteem, with the progressive intrusion of other problems such as financial hardship and strained relationships.

Cognitive behavioural approaches aim to improve the way a person manages and copes with their pain. Cognitive therapy helps identify negative thinking patterns and the development of effective challenges, while stretching and exercising improve physical functioning. The use of relaxation training and the careful planning of tasks and daily activities enable the person to take back control over their lives, do more and feel better. (Pither, 2004)

---

broken down into small steps, and people can feel a sense of achievement when they achieve success with each small step. This is important when people have long struggles to deal with situations such as rehabilitation after a stroke, or making the changes to live a drug-free life.

Many issues that people face cannot be eradicated. For instance, they cannot change the abuse they experienced in their childhood, or ignore an illness such as schizophrenia or multiple sclerosis. However, the way they *think* or *act* in relation to these issues can be changed. Cognitive and behavioural approaches give people a range of tools and techniques to change their habits, thoughts and behaviours, break the old associations they have and learn new ways of responding to their situation. Habits are not easy to break, as anyone who has ever tried to go on a diet or stop smoking can testify. However, it is possible to make changes armed with a clear plan, motivation and the right support.

Humanist perspective

The humanist perspective was developed from the 1950s onwards in the USA and Europe, in response to the limitations of the psychodynamic and cognitive/behavioural models. Many counsellors and therapists had trained in and worked with these models, but found that many of their clients still did not make long-lasting changes in their thoughts or behaviour. They perhaps gained insight during psychoanalysis, but were not able to put this into practice in their current relationships. Or they made changes to their thoughts and actions after cognitive behavioural therapy, but then they fell back into their old patterns when they met an obstacle, or became less motivated when they did not have the regular support of a therapist.

The humanist approach is holistic: theorists felt it was important to look at ALL aspects of a person's life – behaviour, thoughts, past and present experiences, spirituality etc. – and not concentrate on just one aspect. They also felt it was important to get away from the doctor–patient type of relationship that had existed in therapy until then, and put the client at the centre of the relationship: the client was seen as the expert in his own life, and it was the role of the therapist to enable him to discover his 'true self' rather than to diagnose him.

The humanist theory of personality and development is based on the person valuing their uniqueness, understanding their perception and being motivated by a positive drive for growth and development throughout their life towards discovering their full potential. Humanists believe that people have free will and can choose how they act: they are not driven by unconscious forces. The concepts in the humanist approach are used by many helping professionals to inform the way in which they work with service users, and by many people who are interested in looking at how they relate to others, because it emphasises the healthy functioning side of human nature, rather than the darker 'sick half' of psychology that Freud considered.

Maslow and the hierarchy of needs

Abraham Maslow (1908–70), who initially trained in the behavioural approach, developed a model which demonstrates the variety of needs that people have as a series of levels in a hierarchy. He suggests that we are motivated to meet the lower level needs first, before we are able to consider fully meeting our higher level needs.

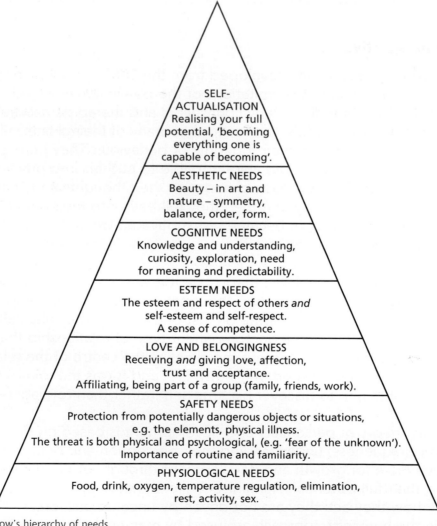

Figure 7.7 Maslow's hierarchy of needs

Maslow does not believe that people have to have *all* of their needs met at one level before they can meet the needs at the next level. However, it is important to have at least partially met the lower needs, or the person will still be expending so much time and energy trying to meet them that they will be unable to meet higher level needs. Also, in any one day, we move up and down the levels in the hierarchy continuously. For example, we go back to the first level every time we think 'I need to get a cup of coffee and a biscuit before I can get my mind round this problem' (physical needs must be met before cognitive) or 'I will just have a quick trip to the toilet before we sit and have a chat' (physical needs before social).

Maslow felt that as long as people are still working to meet the four lower level needs – physical, safety, love and esteem – they are just existing. It is only when people are meeting their three higher level needs that they can be said to be thriving. People do not reach self-actualisation once and stay there: it is part of a continual process of remaining motivated to be all we can be, adapting to the changes in our inner needs and outer experiences. The Olympic gold medallist has reached the top of their sport, but then they create a new goal to gain a second gold, or increase their speed. According to Maslow's model of motivation, it is the nature of human beings to want to grow and develop: that is what motivates us to find a variety of ways to meet our many needs.

Maslow's model reminds us that we have many needs, but in care settings it is sometimes only the basic ones which are met. If people are healthy and feel safe, then that is a good start, but all of us have a right to stretch our minds, find things we enjoy that broaden our horizons and take part in activities where we feel challenged and fulfilled. Whether in a short-staffed residential unit or living at home with inadequate support, many people (staff as well as service users)

Practice focus: the impact of temporary relocation on residents in a care home

One study looked at the stress and strain on residents, staff and relatives in a residential home when they had to be temporarily relocated to allow a refurbishment programme. Despite planning, consultation and reassurances, residents became anxious and problems arose because established cultures which existed within the separate homes changed, and many of the aspects of location, staffing and social contacts which provided security and comfort were lost (Wyld, 2002). Is there anything else the staff could have done, knowing about Maslow's hierarchy, to prepare the residents for this change?

feel they are just surviving, rather than thriving. Maslow's model reminds us that the fulfilled human being would be able to consider development on all seven levels.

Rogers and the person-centred approach

Carl Rogers (1902–87) initially trained as a psychiatrist in Freud's psychoanalytic approach, but eventually felt that it was a limited way of working with clients. From his counselling work, Rogers discovered that the key element to helping someone change was the *relationship* which the therapist had with them, rather than any techniques which the therapist used. He studied and developed this idea, putting the client (the 'person') – rather than the therapist – at the centre of the counselling process.

Rogers believed that you need to look at the whole person from their point of view, in order to understand why they act the way they do. He believed that we lose touch with our organismic self as we grow up, due to all the pressures and influences on us. Our self-image and ideal self have been influenced by the many conditions of worth we have been given – from our parents (I will love you if you: go to church, act like a proper good girl, be tough like a boy should be etc.), school (clever kids are not cheeky) and friends (you have to dress/act/talk like this to be part of our group).

Rogers does not say that this is only a negative process. However, Rogers is concerned that the conditions of worth and lack of positive regard which people receive throughout their lives, can mean that they develop an external locus of evaluation. That means that when it comes down to it, they are not really sure what they feel or think about themselves, their relationships or their life because they have always just gone with the flow, fitted in with what their family/friends/society expected of them. For much of our life, this is an easy enough, if habitual and unfulfilling, way of living.

When a situation comes along that disturbs our equilibrium (such as illness, an accident, or being victim of a crime), we become unsettled, ask different questions of ourselves and make different demands on other people. Although we can often come through these situations, sometimes we need the support of someone who will offer us unconditional positive regard and empathy: they will listen to us without judging us. If they do not put conditions on us about how we should think or feel, we have more chance of making decisions from an internal locus of evaluation. We are more likely to develop a clear and honest self-image (accepting both the positive and negative aspects of ourselves) and a realistic ideal self (not based on what family/magazines/celebrities say is

Organismic self	Our 'true' self; what we would have been without all the influences/pressures on us.
Self concept:	The picture we have of ourselves. This is made up of three inter-relating parts:
❑ Self image ❑ Ideal self ❑ Self-esteem	How we see ourselves at the moment How we would like to be How we feel about ourselves.

Your self-esteem is likely to be high if your self-image and ideal self are close; your self-esteem is likely to be low if the way in which you see yourself and what you would like to be are very different.

Unconditional positive regard	Accepting someone for who they are, not judging them (either as good or bad)
Conditions of worth	Expectations people have about what other people should do before they will love/respect/admire/care for them.
Empathy	Understanding someone; seeing the world from their point of view.
Locus of evaluation:	The place you make decisions from; this can be either:
❑ Internal	From inside yourself: from your own point of view and based on your own opinion.
❑ External	From outside, based on, or being influenced by other people's point of view or opinions.

Figure 7.8 Key concepts of Carl Rogers and the person-centred approach

important). Therefore our self-esteem will increase as we live a life which is nearer to our true, authentic and genuine organismic self. Some people may need the support of a counsellor, therapist or other helper to help them through this process. For others, a supportive friend or care worker is the catalyst to change in their life. If people are offered unconditional positive regard, there is a chance that they will feel safe enough to explore and express their true feelings and opinions.

Practice focus: quality of life for people in care homes

Research based on interviews with people living in care homes, many of whom had dementia and/or communication difficulties, found that they were not being given the chance, literally, to be themselves. People need to be able to express themselves, and their quality of life is inhibited if they are not able to feel at home and comfortable in expressing a sense of self positively. Paying attention to how they look, valuing their possessions and showing that they like to have some personal space, all add to how they see themselves.

The sense of one's self is important in the relationships that people sustain with other residents in the home and with their families. Trips outside the care home are rare, and this confinement increases the risk of being cut off from past associations with neighbours and friends. Ordinary activities like window shopping or going for a pint are no longer possible. The quality of life of residents is determined almost wholly within the home, but over-worked carers have limited opportunities to spend time with and listen to the residents. (Tester, 2004)

ACTIVITY 7.3

What steps could be taken to improve the variety of interactions that the residents might have? What links with the community (schools, library etc.) might they need to develop? What role might befrienders play in this situation? What other changes might be implemented so that the residents can express their individual choices and preferences?

Themes in psychology: grief and loss

A number of writers have looked at the particular changes which we undergo during periods of grief and loss. Most of the models are presented as a series of stages a person has to go through. Elizabeth Kubler Ross (1926–2004), working with people with terminal illness, identified five stages that a person might go through when facing up to their situation: denial, anger, bargaining, depression and acceptance (1989). Colin Murray Parkes (1998) looked at the process of grieving after a loss, and suggested a person might go through a four-stage process: numbness, searching and pining, depression and recovery. William Worden (2003) identified this grieving process as a series of four 'tasks' which a person has to go through: Task 1 – to accept the reality of the loss, Task 2 – to work through the pain of grief, Task 3 – to adjust to the environment in which the dead person is missing and Task 4 – emotionally to relocate the deceased person and move on with life.

These models are guidelines to general trends of adaptation: it is not compulsory for someone to go through all stages; the time spent in any stage will vary widely and people may move back and forward through the stages. However, it is useful in care settings to be aware of the general patterns so we can understand and assist others to deal with the stage which they are experiencing. It also helps people understand that the feelings they are having, which are often quite intense, are likely to pass in time.

Adam, Hayes and Hopson: Transition and self-esteem

A transition is the period during which an individual goes through some kind of change, either associated with expected events (adolescence) or unexpected (accident, redundancy, loss). This model links the stages involved in a transition to the effect it can have on a person's self-esteem. It shows how a person's ability to cope with the various stages may be affected by how they are feeling about themselves at the time (Figure 7.9).

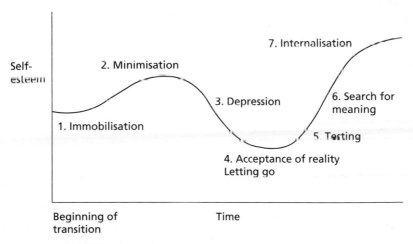

Figure 7.9 Self-esteem changes during transitions (Adams *et al.*, 1977)

Practice focus: grief and crime

Grief can affect our behaviour in many ways, depending on the life stage which we are going through. In one study, a significant link was found between loss or rejection and criminal behaviour in children and young people. The research found that 68 per cent had experienced family breakdown resulting in permanent loss of contact with one or more parents, and 42 per cent had experienced outright neglect or rejection by parents and carers. (Kerr, 2004)

SOCIOLOGY

Most people recognise the importance of psychology when they first read the different theories. They can see that it helps them to explain their own behaviour and understand why other people act the way they do. When it comes to reading about sociology for the first time, it is sometimes more difficult to see the link to our own lives as clearly. Sociologists talk about systems and structures, and it is difficult to relate this wider level so readily to our own experience.

However, it is fascinating to consider what sociologists can tell us, because they are interested in how we act when we are with others, and the influences upon us. Many of these influences are not immediately obvious to us, but they affect our lives greatly. Sociologists look past individualistic answers (people are poor because they are lazy) and common-sense explanations (suicide is the behaviour of an individual who is mentally ill) to look at the structures of inequality and the influence of factors such as family, gender and religion on our individual decisions. Many things accepted as 'truth' are not based on evidence. For instance, figures from the 2001 census revealed that 9.9 per cent of the population are from ethnic minorities, whereas a MORI poll found that people estimated that ethnic minorities comprised 22.5 per cent of the total population.

There are four main sociological perspectives: functionalism, conflict, symbolic interactionism and feminism. The first two are known as macro-sociological approaches because they look at the influence that social systems and power structures have over the individual. The symbolic interactionist approach is considered a micro-sociological approach because it emphasises the influence that individuals have in creating society. Feminism draws on both macro- and micro-sociological perspectives.

Socialisation	The process whereby people learn how to behave in society; how culture is transmitted from generation to generation.
Culture	The way of life in a system such as a society or an organisation.
Rules	Written regulations about what people should do, e.g. laws or policies.
Norms	Unwritten rules about acceptable behaviour, e.g. queuing.
Values	The beliefs or attitudes upon which rules and norms are based, e.g. it is wrong to kill.
Roles	The part people play in the different groups they belong to. They can be ascribed (given), e.g. daughter, or achieved (chosen) e.g. boss.
Status	A person's position in society and the respect which this commands.

Figure 7.10 Key concepts in sociology

Functionalism

Like many of the first sociologists, Emile Durkheim (1858–1917) lived in a period of great change. The developments of the industrial revolution meant that many people moved from living and working in the country to working in the factories and living in the slums of the towns. The old ties that used to bind people together were broken – there was not the same sense of community in the new urban areas, nor the same strong moral guidance from the church, and people did not have extended family to rely on for practical, financial and emotional support. In the days before the welfare state, if you did not work, you ended up in the workhouse or destitute on the streets.

Although Durkheim was the initial theorist of the functionalist approach to sociology, many people, such as Robert Merton (1910–93) and Talcott Parsons (1902–79) have developed his ideas. Durkheim believed that all parts of society have a function (or part) to play, in order for society to work well. The easiest way to understand this is to compare society to the human body – if any organ is not working properly, then the whole body is affected. In a society, aspects like

Functional	Anything that works to benefit the system it is part of.
Dysfunctional	Anything that works to disrupt or disturb the system it is part of.
Consensus	Agreement; in this case an agreement in society about the rules and norms.
Chaos	What will happen to a system if too many parts are dysfunctional.
Harmony	What will happen to a system if the parts are functional.

Figure 7.11 Key concepts in functionalism

Practice focus: protecting children

There has been a cultural shift in our values and norms about how children should be treated, and this is having far-reaching implications on other aspects of society such as education, health and crime, as the following excerpt describes:

There is a growing concern that young people have greater difficulty than previous generations in bouncing back from adversities, and are less resilient. In recent decades, the identification and elimination of risk have become a dominant preoccupation of childcare professionals and parents. This has certainly resulted in many benefits, especially relating to the physical health of children. Unfortunately, children's emotional and mental health appears to have declined in all developed countries over the same period. If we imagine an average British child today, compared with 1970, today's child would be less likely to be injured in a road traffic accident, less likely to die from measles and more likely to live long enough to draw a pension. Conversely, today's child would be more likely – if they are male – to commit suicide and have a behavioural problem and – if they are female – to self-harm and be depressed. Children have been protected from road traffic accidents by being driven to school, but exposed to the risk of obesity and early death through coronary heart disease by the resulting lack of exercise. (Newman, 2003)

ACTIVITY 7.4

In the practice focus above, how does a functionalist perspective assist your understanding?

the family, education, industry, the media and the law, all need to operate efficiently if a society is going to thrive and develop. When one aspect of society stops working well (e.g. there are too many strikes in industry or there is a high crime rate) then society comes under strain and, if the situation is not sorted out properly, that society could collapse.

Functionalists believe that everyone needs to conform to the rules, norms and values in a society for that society to function well. If there are people who disagree with the rules, norms and values, they are seen to be dysfunctional. If too many people are dysfunctional, there will be chaos in society. Society tends to react to people who threaten the harmony and stability of society in two ways – removing them (e.g. imprisoning, banishing or killing) or re-educating them. Sometimes behaviour which would appear to be dysfunctional might also be useful for society because it helps confirm the rules, norms and values. Also, it might help society gradually change if people constantly challenge the existing rules, norms and values.

This model can be used to study systems smaller than society such as schools, hospitals and even families, because the same principles apply to any system. For example, a disruptive pupil will be suspended from school, removing them from the system. It is likely they will have a meeting with guidance staff and others to discuss how they can learn to fit in better at school and learn ways to behave in an acceptable manner.

Conflict perspective

Karl Marx (1818–83) developed the conflict perspective, which is based on the premise that society is made up of groups which compete for scarce resources (money, jobs, housing etc.) and who are therefore in competition to see who can gain the most. This means that the basis of society is conflict (not consensus as functionalists would suggest), and that all societies will be in a state of continual change as groups fight to maximise their position. Conflict theorists suggest that it is the group which holds most power in any conflict that will gain the most in the situation, and that groups who hold power will organise society in such a way that they maintain power.

Conflict	Caused by competition between groups for scarce resources.
Constraint	The actions used by groups in power to impose their views on others.
Power differentials	The difference in power between groups in society.
Change	Inevitable part of society due to conflict.

Figure 7.12 Key concepts in conflict theory

Marx was writing at the time of the industrial revolution when the capitalist system was developing in Europe, and he described the two main competing groups or classes: the bourgeoisie – those who owned the means of production (factories, shipyards etc.) – and the proletariat – the workers who sold their labour to the bourgeoisie. The bourgeoisie, or their supporters, were the only ones elected to parliament at that time because of the way the voting system was organised (remember, women did not gain the vote until 1918, and there were not full voting rights for all adults in the UK until 1928), and so they passed laws which were favourable to them. It was only with the development of the trades union movement and the Labour party that laws were passed to safeguard the rights of workers, develop health and safety systems, reasonable working conditions, universal unemployment benefits and so on.

Ralph Dahrendorf (born 1929) is one of many writers who have developed Marx's ideas. He believes that change is continuous and normal in society, and in fact the surprising thing in a society would not be the presence of conflict but the *absence* of conflict. He is also interested in the notion of constraint, or the way that people impose their will on others and restrain their actions. Today's society is much more complex than Marx could have imagined, and many other divisions apart from class are now recognised as having a big impact on the status and opportunities of people in society, as discussed in 'Research focus: inequality', below. Dahrendorf also saw that people could be in the position of power in one situation, but be constrained in another. For instance, a woman might have power in her role as a mother over her children, but be constrained by the demands of her employer at work.

Many service users belong to groups in society who have been disadvantaged and oppressed. Many of these groups have struggled for years to challenge the power of law-makers and law-enforcers, using techniques such as campaigns, awareness raising, protest marches and civil disobedience (e.g. people with disabilities chaining themselves to the Houses of Parliament in 1994 and 1995 in order to raise awareness of the need for disability discrimination legislation), because people with power do not tend to give it up easily. It takes much effort to overturn existing laws and power structures, but it has now been done successfully by many groups. In care settings, service users and organisations have made a considerable effort to look at the power structures and minimise the power imbalance through the use of advocacy, service user committees and consultation.

Research focus: inequality

Equality legislation has existed in Britain since 1975, but there are still major inequalities between different groups in society. A Disability Rights Commission survey in October 2003 discovered that 73 per cent of disabled people with mobility and sensory impairments in Great Britain said that they have difficulty accessing goods and services. The main physical barriers were steps at the entrance to buildings, negotiating heavy doors and parking spaces for disabled drivers being used by non-disabled drivers (Chowdhury, 2003).

A study in 2004 revealed that despite the large number of black players in top football clubs, every member of the English FA and the 92-strong FA council is white. Less than one per cent of positions off the field – whether in boardrooms, management or coaching staff – and fewer than two per cent of supporters are non-white (CRE, 2004).

Although women make up 51 per cent of the population, they make up only: 23 per cent of top management posts in the civil service; 18 per cent of MPs elected in June 2001 to Westminster; nine per cent of editors of national newspapers; seven per cent of senior police officers and six per cent of high court judges (EOC, 2004).

ACTIVITY 7.5

The three main equality bodies – the Equal Opportunities Commission, the Commission for Racial Equality and the Disability Rights Commission – are involved in campaigns to promote awareness of discrimination, such as that described above, and to monitor the legislation and encourage organisations to make changes. Although created by the government, they are independent and highlight areas that the government and other organisations need to change in order to achieve equality. They all have excellent websites which have up-to-date information and articles.

Click onto the CRE, DRC and EOC websites and discover which campaigns and initiatives they are currently involved with in order to challenge the inequalities which still exist.

Symbolic interactionism

Symbolic interactionism is a micro-sociological approach which emphasises the role that our day-to-day interactions play in creating our ongoing reality. This is different from the macro-sociological view which states that individuals are influenced by the wider structures of society. George Herbert Mead (1863–1931) was one of the original writers in the symbolic interactionist perspective. Other writers who have contributed to this perspective include Max Weber (1864–1920) who developed social action theory, and Howard Becker (born 1921) who developed labelling theory.

Self	The person; their picture of who they are.
Symbol	Tools of communication; words, dress, accent, jewellery, gestures etc.
Interaction	A situation where there is communication between two or more people.
Significant other	A person who has a special role in our life, e.g. a parent or partner.
Generalised other	People who influence us but do not have a significant role in our life.
Labelling	The process by which we build up a picture of ourselves, based on descriptions or 'labels' given to us by others. A label is more likely to stick if it is given publicly, frequently or by more than one person in one situation. A label can be negative or positive.
Self-fulfilling prophecy	The tendency to act in a way that people have told us that we will, or that people expect us to.

Figure 7.13 Key concepts in symbolic interactionism

This is a much more dynamic model of human behaviour and social relationships than the macro perspectives. This is ideally suited to care work, because people in care settings are often going through some transition in their life, or hoping to change things. It proposes that people create their shared reality every time they meet, so there is a chance that any interaction may lead to change. We communicate through the use of symbols: the clothes we wear, the language we use and the accent we have all give signals to the other person about who we are. We pick up these signals from others and judge them on the basis of how we interpret their symbols.

This is most obviously seen when teenagers dress as part of a 'tribe' and go to nightclubs associated with their group to listen to a particular type of music, or when football supporters dress in their team colours and chant their songs. But it also happens more subtly in all our interactions. We are generally more influenced by our interactions with significant others than we are by generalised others who do not play such an important part in our life. For example, if someone has been labelled as a troublemaker and slow learner in school, they

---

Practice focus: children who sexually abuse

Up to a third of all child sexual abuse is carried out by children and young people. This has been recognised for over a decade, but the professional response can vary widely from area to area. A social worker was concerned about where to place Stephen (not his real name), a seven-year-old boy who had been sexually abused by his 14-year-old brother. However, when it was discovered that Stephen had started to behave in a sexually aggressive way to his four-year-old brother, his social worker sought to place him in the same foster placement as his older brother. The reason given was that he had now crossed over the line between victim and perpetrator.

This type of pigeonholing does not help address the complex interplay of factors which influence the behaviour of children when they are unable to control where they live and whom they live with. Labelling Stephen as an abuser invalidated any concern about his own vulnerability. In the past, responses to child sex offenders were heavily influenced by theories about, and approaches to, adult sex offenders. Much work is now being done, particularly in the voluntary sector by organisations such as NSPCC and Barnardo's, to provide services which respond to the particular needs of young people (Hackett, 2004).

ACTIVITY 7.6

Can you think of a situation from your own experience where a label has been allocated that has limited a person's options and become a self-fulfilling prophecy? Do you know of services where people are actively challenging the labels that have been given to them?

may have stopped attending classes and thus confirmed the expectations of others that they were stupid, ended up unemployed and started drinking heavily (self-fulfilling prophecy). Later in life, they might attend a rehabilitation centre and meet an inspiring group worker (who becomes a significant other) whom they like and who feeds back to them on how well they contribute to the group (positive labelling). The person is likely to develop a more positive sense of self through these new interactions. Their actions are now more likely to lead towards a more positive future.

Feminist perspective

One thing that all sociologists had in common until relatively recently was that when they spoke about people, they often just meant 'men'. So the society they studied and wrote about was that of men – in politics, at work, at leisure. A description or analysis of the role that women played in society was largely missing from the work of Durkheim, Marx and others. Women were the invisible presence that made possible all the 'important' work, wars and struggles which men carried out. Since the 1970s, many academics have redressed this imbalance by researching women's historical role in work, war and the family, as well as carrying out research into the lives of women in modern society.

A feminist approach is one which reminds us that women are a factor in any situation that sociologists might study, and that their behaviour, thoughts and

Patriarchy	The system of male oppression of women, as structured in areas of society such as the law, family, economic system, sexual relations, medicine etc.
Social construction of gender	The idea that girls and boys 'learn' to become feminine or masculine, as opposed to the idea than maleness or femaleness are determined mainly by biology.

Figure 7.14 Key concepts of the feminist perspective

feelings must be considered alongside those of men. Much feminist research is macro-sociological because it looks at the patriarchal system: the way in which society is structured to perpetuate the dominance of men. It has examined the role of laws which historically kept women in an inferior position, not allowing women the same rights as men with regard to owning property and being allowed to vote. Now that women in general have established a much stronger legal and social position in society, feminist approaches can look more closely at the micro-sociological detail of women's lives and particularly at the multiple oppressions women might face who are also black, disabled, drug users etc.

Much research has been done by feminists into the process of socialisation, looking at the way people 'learn' their gender from their family, television, magazines etc. Although some of the physical differences between males and females are clearly biological, feminists argue that the concepts of masculinity and femininity are socially constructed. That is, the idea of what it is to be an 'ideal man' or a 'perfect woman' is not fixed and has not remained constant. Indeed, they have changed over time and vary in different countries and cultures.

The family

Sociology emphasises the importance of groups in our development as human beings. The first group that most of us are part of is the family, and the structure of the family has changed dramatically in the last hundred years. This process has been greatly influenced by the changing role of women in society, the existence of contraception which enables women to control when, and if, they have children, and greater opportunities for women in the workplace.

Types of family structure include:

- **Extended family**: where more than two generations live together, or more than one family linked by marriage, e.g. two brothers with their wives and their mother.
- **Nuclear family**: mother, father and one or more children. However, it is interesting to note that 31 per cent of parents who live together are unmarried but co-habiting. This varies greatly between areas, from 12 per cent of families in some areas to almost 50 per cent in other areas.
- **Single-parent family**: mother or father with one or more children. Fifteen per cent of babies born in 2000/1 live with just their mother. Of these, nearly half see their father at least once a week, though nearly four in ten have no contact at all.

❏   **Reconstituted family**: where one or more parents bring children from a previous relationship. The most rapidly growing family type is the step-family. Most children remain with their mother following divorce or separation, so most families have a step-father rather than a step-mother. 'Social' rather than 'biological' parenting is an important new phenomenon in family life. Seventeen per cent of fathers born in 1970 are step-fathers, nearly double the number born in 1958. In 1965, the average seven-year-old child lived with 2.1 other children, and only one per cent were living with step-siblings. Nearly 40 years later, the average seven-year-old lives with only 1.5 other siblings, of whom ten per cent are step- or half-siblings.

The fact that many more women choose to work means that alternative arrangements have had to be developed to look after children. Of babies born in 2000/1 nearly 50 per cent of the mothers go out to work. When mothers are at work, about 40 per cent of the babies are looked after by their grandparents and about 70 per cent are regularly looked after by their grandparents at other times. If mothers do not go out to work, their babies spend about ten hours a week being looked after by someone other than their parents. If the mothers do work, then the babies spend about 22 hours with someone other than their parents. This has created a need for childcare facilities on a scale unprecedented 50 years ago.

Another demographic change is that the road to adulthood is getting longer, with the trend now being for young people to continue in education and postpone independence until they are 24 years old. This is causing problems, both for parents with limited financial resources, and also for young adults who want to be able to make and act on their own decisions. However, further education students who could not live at home and had no family support were more likely to drop out of courses (Stewart and Vaitilingam, 2004). Many middle-aged people also have to care for their elderly parents who are now living much longer. As women are still the main carers in most families, the responsibility falls more heavily on them as mothers, daughters and partners to care for other family members in need.

Sociology and psychology in action: poverty

Poverty is one of the issues in society which needs to be understood from both psychological and sociological perspectives in order to tackle the causes and provide meaningful solutions. The children of people raised in poverty are also more likely to experience poorer outcomes. Children raised in poverty are, as adults, more likely to be unemployed or to be in low-paid employment, more likely to get in trouble with the police and are at greater risk of alcohol and drug abuse. Some of the factors which influence these life chances:

❑ Babies born into poorer families are more likely to be born prematurely and to be of low birth weight. The implications of this include a greater likelihood of impaired development and of certain chronic diseases later in life.

❑ Children in poorer families are more likely to experience illness, with a greater risk of respiratory infection, gastro-enteritis, dental caries and tuberculosis.

❑ Children from poorer backgrounds are less likely to do well at school, leaving school with fewer or no qualifications and less likely to stay on in the sixth form (CPAG, 2001).

In March 1999, the Prime Minister, Tony Blair, pledged to eradicate child poverty in Britain within a generation. This is a major commitment, given the number of factors which are related to poverty. In the UK, people can become poor as a result of social and economic processes such as unemployment and changing family structures. Low pay is common for young people, women and employees from some ethnic minority communities. After separation and divorce, mothers with children often experience a drop in income. Time spent caring for children and a lack of work skills and experience can affect their ability to take on paid work. People with disabilities are also at risk from poverty because of extra disability-related costs and low incomes. Many unpaid carers give up work to provide assistance to an elderly or disabled person and so are also on low incomes, often bearing some of the financial costs of disability.

Changes in the labour market can influence the scale of unemployment, in turn affecting poverty: unskilled workers are five times more likely to become unemployed than professional workers. Poverty is not evenly spread across the country: the UK ranks second only to Mexico in the industrialised world in terms of its regional inequality. For example, 22 per cent of households were without work in the north east of England, compared to 11 per cent in the south east (Flaherty, 2004).

There are a number of policy changes which will need to be delivered in order to meet the aim of eradicating child poverty. Many of them are at societal level: employment is the key tool in the government's anti-poverty strategy, but basic problems of the availability and sustainability of jobs in certain areas remain. However, because of low pay and part-time work, even employment itself does not guarantee a route out of poverty, and many people rely on top-up benefits.

The Child Poverty Action Group is a pressure group which aims to press the government on the following structural and institutional measures to help eradicate child poverty:

- ❑ Campaign for child benefit to remain at the heart of child poverty strategy and to be regularly updated to ensure child poverty targets can be met.
- ❑ Press for proposals (e.g. through the tax system) to deliver more income to the poorest families.
- ❑ Challenge the government to ensure work pays, and to provide adequate support to those for whom paid work is not possible.
- ❑ Press for effective proposals to tackle poverty in black and ethnic minority families.
- ❑ Work with others to ensure asylum-seeker children are guaranteed an adequate amount to live on (CPAG, 2004).

At the individual level, ideas from psychology are useful when working with people in unemployed workers' centres, lone parent training agencies and local economic initiatives. Many 'return to work' courses include activities such as confidence-building, assertiveness and goal-setting. These types of activities help to motivate people to think and act in new ways, and aim to increase the self-esteem of people who have been out of the job market. However, no amount of group work will help a person to gain employment if there are no childcare facilities or jobs available in their area. If poverty is to be tackled successfully, changes at individual, family and societal level need to be achieved in order to enable the children of today and the adults of tomorrow to break out of the cycle of poverty.

SUMMARY

Psychology helps us to explain and understand motivation, personality and development, but it presents an overly individualistic analysis of the world. If we took ideas from psychology alone to explain mental illness or discrimination, then the conclusion would be that the only meaningful changes that can be made to people's lives is at the personal or emotional level. Sociology adds a structural dimension which emphasises the role that our upbringing, place in society and the structures of power in society play in the way we live our life. In order to understand any situation fully, an understanding of both perspectives is most useful. Individual changes may appear to be easier to achieve at times, but long-lasting change will often occur only if there are wider changes in our family, workplace, community or society. Through research, both psychology and sociology help us define problems, patterns and trends more clearly and suggest some options for action. In care settings, new solutions to issues based on psychological and sociological research are being developed every day, putting theory into practice.

FIVE KEY POINTS

1. Human development and behaviour are influenced by a number of factors including genetics, personality, perception and the family, friends, community and society in which we are brought up.
2. Every individual is unique and human behaviour cannot be predicted. However, psychology and sociology give us tools which can help us to understand behaviour, respond to it and plan appropriate changes.
3. There is no single theory which can explain every aspect of human existence. All theories offer only a limited explanation, and most people use information from a range of different theories to understand and respond to any situation.
4. All psychological and sociological theories are based on evidence which is refined and developed as more research is carried out and applied in a range of different settings.
5. Good care practice, based on sound underpinning knowledge, is now more easily shared through a range of accessible media which include magazines and the internet.

THREE QUESTIONS

1. Why is it useful in a care setting to know about a range of psychological theories?
2. What does a sociological approach add to an understanding of issues such as poverty, addiction, ill health or discrimination?
3. How can you keep up to date with new findings in psychology and sociology?

RECOMMENDED READING

MESSER, D. and JONES, F. (eds) (2001) *Psychology and Social Care*. London: Jessica Kingsley publishers. Twenty-five chapters which discuss in detail psychological theories and techniques as applied to social care issues, such as substance use, dementia, brain damage and child abuse.

MOORE, S. (2000) *Sociology Alive*, 3rd edn. Cheltenham: Nelson Thornes Ltd. A very accessible discussion of issues such as socialisation, research, deviance, poverty and families.

KEEGAN, G. (2002) *Higher Psychology: Approaches and Methods*. London: Hodder & Stoughton.

HAYES, N. and ORRELL, S. (2003) *Psychology: An Introduction*, 3rd edn. Harrow: Longman. Good introduction to the basic themes in psychology.

RELEVANT WEBSITES

There is an enormous number of relevant internet sites. The best general one to start a search for sociology- and psychology-related information is: www.sosig.ac.uk – the social sciences information gateway

Other general sites with a range of information and links to other sites are:

www.sociology.org.uk – site with links to issues on family, inequality etc.

www.feminist.org – links to feminist research worldwide

www.theory.org.uk – very user-friendly site about sociology applied to modern culture.

CHAPTER 8

A PERSON-CENTRED APPROACH TO ASSESSMENT AND CARE PLANNING

Sylvia Brewer and Janet Miller

> **People are done to rather than with, and their own contribution is often wasted or unsought.**
>
> (Ritchie, P *et al.*, 2003)

By the end of this chapter you should be able to:

- ❏ understand and apply a model of care based upon assessment, care planning, implementation and evaluation/review
- ❏ explain a person-centred approach to assessment and care planning
- ❏ understand and apply theories of need and explain the importance of a needs-led approach
- ❏ understand the importance and content of risk assessment
- ❏ understand different approaches to assessment and care planning
- ❏ understand and use a range of care planning tools, including care planning meetings and 'maps'.

The content of this chapter provides underpinning content and context for all care qualifications. It relates especially to the following units:

NVQ and SVQ Level 3 Units HSC36: Contribute to the assessment of children and young; 328: Contributors to care planning and review; 329: Contribute to planning, monitoring and reviewing the delivery of services for individuals.

HNC Care/Social Care Units – e.g. Social Care Theory for Practice.

INTRODUCTION

Assessment and care planning are part of a dynamic perspective that focuses upon the needs of service users and ways of meeting these needs. Initially in this chapter a model of care is outlined that reflects the context in which practice takes place, and assessment, planning, implementation and evaluation as a continuous process. The care plan can be compared to a

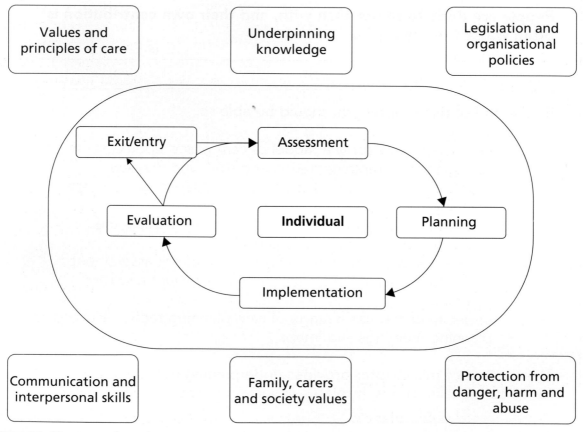

Figure 8.1   The context of care planning

ACTIVITY 8.1

Start with yourself and answer these questions:

- ❏ What does planning mean in your life?
- ❏ What needs do you have?
- ❏ Do you have dreams and aspirations? What are they?
- ❏ What is most important to you?
- ❏ What support do you need?
- ❏ What impact has your history had on your life?
- ❏ Imagine where you would like to be in a year from now and make a picture (a plan, map or drawing) that reflects how you might plan to achieve this.

giant jigsaw with the service user and others, including the care worker, identifying and fitting the pieces together to create a picture of needs, wishes and dreams and how these will be met and achieved. The whole process can be seen as a helping cycle, with the individual firmly at the centre, as illustrated in Figure 8.1 (The context of care planning). This figure illustrates the various aspects of the context in which helping happens, ranging from the underpinning value base, knowledge and skills of workers, to the legal system in which you must operate and the remit of the organisation in which the work takes place.

In recent years, a person-centred approach has transformed the way in which assessment and care planning are carried out and the ways in which care is delivered. This approach *seeks to mirror the ways in which 'ordinary people' make plans* (Sanderson, 1997) and is discussed in greater detail as the chapter unfolds. The most important thing that it does is to remind you constantly that individuals must not only be included in their assessment and care planning, but that they are experts in their lives. Care workers can facilitate the process by enabling the individual to contribute their viewpoint, by providing information and advocating on the individual's behalf, but it is the individual's assessment and plan, not the worker's.

ASSESSMENT

Assessment has been defined as:

> A tool to aid in the planning of future work, the beginning of helping another person to identify areas for growth and

change. Its purpose is the identification of needs – it is never an end in itself.

(Taylor, B and Devine, T 1993)

This is the initial stage, but also a stage that is revisited throughout the helping process, when a picture is developed of the individual's circumstances and what is required to meet their needs. Assessment is an ongoing process whereby the service user, care workers and relevant others work together to understand and identify needs, and make sense of the service user's situation. It is a basis for planning what has to be done to meet this person's needs now and in the future.

The importance of assessment cannot be overstated. There is evidence that in many instances of failure to protect or adequately help individuals, there was poor assessment with insufficient attention paid to the service user's views and needs.

Lord Laming (2001) in the 'Victoria Climbie Inquiry' states:

> . . . had there been a proper response to the needs of Victoria when she was first referred to Ealing Social Services, it may well be that the danger to her would have been recognised and action taken . . .. The dreadful irony is that these services knew little or nothing more about Victoria at the end of the process than they did when she was first referred . . ..

And in 'It's everyone's job to make sure I'm alright', we read:

> Where children were not protected or their needs were not met this was often the result of poor assessments.

(Scottish Executive, 2002)

Under community care, disability, carers' and children's legislation, other people in the service user's network may be entitled to assessment in their own right. Carers' needs, for example, are often overlooked or minimised if they are an add-on to someone else's assessment, but where the assessment focuses upon the carer, a completely different picture of their needs may arise. Anna, the mother of a child with disability, felt that although she had participated in her daughter's assessment, her own needs had been overlooked. She asked for an assessment in her own right. The social services department stated that her needs had been taken into account in her daughter's assessment. However,

---

Ten essential points about assessment and care planning

1. It is the service user's assessment and plan, not the worker's or anyone else's.
2. Needs, not availability of services, must determine the nature of the plan; it must not be service-led but needs-led.
3. Assessment and care planning rest upon the care value base and the development of positive relationships.
4. Assessment and care planning are not just about the 'big' things in life but also about the minutiae of everyday life.
5. Participants in the process must work in partnership with the service user and one another.
6. Evaluation must be built into the assessment and care planning process.
7. Good risk assessment plays a vital part in protecting individuals from danger, harm and abuse.
8. Assessment should be based upon accurate, up-to-date information. It is important to distinguish fact from opinion or intuition.
9. Avoid labels and sweeping statements, e.g. in relation to behaviour that challenges.
10. It is helpful to have one worker who coordinates the assessment and care plan and is a key person for the individual.

Anna insisted upon her right to her own assessment, and participated in an assessment focusing on her needs and not those of her daughter. It was in this way that she became a member of a parent's support group, received counselling and additional days of respite in order to update her computing skills in preparation for a return to work. None of the needs that led to the provision of this help had been identified in her daughter's assessment.

The concept of need

The concept of need is central to the process of assessment. As described on page 202, Maslow (1954) categorised need into a hierarchy, which is normally shown as a pyramid. The categories of need identified were:

- physiological – e.g. to eat and drink, be warm
- safety – to feel safe, secure and free from danger
- social – to belong and be loved

❏ esteem – to gain recognition as a valid individual, to achieve and be competent
❏ cognitive – to know, understand and explore
❏ aesthetic – to achieve symmetry and order and appreciate beauty
❏ self-actualisation – to realise potential and find fulfilment.

Maslow maintained that it is only when basic needs for food, warmth and shelter are met that people can begin to move up the hierarchy.

Bradshaw (1972) produced a taxonomy of need, still widely used, which sets out different types of need that have different consequences for services. These are:

❏ normative need: defined by an expert or professional
❏ felt need: what people feel they would like; sometimes not even verbalised, sometimes verbalised as a want
❏ expressed need: where felt need is turned by some action (e.g. applying for a service) into a request or a demand
❏ comparative need: where people are in need if they suffer the same conditions as others did who now receive a service

Felt needs or wants are very often lost in the assessment process. A person-centred approach *begins* by attempting to find out what people want. It may not be possible for a person to receive everything they want, but it is very relevant to planning to know what people's preferences are. When looking at people's wants, it is important to find out what their hopes and fears are. These are referred to as dreams and nightmares in the vocabulary of person-centred planning. Dreaming can give people the energy to achieve more than just meeting their needs, and fears or nightmares tell us what must under all circumstances be avoided.

The SPICE model is another way of looking at needs: social; physical; intellectual; cultural; emotional. In this chapter spiritual needs are added to this model, making it SPICES, emphasising that all areas of the individual's life must be taken into account in an assessment. The various ways of looking at need are summarised in Figure 8.2.

The models of need in practice

Following an incident at a garage forecourt, police officers phoned the care and education centre where David, aged 15, was living, to ask someone to collect him. He was in a very distressed state, as was the owner of the garage. David had gone to the garage forecourt and kicked dents in several cars.

David's father, who was West Indian, had died a year ago and his mother, June Stewart, who is white, had been unable to cope with his increasingly disruptive behaviour. He had been excluded from school several times and was eventually accommodated at Sidlaw House, a care and education centre in his home town. He had been making some progress but staff were very concerned about a recent deterioration in David's behaviour and educational progress. At this time, David has not been charged with an offence, but the police are under pressure from the garage owner to charge him. David's mother, who now lives alone, has been feeling constantly depressed and very disappointed that she has been unable to help or to understand her son.

ACTIVITY 8.2

Using both Bradshaw's and Maslow's models of need, identify how you could work with David and Mrs Stewart to enable them and you to understand their needs. Possible areas to consider in Maslow's theory are:

- ❏ security/safety needs
- ❏ social needs
- ❏ esteem needs.

Possible areas to consider in Bradshaw's taxonomy are:

- ❏ normative need
- ❏ felt need
- ❏ expressed need
- ❏ comparative need.

ACTIVITY 8.3

What other needs in Maslow's hierarchy should be met, and are these being met for both David and Mrs Stewart? If not, how could they be met?

Maslow

- ❏ **Security/safety needs:** David's safe and secure world was shattered when his father died. He may need a re-establishment of boundaries and the security of knowing that people care about

Figure 8.2 Some concepts relating to human needs

him. He seems to be angry and unhappy and does not know why. He probably needs counselling to help him to deal with loss, guilt, issues of identity, pain, anger or any number of feelings he may be experiencing. In order to improve his life, a plan could be developed with David to help him to find ways to deal with his loss that do not involve illegal behaviour and the ruination of his relationships.

- ❑ **Social needs**: David now lives at the care and education centre away from home. Work with both David and his mother may enable them to understand what in David's behaviour is due to loss, what is just normal teenage behaviour, and what needs to be changed so that they can have a more satisfactory relationship and that David can eventually return home and pick up positive friendships that he had before leaving his neighbourhood. He may also need encouragement and support to participate in the activities of the care and education centre.

- ❑ **Esteem needs**: David's loss of his father and loss of control over his feelings and his life seem to have resulted in a reduction in David's self-worth. He vents his frustration, pain and anger through damage to property, and then feels even worse about himself. An understanding of esteem needs may help him to understand what is happening, perhaps to make some reparation for the damage he has done and to achieve his potential.

Bradshaw

- ❑ **Normative need**: The police took David to the police station because he had committed an offence. They phoned care workers because he was accommodated in a care and education centre and was in a distressed state. Care workers recognised his behaviour as possibly resulting from loss and unresolved anger about losing his father. Here the professionals are defining need in terms of norms or standards of expected behaviour.

- ❑ **Felt need**: David wants to show how angry he is; he seems to want help but he does not really know how to ask for it, and to feel better about himself.

- ❑ **Expressed need**: David's expression of need does not really meet his need. He kicks dents in cars to express his need for some understanding of his loss and consequent anger.

- ❑ **Comparative need**: David's need for emotional help has been neglected by the care and education centre, whereas the needs of other young people in similar circumstances have been met. He probably needs some counselling to help him to resolve his difficulties. It is likely that he will need a service as long as his need for help is recognised. An assessment with David of his need will help to identify and define what help he can be offered. He also needs to appreciate that there were consequences of his actions and people who were affected by them.

ACTIVITY 8.4

Now look at David's needs in terms of the SPICES Model. What do you think David's needs are in relation to this?

ACTIVITY 8.5

Choose one of the case studies below or a case study of your own, and analyse it in terms of two of the above models of need.

George

George is 86 and lives alone in his own home, but after a stroke he is finding it increasingly difficult to cope. His wife died three years ago and his only child, a son, lives in New Zealand. George sometimes forgets to eat, occasionally forgets to turn the gas ring off after cooking a meal, is sometimes incontinent because he cannot move fast enough to reach the toilet, and he never goes out. What do you think George's needs might be? Look at George's needs in terms of Maslow's hierarchy, Bradshaw's taxonomy of need, and the SPICES model.

Kathy

Kathy has a learning disability and very little speech, and lives in a house with three other women who also have a learning disability. They are supported by care workers on a rota basis. Kathy moved here from a large hospital, where she had lived for 30 years. She is now 63 years old. Initially, Kathy found it very difficult to live in an ordinary house but now she seems much happier, enjoys going for walks with her support workers and looking at shops. She is learning slowly to do a few tasks around the house, and has chosen as her special job to pick up mail from the letter box in the mornings. She is very proud of this achievement. What do you think Kathy's needs are? Look at Kathy's needs in terms of Maslow's hierarchy, Bradshaw's taxonomy of need, and the SPICES model.

Risk assessment

Do you ever take risks? Have you ever exceeded the speed limit or crossed a road when a car was coming? Do you smoke, eat too much sometimes, drink too much sometimes, sunbathe? Who does not take the occasional risk? Risk assessment has already been examined in relation to health and safety, but a slightly different slant is put upon it in the assessment and care planning process. The aim is not totally to eliminate risk. Too much emphasis on risk leads to undue restriction, whereas too little means that people are insufficiently protected. Striking the 'right' balance and ensuring that decisions made are defensible and as good as possible for the people concerned are the important factors.

Risk can be defined as the likelihood that something will happen. In care work, risk is associated with the likelihood that something negative will happen. It is useful to look at three kinds of risk:

1. risks that people pose to others
2. risks that people are exposed to, especially if they are vulnerable
3. a combination of being exposed to risk and posing risk at the same time, e.g. people with a mental illness who fail to take their medication may pose a risk to others and be exposed to risk themselves.

There are several key questions that should be answered in risk assessment. What do you think these may be? You may have thought of some or all of the following:

- ❏ What are the risks?
- ❏ What is the likelihood of negative consequences?
- ❏ Under what circumstances is risk most likely to occur?
- ❏ What are the probable effects of the risks?
- ❏ Who may be affected by the risks?
- ❏ What is the individual's view of the risks and their preferred action?
- ❏ What are the views of others affected by the risks, including you?
- ❏ What would be the possible effects of taking different courses of action, or no action at all?

How do you decide what the risks are and what to do about them? In everyday life you probably use a mixture of past experience and knowledge about what

ACTIVITY 8.6

Look at the case study of George above (page 232) and try to answer all of the above questions.

happens in certain situations, based upon what you have read or heard somewhere. You can hardly fail to know that smoking is bad for you if you wake up every morning with a hacking cough, become breathless after going up the smallest hill, and read statistics in the newspaper or in medical journals that relate smoking to many illnesses. If you have only the experience and not the knowledge, you may put your state of health down to other causes. You may have the knowledge with or without negative health consequences, and still decide that you will smoke because for you the pleasure outweighs the consequences, or because you cannot stop without some help. In the case of smoking there is some degree of predictability about the likelihood of harm occurring, because there have been statistical studies that illustrate the links between smoking (and passive smoking) and ill health. Similarly, there have been studies that show that people who offend have often offended before. In neither of these cases though does it automatically follow that because you smoke you will experience ill health, or because you have offended you will re-offend. There is only a likelihood. In the case of child abuse, Professor Cyril Greenland (in Jay and Doganis, 1987) set out a high-risk family checklist (see page 175), in which many of the factors listed were stress factors. He saw that the greatest value of this checklist was to raise warning signals, and to indicate where child abuse may occur and where stress could be relieved. It did not follow that where families had features on the checklist they would abuse; indeed most of them did not, even though they experienced significant stress. It illustrated only that research with abusers identified these factors more often in abusing families than in non-abusing families, not that families with these characteristics would necessarily abuse.

Predicting risk is therefore a risky business. A holistic approach is advocated in which knowledge, experience, assessment of need, results of relevant research and a team and collaborative approach combine to enable individuals and workers to evaluate what the risks are, what the consequences may be and what actions should and could be taken to minimise risk without unduly restricting freedom of choice. A reflective and critical approach to care practice is required that looks at all of the options and possibilities before decisions are reached. These are incorporated into the plan of care.

Single shared assessment process

> Why do we have to tell staff from health and social services the same
> things over and over and over again?
>
> (quote from carer)

Shared or joint assessment is being introduced as a statutory requirement, to
overcome problems associated with several similar assessments being done
with the same individual from different organisations and/or workers. It
involves having one shared assessment. The aim is to avoid duplication
and to promote an effective response to meeting needs. It requires
collaboration in approaches to assessment, and joint structures for
assessment to be in place. There is a danger with this process that it becomes
too clinical and service-led. It is therefore very important that it takes
place within a person-centred approach, with and not for the individual
concerned, and focusing upon the individual's needs and not the availability
of services.

For example, in Sheffield the introduction in 2001 of the Single Assessment
Process marked an important step in the care provided to vulnerable adults. It
resulted from sustained partnership working between the council's housing and
social services, Sheffield's national health service trusts and the voluntary sector
(www.sheffield.gov.uk).

In the Green Paper 'Every Child Matters' (Department of Education and Skills,
2004), it is proposed that a common assessment framework is developed across
services for children and young people, covering special educational needs,
connexions, youth offending teams, health and social services. The aim is for
basic information to follow the child, to reduce duplication.

The Care Programme Approach (CPA)

Although this approach does not differ significantly from the general assessment
and care planning approach of this chapter, the Care Programme Approach is
mentioned since it applies to the assessment and support of people with mental
health difficulties outside hospital. It has been introduced to provide one
integrated process of identifying and addressing need. The CPA process has
four stages:

1.   A systematic assessment of the person's healthcare and social care
     needs.

2. The development of a care plan agreed by all involved, including the service user and any formal and informal carers, as far as this is possible, and addressing the assessed needs.
3. Identifying a key worker to be the main point of contact with the person concerned and to monitor the delivery of the care plan.
4. Regular review of the person's progress and the care plan, with agreed changes to the plan as appropriate.

The Looking After Children (LAC) system

The LAC system is a set of documents published by the Department of Health to provide an integrated system of assessment, planning, review and monitoring of the services to looked-after children (Parker *et al.*, 1991). This applies to children who are 'accommodated' as part of a family support service, with parent(s) retaining parental responsibility, and also to children for whom the local authority has acquired parental responsibility. There are two closely related parts to the LAC system: information planning and review forms, and assessment and action record. The assessment and action record (AAR) focuses on development across seven dimensions of the child/young person's life. These are:

1. health
2. identity
3. social presentation
4. emotional and behavioural development
5. education
6. family and social relationships
7. self-care skills.

The assessment is addressed to children and young people. For example, for 10–14-year-olds in the education section, the following explanation is given:

The questions in this section are designed to find out if you are getting the help you need to make sure that you do as well at school as you are able to and that your education is being properly planned. They are also meant to find out if you have opportunities to learn special skills and to take part in a wide range of activities in and out of school.

At the end of the whole record there is a summary of work to be undertaken, by whom and by which dates, which is presented at review meetings. As well as providing additional protection for looked-after children, one of the aims of the LAC system is to improve life for a group who have for too long under-achieved in education and have lacked opportunities to reach their potential.

ACTIVITY 8.7

For one area of work that interests you, find out what local arrangements are or will be in place for the assessment of vulnerable adults and children and young people.

THE CARE PLAN

Planning goes past assessment and description: it points to action – action by and for the person.

(Ritchie, P *et al.*, 2003)

The Social Care Association in 'Introduction to Care Planning' (2000) says the following about a care plan:

A care plan is an action plan in working with service users. As plans are written down and shared with users, they emphasise the contractual nature of the service provided.

Planning is a practical activity that:

- ❑ gives a sense of purpose to meeting needs
- ❑ takes action in advance of any problems
- ❑ ensures that service users do not get overlooked

Plans can be staged according to which needs are to be met in what timescale. For example, there will be some needs to be met immediately, some in one month, some in three months, some by next year and some which will be worked towards at some point in the future. The essential features of a care plan, from the above definition and the preceding discussion of assessment, are that:

- ❑ It is the basis for action (not just a paper exercise).
- ❑ It is written down.
- ❑ It is shared with the service user.
- ❑ It is a contract – providers and users agree about what is to be done by whom.
- ❑ It is a practical activity.

❑ All team members should be working to this plan which is the service user's, not theirs.

❑ The plan should state specifically what is to happen, who should be doing what and in what timescale.

❑ Monitoring and review of the plan should be built into the planning process.

❑ The plan should clearly identify any statutory/legal requirements, implications or constraints. For example, some care plans for children incorporate a supervision requirement which is legally enforced by the courts or, in Scotland, the children's panel. Any other likely constraints which may affect the care plan should be detailed.

Models used in the care planning process

The above discussion has drawn heavily upon two models of planning: the exchange model and person-centred planning. Both of these emphasise the importance of placing the service user at the centre of the planning process. However, person-centred planning goes much further than this, and presents exciting possibilities for the service user to make supported choices ranging from who attends planning meetings to how the future is to be lived. It is a holistic approach that does not negate the need for assessment in the sense set out above, but goes beyond the results of many assessments that may or may not provide services to meet needs, and which do not really look at the possibilities and potential for every aspect of life.

The exchange model

The exchange model is described in Coulshed and Orme (1998) and emphasises an exchange among service users, carers and workers of their knowledge and skills, including knowledge of methods of helping and of resources and skills in the process of problem solving. The model recognises that people with needs and those in their network know more about their problems than any worker who comes along to help them, though workers have their own areas of expertise. The process of producing a plan is an exchange among everyone involved and should be multi-disciplinary in nature. A plan emerges which is a balance sheet of everything that has been presented. One person, usually a keyworker or social worker, coordinates the plan and negotiates agreements about who is to do what for whom in what timescale.

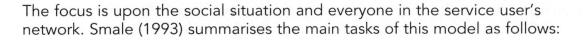

The focus is upon the social situation and everyone in the service user's network. Smale (1993) summarises the main tasks of this model as follows:

❑ Facilitate full participation in the process of decision making.
❑ Make a 'holistic' assessment of the social situation, and not just of the referred individual.
❑ Help create and maintain the flexible set of human relationships which make up a 'package of care'.
❑ Facilitate negotiations within personal networks about conflicts of choices and needs.
❑ Create sufficient trust for full participation and open negotiations actually to take place.
❑ Change the approach to all these broad tasks as the situation itself changes over time.

This approach to care planning is especially useful where there is a need for the provision of services, or where there is some statutory responsibility towards the service user, as in the case of looked-after children or vulnerable adults. In these instances, the individual is central and is enabled to choose as far as this is possible, but the individual may also need protection, sometimes through the recommendation or order of a court or children's panel. People in the service user's network are also taken into account in developing a plan. This approach is person-centred in that the main aim is to focus upon meeting the needs of individuals. It differs from person-centred planning, which is a particular way of working outlined below, that aims to empower people to make changes in their lives.

Person-centred planning

(Most of the following section is produced with permission from SHS Ltd, Edinburgh.)

> Be careful what you ask for – you might just get it! Person-centred planning used to be something counter-cultural, done by eccentric outsiders with coloured pens and strange ideas about having people in the room when decisions are being made about their lives.
>
> Now it's government policy.
>
> (Ritchie, P 2003)

Person-centred planning has developed from ideas presented by O'Brien and Lovett (1992), mainly in relation to people with learning disability who are now beginning to find a place 'in the community', often after spending many years in hospital. Some of its central ideas, however, can be transferred to care planning in general and can be useful with any service user who wants and is in a position to make changes in his or her life. It is an exciting advance upon traditional models of care planning, moving away from professionals organising the process towards placing as much control and decision making in the hands of the service user as possible.

Various forms of care planning are based upon the person-centred approach, including personal futures planning and essential lifestyle planning and many agencies, among them, the Richmond Fellowship, People First and even social services and social work departments. These are embracing person-centred planning as central to their work. The Valuing People White Paper (Department of Health 2001) translated person-centred planning into government policy. The potential of this approach for empowering service users is enormous and exciting, and for this reason it is given considerable space in this section of the book.

Three ways of working which are essential to the person-centred planning process are now considered. These are:

- ❑ sharing power
- ❑ building a shared picture
- ❑ building a capacity for change.

Sharing power is not always easy, especially when service users have experienced many years of powerlessness in institutional settings. For this reason, planning may have an educational element, showing and informing the person about what is possible. It may also require enormous patience and a very positive belief that the person is capable of growth and participation. The use of visual materials is one of the ways in which people are empowered and can begin to build a shared picture of their future.

Building a capacity for change may involve investigating and utilising community resources in creative and new ways. Here are some ways in which agencies share power and build up a shared picture. Outlook (Kirkintilloch) asks the service user whom he or she wishes to invite to a planning meeting, and the meeting is at the user's and not anyone else's pace. Figures 8.3 and 8.4 illustrate the person-centred planning process, looking creatively at how meetings can take place and how decisions can be made in the most empowering way.

Essential Lifestyle planning looks at the best possible day and the worst possible day for the person, going right through a 24-hour period and looking at every

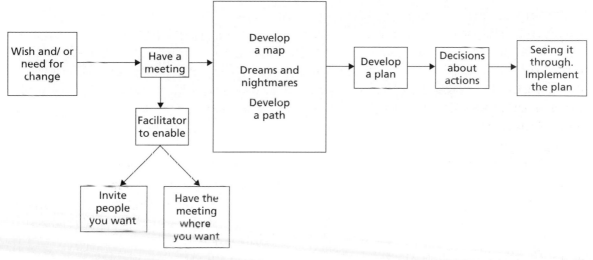

Figure 8.3 Person-centred planning

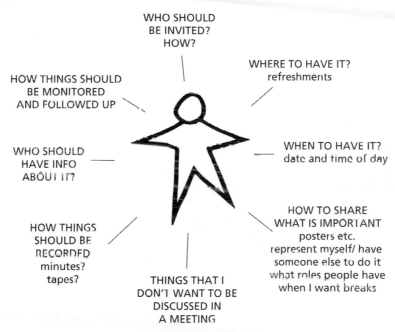

Figure 8.4 When a meeting is needed . . . (reproduced with permission of SHS Ltd, Edinburgh)

detail. The important thing about this is that it focuses attention upon the small details of life, such as what this individual likes for breakfast. Other tools of person-centred planning are the use of 'maps' and 'paths'. Maps in this sense are tools to help individuals, organisations and families find out the best possible way for them to move into the future. Bill's map below illustrates the outcome of this process.

Figure 8.5 Bill's map

Path

> Path is there when a situation is complex and will require concerted action, engaging other people and resources, over a longish period in order to make an important vision real.
>
> (Pearpoint, J *et al.*, 1993)

Path generally has the following steps, ideally worked through by the person, the people he or she wants to invite to meet together to help with the path, and two facilitators experienced in person-centred planning, one of whom is there to write or draw the process:

Step 1: The dream
This is the person's vision for the future.

Step 2: Sensing the goal
Participants imagine a year into the future and goals are recorded that are positive and possible.

Step 3: Now
What is it like now and what are the tensions around getting to where the person wants to be? This gives energy and dynamism to the process.

Step 4: Enrol/Who is on board
Who might help; who might stand in the way. How can the latter be won over?

Step 5: How are we going to build strength?
How can the group maintain strength and commitment to the goals, e.g. by supporting one another?

Step 6: Three-six-month goals
Interim goals are set within a realistic timescale.

Step 7: First steps
First steps are identified and the next meeting date is set.

Circles of support, described in Chapter 9, are often used to enable achievement of the path. Below is a summary of what person-centred planning is moving from and towards (Figure 8.6), adapted from Sanderson, H (2003).

Moving from	Moving towards
clinical descriptions of people	seeing people as human beings
professionals being in charge	sharing power
professionals inviting people	the person choosing who attends meetings
meetings in offices at times to suit professionals	meetings in a venue chosen by the person, when it suits her/him
meetings being chaired	meetings being facilitated
not asking what person wants	encouraging person to dream
assuming inability	looking for gifts in people
filing plans away	giving the plan to the person
writing notes of meetings	graphic facilitation of meetings
professionals putting plan into action	all team members having some responsibility for implementing plan

Figure 8.6 Moving towards person-centred planning

ACTIVITY 8.8

Brent's plan

Brent is 24 years old, black and proud of it, in a wheelchair because of paraplegia following a diving accident on holiday. There is nothing wrong with his mind, though he is frustrated and confused about what the future holds. He is due to be discharged from a rehabilitation centre. The workers involved in his care all have a meeting since they are concerned that he cannot possibly go back to his second floor flat where he lived alone before his accident. A plan is needed for his future. They discuss with great concern what would be best for Brent and conclude that a place at a voluntary organisation supported housing scheme, some distance from his family and in a predominantly white area of the city, will suit his needs best. There is currently a vacancy. They think the advantages of the support that can be offered in the scheme outweigh any disadvantages. They invite Brent into the end of the meeting to tell him what they think would be best for him.

Aisha's plan

Aisha is also in her twenties. She has a learning disability that has so far prevented her from living independently. She lives at home with her mother, father and younger brother. She has a white mother and an Asian father, who have always supported her to do as much as possible for herself and would like her to have a future that is as fulfilling as possible. They also think that it would be very difficult for Aisha if she left home. At her day centre Aisha has become increasingly awkward recently and seems to be frustrated for some reason. Aisha is asked if she would like to invite some of her friends and family to a meeting to help her to look at what she would really like to be doing, what thoughts and dreams she has about the future and whether anything is troubling her at the moment. Aisha welcomes this opportunity and a date is set for her meeting. She invites her mum and dad, her brother, two friends from the centre, her next-door neighbour, her keyworker and a student who is on placement at the centre. Aisha is asked where she would like the meeting and chooses the lounge at the day centre, which is booked for the date they agree upon. Aisha's keyworker explains that the meeting is all about her and that everyone will be working together to help Aisha make decisions and choices that she wants.

Look at the two short studies above and grade them on a scale of one to five in relation to how person-centred they really are; zero is not at all, one is a bit and five is very. Give four reasons from each study why you think they are person-centred or not.

Figure 8.7

SUMMARY

This chapter has examined assessment and care planning as part of a process of person-centred care that places the individual firmly at the centre. Assessment should not only be needs-led but also person-centred and collaborative. Consideration has been given to theories of need, such as those presented by Maslow (1954) and Bradshaw (1972). Two models of assessment and care planning have been examined: the exchange model and person-centred planning. The exchange model emphasises partnership and exchange by all participants. Person-centred planning is particularly helpful for people who wish or need to make changes in their lives. It places and keeps the focus firmly upon this individual, their choices, needs, wishes and dreams for the future, and how to discuss and reach these in creative ways.

FIVE KEY POINTS

1. Assessment, care planning, implementation and review are part of a person-centred model of care that places the individual firmly at the centre.
2. Assessment should be needs-led, not service-led.
3. Maslow's, Bradshaw's and the SPICES theories of need can help you to understand need from different perspectives.
4. Two models of assessment and care planning have been explained: the exchange model and person-centred planning.
5. Person-centred planning challenges approaches that exclude and marginalise people by including them and empowering them to take control of their own lives.

THREE QUESTIONS

1. What do you think is important about a person-centred approach to assessment and care planning?
2. Distinguish between a person-centred approach and person-centred planning?
3. With one individual, apply what you have learned about the process of assessment, care planning, implementation, and review and identify what values, skills and knowledge you drew upon to assist you.

RECOMMENDED READING

COULSHED, V. and ORME, J. (1998) *Social Work Practice*, 3rd edn. Basingstoke: BASW Macmillan. Although the title refers to social work, the clarity of this book in explaining the essentials of assessment and care planning makes it very useful for anyone working in the care field.

SANDERSON, H. *et al.* (1997) *People, Plans and Possibilities*. Edinburgh: SHS. A brilliant book with lots of practical guidance about putting person-centred planning into practice.

SOCIAL CARE ASSOCIATION (2000) *Handbook*. Surbiton: SCA. A mine of easily accessible information on many social care topics, including assessment and care planning.

CHAPTER 9

IMPLEMENTING CARE PLANS – APPROACHES TO HELPING AND THE PROMOTION OF WELLBEING

Janet Miller, Sylvia Brewer, Margaret Crompton and Robin Jackson

> **I have lived in a wonderful residential care home . . .. Thanks to the staff here I can face the future with confidence.**
>
> (Service user statement)

By the end of this chapter you should be able to:

- ❏ develop ways to help and promote the wellbeing of individuals
- ❏ understand and apply team work and collaborative work
- ❏ promote spiritual wellbeing
- ❏ understand some approaches to challenging behaviour
- ❏ help to develop networks and circles of support
- ❏ understand and apply task-centred work
- ❏ use theories of resilience to assist you in your work
- ❏ develop group work skills
- ❏ understand what advocacy is and how it can be used.

This chapter provides underpinning content and context for all care qualifications. These include:

NVQ and SVQ Units – HSC331: Support individuals to develop and maintain social networks and relationships

HSC337: Provide frameworks to help individuals to manage challenging behaviour

HSC326: Contribute to the prevention and management of challenging behaviour in children and young people

HSC350: Recognise, respect and support the spiritual wellbeing of individuals

HSC367: Help individuals identify and access independent representation and advocacy

HNC Health and social care units from various examining bodies:

Social care theory for practice

Supporting spiritual wellbeing

Ensuring best outcomes for individuals.

INTRODUCTION

Implementing care plans means making a reality of the care plan and putting into practice its content. Much of the work that care workers do in relation to implementing care plans does not require complicated theory or advanced practice techniques. If person-centred planning is being used, this may require a great deal of flexibility and creativity in implementation. Whatever the process used to reach the implementation stage, you must not lose a focus on the individual service users, their voices and choices. Thinking reflectively and using resources, including yourself, in the best possible way to meet the needs of service users are of prime importance. Although the examples given in this chapter refer to people in particular settings, the content applies to people wherever they receive a service: in their own homes, in small homely settings, larger care homes, day centres or just dropping in for a particular purpose. It is only possible in this chapter to consider some of the many methods and tools that may prove useful in implementing care plans and promoting the wellbeing of individuals. Through your learning you may adopt different ways to work, but

ACTIVITY 9.1

Begin where you are at the moment. What skills do you already have that you can use to implement care plans?

whichever way you work, it is necessary to ensure that the care value base underpins everything you do.

When some care workers were asked what they did that they thought was helpful to people, here is what they said:

- ❏ If you build a relationship, that wins hands down. They learn to trust you.
- ❏ When you know there is a real issue, you try to be there for them and support them through it if it is a bad time.
- ❏ Listen to them.
- ❏ Follow through person-centred plans by ensuring you put them into practice and evaluate them afterwards.
- ❏ Encourage people with their hobbies and interests.
- ❏ Use your sense of humour.
- ❏ Take an active interest in the people you work with.
- ❏ Be genuine with them. They can pick a fraud a mile off.
- ❏ When helping people, such as with bathing, always talk to them and ask how their family are doing or whoever is important to them.
- ❏ Help with life story books so that they have a reminder about who has been important to them and important places, holidays and so on.
- ❏ Use and develop skills you already have. One worker said the following:

   I used to be a hairdresser and when we're going on an outing I ask if if anyone wants their hair done. Lots of them do. While you are doing their hair or their nails, you talk to them and they tell you all sorts of things they would never usually because they are so relaxed.

Without really realising it, these workers were bringing many skills that were helpful in implementing care plans, many of them related to communication and relationships discussed in Chapter 4 and care planning discussed in Chapter 8.

These included:

- ❏ listening and building a relationship
- ❏ using a model of care practice based upon assessment, care planning, implementation and evaluation
- ❏ using person-centred planning as an approach in its own right
- ❏ providing support
- ❏ using practical skills alongside talking to people
- ❏ promoting activities including hobbies, interests and life story books
- ❏ transferring skills which they already had to the helping situation.

All of these are relevant to helping and promoting wellbeing, the subject of this chapter.

PROMOTING WELLBEING

The Oxford Dictionary defines wellbeing as the state of being comfortable, healthy or happy. It involves meeting all of the needs identified in the SPICE theory outlined on page 228: social, physical, intellectual, cultural and emotional needs. Although meeting spiritual needs may be deemed to come into several of these categories, separate consideration is given to this aspect of care work.

Promoting wellbeing is not only a desirable outcome but is also included in legislation. The new Children Act 2004, for example, places a duty on agencies to collaborate to improve the wellbeing of children.

The care environment

In care practice, things that you do to provide a good environment for people, both in their own homes and in other care environments, contribute greatly to this sense of wellbeing. Of foremost importance in this are the workers, their attitudes, values and the way they work. Davis (1992) also talks about creating environments that appeal to the senses. These may be: places that look good with things in them chosen by the people who live there; meals that taste delicious and meet people's cultural needs and choices; a homely, pleasant smell and the use of aromas, such as fragrant candles, as a form of therapy; sounds that people like to hear, including music of their choice, and a reduction of loud noises such as banging doors and shouting that can raise stress levels and sometimes lead to challenging behaviour; things that feel good to touch such as fabrics on beds and furniture, clothes chosen by the individual, animals to stroke, and places that feel warm and welcoming.

ACTIVITY 9.2

Imagine that you have the task of setting up a day centre for older adults, children or people with learning or sensory disability. Make a list of ten things that you regard as important in establishing an environment that promotes wellbeing.

Barbara Kahan (1994) was a great advocate for the needs of children, and wrote that:

> children care about shabby, run-down buildings, lack of privacy in bedrooms, showers, toilets and bathrooms. They recognise them as indicators that they are undervalued and that their needs have been overlooked.

It is not just children but everyone who feels undervalued in such an environment.

Reducing pain

James Anglin (2002) researched group care environments for children and young people, though his findings can be applied much more widely. He was especially concerned about the effects of emotional and physical pain on people, and felt that care workers often ignore pain or underestimate how much pain people are in or have experienced. Ignoring this pain and failing to deal with it often means that the work that care workers do is not as effective as it might be. Much trouble is often an illustration of pain-based behaviour and is glossed over. The terms 'disturbing' or 'challenging' are often used when in fact behaviour is a response to pain. All too often, care workers inflict more pain on people through, for example, removal of privileges, creating secondary pain added to the primary pain, fostering a cycle of conflict. The care worker can make some if not all of a contribution to the reduction of pain through recognising its existence, building positive, helping relationships, listening to the individual's verbal and non-verbal communication, responding sensitively and with empathy, and through creating positive care environments.

Developing a sense of normality

Anglin also emphasised the importance of developing a sense of normality. In care establishments, there is the paradox that people are not in a normal place but can develop a sense of normality within it. Homes can create a sense of place. There needs to be something that feels homely. People need to be given a sense of belonging, personal power, hope, opportunity, connection, dignity and a sense of having mastery. Some of the things that Anglin found can make a difference are:

- ❏ listening and responding with respect
- ❏ building rapport
- ❏ establishing routines and structure
- ❏ instilling commitment
- ❏ offering people emotional support
- ❏ challenging people's thinking
- ❏ sharing power and decision making
- ❏ respecting personal space
- ❏ encouraging potential
- ❏ providing resources.

These things also apply to people who receive a service in their own homes.

The organisational environment

Creating positive living environments does not take place in a vacuum. It depends to a great extent on the organisational environment in which the promotion of wellbeing takes place. A value base and positive ethos are a starting point in this. As Kinsella (1993) has pointed out:

> Effective organisations have clear philosophies that are known throughout the organisation, and that shape everything that the organisation does. This culture is passed on to new workers in a variety of ways and is reinforced through training, support and supervision, and the very way everyone in the organisation talks, writes and acts.

Also important to this are team work and collaborative work.

Team work and collaborative work

> **. . . team work should never be regarded as an optional extra in this sort of work: it is the heart of the matter.**
>
> (Ward, 1993)

Collaborative work is all about working together to achieve the best possible results for service users and carers. It takes place within teams and between teams and organisations. Thus, team work is part of collaborative work, and the whole of collaborative work involves all of the networks that need to work together to provide services to individuals. As a starting point, team work is examined, followed by a consideration of the bigger picture that contributes to a collaborative approach.

A team is not just a collection of people called a team. Being a team involves much more than that. It requires that people work together, sharing a value base and aiming to achieve agreed goals. Teams are necessary when people work together to cope with complicated, complex or difficult situations where no single person can do all the work or come up with all the solutions. To be really effective, team members need effective leadership that encourages and supports them to feel like a team, to think like a team and to act like a team.

Teams vary enormously according to the functions they perform, how they are led and how they go about achieving their goals. There is no one right way to do team work, though there are many features of a 'good' team which are outlined below. There are certainly some wrong ways to do team work. These may include: too much individual work at the expense of working together, creating inconsistency for workers and service users; gossip and rubbishing the work of some team members behind their backs; no clear system for allocating work; workers played off against one another; a lack of clarity about values and goals; workers not listened to or supported by management. Mix all of those together and imagine the consequences.

ACTIVITY 9.3

Examine a team of which you are or have been a member. What are the features that make it, or could make it, a 'good' team, both for meeting the needs of service users and for you as a worker?

In Activity 9.3 above, some of the things you may have mentioned are:

- ❏ feeling valued and valuing the contributions of team members, service users and carers
- ❏ having opportunities to share in decision making and the allocation of work
- ❏ having opportunities to discuss openly how the team is doing and how the work could be improved
- ❏ feeling that everyone is pulling together to reach the same place
- ❏ supportive managers and colleagues

- ❑ positive staff meetings that tackle the needs of service users and team members
- ❑ regular, meaningful supervision
- ❑ a willingness to address and resolve conflicts through discussion and negotiation.

Your list may have been different, but if the experience of team work was a positive one, it probably contained some of these features.

ACTIVITY 9.4

Look at the account below and identify five positive aspects of the team.

The Rural Emotional Support Team (Rest, Staffordshire) offers a mental health outreach service to the agricultural community of mid and south Staffordshire. The team focuses on values, working to people's care plans and using an assertive outreach model. Team members are all equally committed to providing a service that meets the needs of mental health service users outside the statutory sector, and share with their service users a background in agriculture.

We listen to clients' viewpoints and recognise what is meaningful and valued to them. For our clients, this is a service that is accessible, culturally sensitive, and provided at a time and place chosen by the clients themselves

(Coates, C. 'My Practice', 12 August 2004. Published by permission of the editor of Community Care)

Effective team meetings

Team meetings should be part of the cement that holds the team together. What do you think makes them effective? Look at the questions below and answer them in relation to a team meeting that you have attended.

Did the team meeting:

- ❑ start and finish on time
- ❑ provide notes or minutes from the last meeting
- ❑ have an agenda to which you had the opportunity to contribute
- ❑ give you the opportunity to discuss how work is progressing and whether it is meeting objectives and goals
- ❑ provide opportunities to look at the problems being encountered and whether you can help one another to reach solutions

- ❏ enable you to see how you fit into the scheme of things
- ❏ provide learning opportunities
- ❏ provide tea/coffee/water
- ❏ take place in a quiet place away from interruptions
- ❏ have a chairperson who enabled everyone to have a say
- ❏ where appropriate, allow for members of different shifts or those who work at different locations to attend?

A good meeting does not necessarily require a 'yes' answer to all of these questions, especially if it has been called for a particular purpose; but over a period of time, meetings need to achieve most of these things if they are to be effective. It is recognised that, in care settings, life and therefore meetings are far from perfect; there may be crises beyond anyone's control, but that is no excuse for not striving towards positive meetings.

Theory and team work

Many theorists have expounded about team work. One of the most notable was Dr R Meredith Belbin who began researching team roles over 20 years ago. He identified nine team roles or types that combine to make an effective team and stated the following about teams:

> A team is not a bunch of people with job titles, but a congregation of individuals each of whom has a role which is understood by other members. Members of the team seek out certain roles and they perform most effectively in the ones that are most natural to them.

> (Belbin, 1993)

The team roles identified by Belbin are:

- ❏ **Completer** – the completer-finisher is a hard-working, conscientious person who pays attention to detail and organisation, is anxious to get jobs completed, and is a necessary complement to more radical members of the team.
- ❏ **Coordinator** – the coordinator's role is to direct the group, bring out the best in other team members and keep team members working towards goals.
- ❏ **Implementer** – implementers are excellent at putting into practice schemes that others have devised. They favour hard work and application but do not become too anxious. They can be very valuable in a team.

- **Plant** – the plant is a creative, innovative person who prefers to work independently, is not usually very team-orientated, though can contribute greatly to the team's success. One plant is enough, and Belbin's research revealed that teams with more than one plant were no more successful than teams with no plants at all.
- **Monitor evaluator** – the monitor evaluator is an intelligent, discerning and objective person, usually content to take a back seat but comes to prominence when a crucial decision is to be made.
- **Resource investigator** – although not a great source of original ideas, the resource investigator is very good at finding out what is available and what can be done to put the team's innovative ideas into practice. Usually a sociable and friendly person, the resource investigator is a curious explorer.
- **Shaper** – shapers are highly motivated people, high achievers who strive to reach the team's goals by whatever means possible. Although they may take a leadership role, they can be impatient and critical. Interpersonal problems can result if there are too many shapers in a team, but they are a very valuable antidote to complacency.

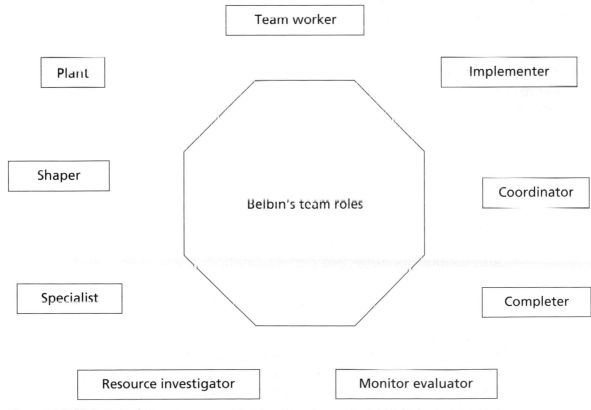

Figure 9.1 Belbin's team roles

❏ **Specialist** – specialists are single-minded, self-starting, dedicated people. They provide knowledge and skills which are in short supply.

❏ **Team worker** – team workers are sociable, caring people, good communicators who recognise the value of all team members and strive to avert team problems. They may combine this role with one of Belbin's other roles and may be a senior manager if the line manager is very goal-orientated and competitive.

ACTIVITY 9.5

Look at a team that you belong to or are familiar with. Try to identify who performs which roles. What is your team role?

Collaborative work

Increasingly there are joint agendas in care which involve collaboration among individuals in the same team and also between individuals and teams who may come from the same or different disciplines. Care, health, housing and education are among the disciplines that are working together to share assessment and care planning in order that there is a minimum of duplication, the most effective use of resources and maximum protection of vulnerable people. Inevitably there are sometimes tensions between workers of different disciplines who work in collaboration, and it is vital that the essential ingredients of effective collaboration are practised here as in any other work. What are the ingredients of effective collaboration? Those which apply to team work have been identified above. Since team work is a form of collaborative work, the points made below also apply to those working within teams.

❏ **Communication and relationships** – communication and relationships are as vital in collaborative work as in any other aspect of care work. The aspects of communication most relevant are: thoughtful, reflective communication; transparency and openness; including service users in decision making; recognising the influences of discrimination and power and avoiding the misuse of these.

❏ **Flexibility** – to work well collaboratively requires adaptability, open-mindedness and a willingness to learn from the skills of others, all of which comprise flexibility.

❏ **Negotiation** – this includes a willingness to discuss issues, consult service users, colleagues, management and members of other teams, agencies and disciplines. Sometimes it involves compromise or confrontation in finding optimum solutions to care.

❏ **Partnership** – this means working with others, and needs a willingness and ability to work alongside all relevant others, especially service users, colleagues and members of other relevant teams, agencies and disciplines. It involves sharing ideas, work practices and information without feeling threatened by others encroaching upon 'your' work or invading 'your' territory, and working together for the good of the service user without being territorial or possessive. This involves all of the preceding skills of communication, flexibility and negotiation, as well as recognition of the boundaries of confidentiality.

❏ **Evaluation** – collaborative work must be accompanied by some form of evaluation. This is the ability to reflect upon all aspects of work in order to evaluate whether they are being used to maximum effect. It means assessing whether what is happening is as good as it can be. Evaluation will also point the way to developing future collaborative work in terms of the next steps to be taken, and who is responsible for which aspects of the work.

Many failures to protect people have been attributed, at least in part, to poor collaboration among individuals and agencies. In the case of Victoria Climbie, there were several opportunities for professionals to communicate across professional boundaries, but this failed to happen in time to save Victoria's life. In 2002, Holly Wells and Jessica Chapman might not have died if agencies had collaborated and communicated with one another in sharing information about Ian Huntley, later convicted of their murder.

ACTIVITY 9.6

Give five advantages of working collaboratively across organisational and professional boundaries.

You may have thought of these or different advantages. Collaboration provides:

❏ improved protection for the individual through sharing necessary information
❏ increased choice
❏ improved access to the 'right' services

❏ better use of resources
❏ improved outcomes based on the needs of the individual rather than the needs of a particular service.

DEVELOPING NETWORKS AND CIRCLES OF SUPPORT

A network sets out the links which an individual has, their nature and frequency. Some people have vast, extensive networks, other people have fairly small networks but feel sufficiently in touch with the world and supported in meeting their needs. It is not necessarily the size of a person's network that is the most important thing but the value of the links for the individual, and whether or not the frequency of contact with others in the network is sufficient to meet need. Many vulnerable people lack meaningful networks because of their marginalised position in society. They miss out on the kind of informal support that is often provided to people who belong to networks.

ACTIVITY 9.7

Look at the links you have with other people and with groups during the course of one week. Draw a diagram of these links, state how often you make these links and rate on a scale of one to five how important they are to you, with five being the most important.

You may have mentioned links with family, friends, social groups, work groups, interest or hobby groups and so on; or you may be quite isolated. Some people choose isolation, but for most people links with others are very important, and isolation is something that happens rather than something that is chosen.

Looking at people's networks with them can be part of the assessment, care planning and implementation process. Where a network is sparse and/or insufficient to meet an individual's needs, work can focus on ways to develop the network as part of the helping process. Have a look at Mary's network in Figure 9.2 and suggest ways in which it could be improved. Mary is 54 years old, has a mild learning disability and now lives alone in the house where she always lived with her mother and father. Both of her parents have died during the past year and many of their friends have now stopped visiting. A couple of people call in occasionally and Mary does her own shopping, where she talks to the shop assistants. She has been making more and more frequent visits to the doctor and appears unhappy, increasingly unkempt and isolated. She complains of aches and pains but does not appear to have any serious illness.

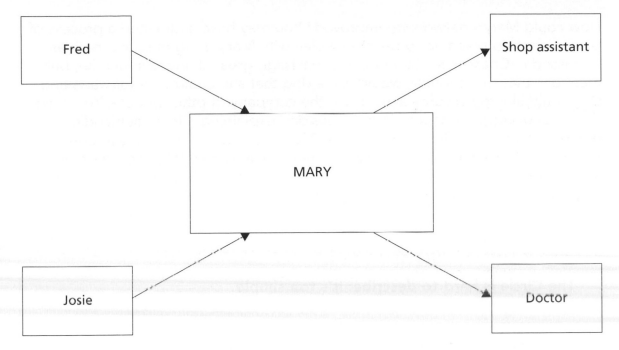

Figure 9.2 Mary's network

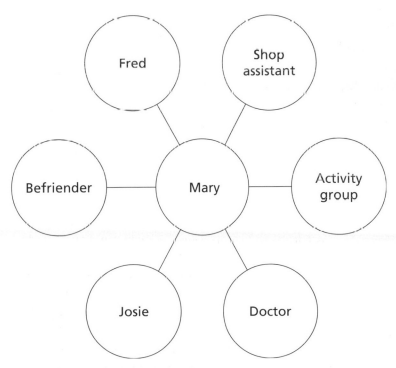

Figure 9.3 Mary's new network

How could Mary's network be improved? You may have suggested a process of person-centred planning to develop a plan with Mary using map and path as discussed in Chapter 8. Mary does not envisage great changes in her life, but mentions that she is lonely, would like a dog that she could take for walks and she would like to do some activities in the company of other people. You make one or two suggestions for Mary to consider, explaining a local befriending scheme and an over 50s activity group. Mary agrees that she will give both of these a try, and a year later she has the network in Figure 9.3, and says how much better she feels. You can see that she is much happier, and her visits to the doctor are far less frequent.

Circles of support

> ### The Circle is hard to describe; it's too simple.
> (Regina DeMarasse in Mount et al., 1991)

Another way in which a person's network can be developed is through a **circle of support**. This idea was developed in Canada, spread to the USA and arrived in Britain in the 1980s. It is often linked with person-centred planning, and is a relatively simple concept that can have a very powerful impact upon a person's life. A circle consists of people chosen by the individual and who voluntarily commit themselves to this person's circle. They may be family, friends, local community members, support workers or anyone else who is prepared to make a commitment to help someone to make changes in their life. They are enabled by a facilitator, who is part of an organisation supporting circles of support, but the

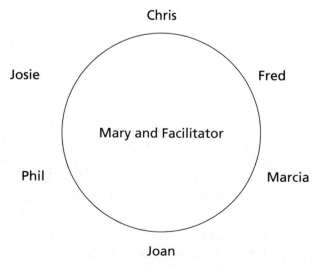

Figure 9.4 Mary's circle of support

> **Example:**
>
> Kerry had a PATH facilitated, which is a person-centred planning tool that focuses on where somebody would like to be in the future and how they are going to be supported to get there. Kerry's circle is made up of her Mum, Dad, brother, brother's girlfriend and two committed keyworkers from Kerry's day service. Initially a dreaming session took place and then those dreams that were seen as positive and possible were set and an action plan made. Kerry was present for about half of the sessions. On the other occasions, she chose not to come in as she often feels uncomfortable and becomes upset if all of her family are present around her. On the occasions that she was not there, the facilitator made it clear to Kerry's circle that the session was based on Kerry's PATH and so was able to continue to guide the process. Also, to encourage Kerry's involvement, the facilitator met with Kerry's brother separately, explaining the process and gaining his views.
>
> (Circles Network, 2004)

control is with the individual and the choices made belong to that individual, the focus person. The group agrees to come together on a regular basis to help the focus person to improve his or her life.

By bringing a group of people like this together, there are often spin-offs for everyone, since everyone gains new relationships and a sense of interdependency. A process of person-centred planning can be used within the circle to help the person to develop a map and/or a path that will fulfil their needs and their dreams. For example, a circle of support for Mary may look like the diagram in Figure 9.4, where individuals have made a commitment to work together with Mary to enable her to meet her needs and achieve her dreams.

CREDO provides another example of the use of circles of support. CREDO is a project which aims to give a voice to young people who have a disability and complex needs. Often these young people are not listened to or are labelled as challenging, and other people make decisions on their behalf. Through circles of support, the CREDO project aims to develop person-centred plans with the young people who are supported by members of the circle, enabling the young people to receive support appropriate to their needs and wishes, rather than being slotted into services because that is convenient for the services.

BUILDING RESILIENCE

The development of ideas about resilience is providing new insights and ways of working with people who are vulnerable. Resilience can be useful both as a tool in the assessment process and in presenting a framework for practice. Like most concepts that are useful, it is not easy to define. It can be seen in terms of a process of becoming resilient, the capacity for being resilient and as an outcome of factors that build resilience. Gilligan (1997) defines it in relation to children as follows:

> . . . qualities which cushion a vulnerable child from the worst effects of adversity in whatever form it takes and which may help a child or young person to cope, survive and even thrive in the face of great hurt and disadvantage.

Other definitions include:

> Resilience is normal development under difficult conditions.

> (Fonagy et al., 1994)

> Resilience is the capacity to transcend adversity.

> (Daniel and Wassell, 2002)

People who are resilient thrive even when the going gets tough. In assessment, it is useful to know how resilient people are and in practice it is helpful to build, or build upon, resilience, so that people can cope more constructively with adverse or difficult circumstances.

Many factors have been shown to contribute to resilience. These can be seen as protective factors that enable a person to cope with difficulties. In the external life of the individual, the following are important:

- ❏ at least one secure attachment
- ❏ supportive networks, which may include extended family and friends
- ❏ positive experiences in the community, or in school or nursery school.

Within the individual, Gilligan (1997) identified the following factors:

- ❏ a secure base providing a sense of security and belonging
- ❏ self-esteem indicating an internal sense of worth and competence

❏ self-efficacy where the individual has a knowledge of his or her own limits and strengths and what can and cannot be changed.

These are summarised as:

I HAVE . . . e.g. people I trust and love.
I AM . . . e.g. a lovable person.
I CAN . . . e.g. find ways to solve problems.

Much of the work which care workers do to promote wellbeing can actually be seen as contributing to resilience. The beginning of this work is a detailed and accurate assessment involving the individual as much as possible. Developing positive care environments contributes to resilience. Networks and circles of support can provide people whom the individual can trust and rely upon, and can enable people to explore ways of solving problems. Cognitive behavioural work encourages the development of positive thought patterns, ways to say 'I can' instead of 'I cannot' and to say that 'I am responsible for my actions and with support can find solutions' rather than 'the way I behave is someone else's fault'. Similarly, a task-centred approach can give people a sense of achievement; promoting spiritual wellbeing can give people the inner strength to cope with some seemingly insurmountable problems. These ways of helping, discussed below, can all contribute to maintaining and building resilience.

One further concept from resilience theory worth exploring is what is called 'mobilising protective strings'. This aspect of practice rests on the premise that work in one area of life can have spin-offs in other areas of life. If work is done in relation to friendships and networks, those networks can in turn encourage a person to develop talents and interests or social competencies. For young people, Daniel and Wassell (2002) identified six such areas or domains as illustrated in Figure 9.5.

Focusing on any one of these can benefit and build resilience in some or all of the other areas.

ACTIVITY 9.8

Suggest how an understanding of resilience could help you to assess and work with a child who is exhibiting disruptive behaviour in the care home in which he lives.

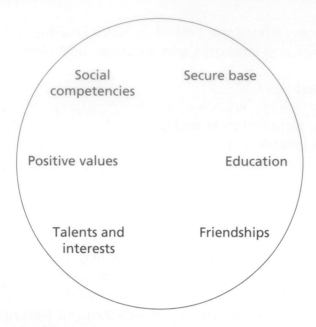

Figure 9.5 Domains of resilience

SPIRITUAL WELLBEING IN CARE PRACTICE

Attending to people's wellbeing means caring for every aspect of life, including physical, emotional, cognitive and social wellbeing. Many people believe in a *spiritual* aspect of life too. Even if you do not believe in this, or do not hold any religious convictions, it is essential to know about, respect, enable, encourage and support the spiritual wellbeing of people with and for whom you work. This includes respecting beliefs which are different from your own, and never colluding with abuse, discrimination, oppression or prejudice.

Some ideas about spiritual wellbeing

People who hold religious beliefs and fulfil religious obligations may regard spiritual wellbeing as inseparable from religion. Other people believe in spiritual wellbeing but do not accept any religious doctrines. Many people, whether as individuals or on behalf of organisations, think deeply about the meaning of such words as spiritual. There are many ways of defining spiritual wellbeing. These examples are all secular, without reference to a deity.

1. The first was prepared by a group of day, foster and residential carers as part of an overall statement about children's needs.
2. The second is from a guide for practitioners working with people with learning disabilities or mental health difficulties.

Children's needs: the carers' view

Physical   to have shelter, warmth, food, sleep

Cognitive   to be encouraged and supported
to receive direct and indirect teaching

Love and understanding

Emotional   freedom and security to try and fail or succeed
to be heard and understood
to be special and treated as an individual
to be accepted by peer groups

Spiritual   to give meaning to life
to be aware of the mysteries of life
to develop one's own beliefs and be accepted for them

(Crompton, 1998)

Spiritual wellbeing

. . . a sense of good health about the essence, the essential self, of one's self as a human being and as a unique individual. Spiritual wellbeing is not so much a state as a process of growth and development. Spiritual wellbeing, feeling at ease with the essential self, happens when people are fulfilling their potential as individuals and as human beings. They are at ease with themselves at a deep level. They have a sense of awareness of their own dignity and of themselves as valuable. They enjoy themselves and have a sense of direction. They can sense this essence in others also and respect them and relate positively to them. They are also at ease with the world around them. . . . The essence of human beings as unique individuals: 'what makes me, me, and you, you?' So it is the power, energy and hopefulness in a person. It is life at its best, growth and creativity, freedom and love. It is what is deepest in us – what gives direction, motivation. It is what enables a person to survive bad times, to be strong, to overcome difficulties, to become ourselves.

(Bradford social services community health NHS trust/Interfaith
Education Centre, 2002)

> **Spiritual wellbeing**
>
> State of wholeness, when every aspect of life is in balance and the person feels confident, creative, fulfilled and integrated, both inwardly and in relation to other people.
>
> It is a process of growth and development that gives to the individual meaning, purpose, direction and value in daily life.

3.   The third is the definition in the Level 3 S/NVQ unit HSC350: Recognise, respect and support the spiritual wellbeing of individuals

These definitions contain many ideas about qualities and experiences which may contribute to spiritual wellbeing. You may find other definitions prepared by individuals, groups or organisations.

ACTIVITY 9.9

❑   The carers thought that love and understanding belonged in all four groups – physical, cognitive, emotional and spiritual. What do you think?

❑   Do you think any of the ideas which the carers listed under physical, cognitive or emotional could also be described as spiritual?

❑   Can you list five words which describe your idea of spiritual wellbeing? Choose words from these definitions or think of others.

❑   Which of these qualities and experiences do you recognise in people with whom you work?

Rights, legislation and regulations

Many official bodies and documents promote attention to spiritual wellbeing. This means that workers are required to know about, respect, enable, encourage and support people's spiritual wellbeing, whatever their own beliefs and attitudes. Here are some examples:

❑   The United Nations Convention on the Rights of the Child (1989) signatories 'recognise the right of every child to a standard of living adequate for the child's physical, mental, *spiritual*, moral and social development' (Article 1).

ACTIVITY 9.10

How are spiritual and/or religious wellbeing promoted in the legislation, standards, and regulations on which your work is based?

Does your agency or organisation fulfil these requirements?

You may need to ask your manager or supervisor to help you find the right documents.

❏ The Education Reform Act (England and Wales) 1988 curricula promote pupils' 'spiritual, moral, cultural, mental and physical development.'

❏ The United Nations Universal Declaration of Human Rights (1948) states:

> Everyone has the right to freedom of thought, conscience and religion; this right includes freedom to change his religion or belief, and freedom, either alone or in community with others and in public or private, to manifest his religion or belief in teaching, practice, worship and observance.

(Article 18)

Expressing and communicating about spiritual wellbeing

Spiritual wellbeing is inseparable from all other aspects of life. If people feel well and supported spiritually, they can find strength to manage difficulties, e.g. illness or bereavement. Similarly, any form of abuse or neglect impairs spiritual wellbeing.

Spiritual impairment is often expressed physically. One worker described a girl whose parents did not love her as 'dis-spirited', with 'no spirit, a shell, no life or verve' and noted that she never smiled. Another described the body language of people whose spiritual wellbeing is impaired as 'dragged down, slumping, their exuberance crushed, his spirit was crushed' (Crompton, 1998).

When people are 'dis-spirited' they have less energy and will to direct towards meeting challenges and overcoming difficulties. When people feel that they are managing well and experiencing achievement, their spiritual wellbeing is stronger. It is important to offer opportunities for people to develop spiritual wellbeing, e.g. by gaining self-esteem through taking part in interesting activities, alone or in contact with other people. Fulfilling tasks and achievements help to develop a sense of being whole people, of contributing to the

ACTIVITY 9.11

How do the atmosphere and activities at your place of work contribute to spiritual wellbeing?

Are people helped to feel respected, valuable and worthwhile?

Do they have a sense of wholeness and dignity?

Do they feel at ease with themselves and other people?

You may think of new ways in which people can be creative and live fully.

community, of being worthwhile, 'the best that I can be'. These may include art, daily chores, crafts, compiling a life story book, dance, drama, gardening, looking after animals, music, physical activity, play, poetry, stories.

The relevance of spiritual wellbeing to care practice

Attention to spiritual wellbeing is relevant in every care context. Here are some ways in which you can support the spiritual wellbeing of people with whom you work:

❑ Recognise ways in which people communicate about feelings and experiences, especially if they are anxious, depressed or dis-spirited, and if they have been abused or neglected.

❑ Provide resources and opportunities for creative and imaginative activities.

❑ Recognise, respect and provide opportunities for peacefulness, privacy, reflection, silence and worship, and protect people's time and space.

❑ Share activities and periods of peacefulness.

❑ Know about and respect people's religious beliefs, and help people to fulfil religious obligations, e.g. attending places of worship, keeping a personal shrine, observing fasts and festivals and celebrating rites of passage.

❑ Observe religious rules about daily care, including diet, dress, hair care and washing, and respect symbolic artefacts such as statues, books and pictures.

❑ Ensure that your attitudes and behaviour are never prejudiced or oppressive and that power and influence are never abused.

❑ Understand and know how to resolve possible conflicts.

Here are three contrasting illustrations of the importance of attending to spiritual wellbeing.

Everyday care

Spiritual wellbeing may be impaired by ignorance of, or thoughtlessness about, religious aspects of everyday care, e.g. diet. Roksana, a nine-year-old Muslim girl in residential care, was distressed because she ate meat which was forbidden by her religion. Her social worker wrote:

She did not wish to be different and this suited staff greatly. Yet, when she had confidence in our relationship, she expressed anxiety and feelings of guilt, she worried about betraying her mother and wondered about punishment from God.

(Crompton, 1998)

The meaning of life

Chances to attend to spiritual wellbeing can come at any time, and with no religious connection. Samantha, aged 27, asked a learning disability day centre support worker, 'Why do you think we are all here?' The worker answered, 'to help us develop skills to work and to make things.' Samantha persisted, 'Yes, but why?' 'Why what?' 'Me, Derek, Fran, Brian, you – why do you think we are alive?' but the worker did not listen to her real question and turned it into an embarrassed joke: 'You are a character! Right everyone, let's have coffee.' The worker lost the chance to show respect to Samantha, to respond to her as a person with dignity and the right to be taken seriously.

(Swinton, 2001)

Staff and students

Sensitivity to people's spiritual wellbeing includes staff and students. A study found that Orthodox Jewish students had difficulty in leaving placements early on Fridays when they needed to prepare for the Sabbath at home, while staff members missed important meetings scheduled on religious holidays (Wood, 1998).

TASK-CENTRED WORK

Task-centred work is one of the ways in which people can be helped to cope with problems. The essence of task-centred work is a focus upon a particular

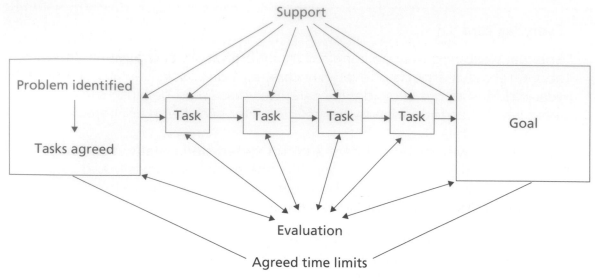

Figure 9.6 Task-centred work

problem, identifying tasks required to tackle the problem, agreeing these tasks and time limits associated with them with the service user, and then providing agreed levels of support to enable the service user to reach the agreed outcome in the agreed time. Problem, tasks, time limits and support are the crucial words. Tasks may be undertaken by any of the people in the situation (e.g. service user, care workers, social worker, family member), but the emphasis is on maximising the participation and independence of the service user. The process is summarised in the diagram above.

Task-centred work is not only about doing tasks. These are part of every care worker's role but may not necessarily be part of a task-centred approach. However, many of the everyday tasks that are undertaken with service users could be used as part of a task-centred approach to resolving difficulties. It may also be used in combination with other approaches such as behavioural work and the use of counselling skills.

Task-centred work can be motivating, but it also needs motivation to begin. Nego-tiation may be needed to agree on what will be tackled, what the goal is and the route to reach it. This is a method that takes maximum account of the service user's views, culture and personal attributes. Task-centred work builds on the service user's strengths and fills any gaps in those strengths through support. It should take account of the individual's networks and the reality of his or her situation.

This work may be carried out with groups and families as well as individuals, and will almost inevitably impinge on others. Working in partnership with the service

> ## ACTIVITY 9.12
>
> A young person with learning and behavioural difficulties expresses a wish to do a college art course. Envisage how a task-centred approach could be used to achieve this wish.

user is crucial to this approach, and reflects the principles of equality and respect.

Task-centred work has been found to be useful where there are:

- difficulties with social relationships
- difficulties in dealing with large organisations
- needs to develop certain skills
- problems of transition from one life stage to another
- situations where there are inadequate resources
- behavioural problems.

It is not suitable for working with people whose problems are really caused by a much broader social problem such as poverty, poor housing or chronic ill health. This approach has been fairly thoroughly researched and therefore rests upon an evidence base confirming its efficacy. There are many advantages to a task-centred approach

- It does not take up vast quantities of time.
- The aim is always known and in sight.
- The strong research evidence (Reid and Epstein, 1997) suggests that this method has a good success rate which can be better than working with a service user on a long-term basis.
- It motivates people to solve other problems in a similar way.
- It increases the service user's ability to cope independently of the worker in the future.

In care practice the achievement of the task is likely to be one aspect in continuing work but can have spin-offs in raising self-esteem and providing encouragement towards a more fulfilling and creative lifestyle.

CHALLENGING BEHAVIOUR AND CRITICAL INCIDENTS

Although the term 'challenging behaviour' is used in the heading, it is not actually about a separate method of working. The term is used because it is common currency. The preferred reference is to people who challenge services.

Example

Fred is usually a cheerful though quiet man who attends a voluntary organisation day centre. He had a stroke a few years ago which affected his mobility and his speech, though he can walk with a Zimmer frame and, if you take the time to listen to his speech, it is comprehensible. For a few weeks now he has been showing signs of being somewhat disorientated and this morning he shouted very loudly, threw his Zimmer on the floor and asked to go home . . . very uncharacteristic behaviour.

The story that eventually emerged was that a new member of staff had assumed that because Fred's words came out slowly, he could not talk. Instead of making the effort to understand him or to find out what his needs were, she had given him a milky coffee and a chocolate biscuit at the morning break. Fred liked his coffee black and hated chocolate. He had tried to convey this information on several occasions to the care worker, but she had been too busy to listen to him. He had had a bad night the night before, had not slept well and was in some pain. Not having the right cup of coffee or a plain biscuit was the final straw. He needed someone to listen to him. Out of sheer frustration he had lost his temper. Although all of the focus may have been on Fred's behaviour, it was actually avoidable if the member of staff had acted differently.

ACTIVITY 9.13

How could the outcome have been changed in the above example about Fred?

Often behaviour that is labelled as challenging is largely caused not by the individual doing the challenging, but by members of staff or others, or by the person's environment. Even where the individual is being a challenge to members of staff, their behaviour may be outside their control, as with people who have dementia, including Alzheimer's disease. It is therefore necessary, where behaviour that challenges is a feature of your work, to look at what lies behind that behaviour. What are the antecedents to the behaviour at issue? It may be found that there is a pattern to the behaviour and that it occurs when there is a particular event or series of events that act as triggers. It may be possible to prevent a situation escalating to the point where behaviour is challenging if changes are made to the way in which you or others react to a service user's behaviour, or if changes are made to their environment.

In many circumstances, even though there may have been a contribution by staff members in escalating a situation, there is work to be done with the service user in developing different responses when they feel frustrated or angry, especially where this frustration or anger is a maladaptive response. In this case, the approach taken will result from an assessment of need and will be set out in the individual's care plan. In the event of an incident where a response is needed *now*, here is some helpful guidance:

> If a serious incident is occurring, then act decisively to disrupt the pattern of activity which is taking place. This is achieved by breaking up the action (using a variety of tactics appropriate to the situation) and diverting attention and energy elsewhere. The sooner the heat can be taken from the situation the better. Do not inflame the situation by adding fuel (i.e. your own emotions) to the fire. Keep calm, act firmly and decisively and, especially when you are only recently in post, *do not hesitate to seek help when needed.*

> (SRC, 1993)

There are also particular ways of working that may be helpful in both the present and the longer term; e.g. programmes that include safe holding require special training and should not be attempted without this.

For many people who challenge, most of the ways of working outlined in this and other chapters may bring about positive change, according to the result of a shared assessment. Use of communication and relationship skills, promoting wellbeing in a number of ways, including spiritual wellbeing, advocating on their behalf, using a task-centred approach, and creating a positive environment, may all contribute to diminishing or extinguishing behaviour that challenges. Using a cognitive behavioural approach as described both in Chapter 7 and below may also be helpful.

A cognitive behavioural approach

A cognitive behavioural approach has its roots in the behavioural theories discussed in Chapter 7 (pages 194–197), which you are advised to read again at this point. Behavioural theories rest on the premise that behaviour and the thought processes associated with behaviour are learned. Cognitive theory is concerned with people's thinking and how that thinking process directs our choices. If the ways people think and behave have been learned, then they can also be unlearned if they are unhelpful to the individual's development and fulfilment. The ABC model described in Chapter 7, page 195, adapted to take account of a cognitive approach, looks like this:

A Activating event   Something happens which
B Beliefs   affects our thinking, which
B Behaviour   affects our behaviour, producing
C Consequences   consequences to thinking and behaviour.

Figure 9.7 illustrates the process that the worker using a cognitive behavioural model needs to understand in order to influence change.

The cognitive approach assumes that we each perceive the world in terms of the meanings we give to it, and how we interpret it will decide our behaviour. If our beliefs and thinking processes are positive, then our resulting behaviour will more likely be positive. If, however, our thinking is negative, then our behaviour is likely to be negative. The 'thinking' stage is often described as our 'self-talk', where we think in words. For example, when trying out something new, if I keep telling myself 'I can do this', I am more likely to succeed than if I tell myself 'this is really hard to do'. What the worker is attempting to achieve is to help the

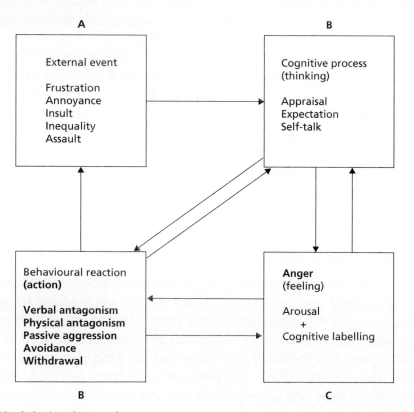

Figure 9.7 A cognitive behavioural approach

Activating event

I am standing in the pub on a hot summer night. The pub is really crowded and people have to manoeuvre carefully to reach the bar. I am just about to take a sip of my drink when another customer knocks into me, causing me to spill my drink. They apologise for knocking into me and check that I am all right.

Belief

I am now free to make an assessment of what I think has happened. My self-talk can lead me to make one of two choices:

1. I can accept that it is very busy and that the person could not have helped bumping into me, or
2. I can make a decision that the person has deliberately bumped into me, causing me to spill my drink.

Behaviour

My behaviour is now determined by my thinking. If my thinking was driven by option 1, my behaviour is likely to be:

1. Accepting the apology, staying calm and continuing my enjoyment of the evening.

If my behaviour is determined by option 2, my behaviour is likely to be:

2. Anger, believing the person did it deliberately to get at me.

Consequences

If choosing option 1, the consequences for me are likely to be:

1. Having a good evening with friends.

In choosing option 2, the consequences are likely to be:

2. Perhaps being involved in an argument, maybe a fight, which may result in my being evicted from the pub and perhaps charged with an offence.

ACTIVITY 9.14

Think of a situation in which a cognitive behavioural approach may be helpful. Outline the steps you would take.

---

individual to understand the possible impact of their thinking patterns on their behaviour, not control their thinking or tell the individual what to think. The example on page 277 helps to illustrate this process.

The cognitive approach aims to slow down the time between the activating event and the behaviour occurring. This then allows more 'thinking time', distancing the action from the behaviour. When taking a cognitive approach, the care worker is trying to understand the service user's thinking processes in order to identify if thinking is functional or dysfunctional.

Using the example of myself in the pub, by choosing the options in route 1, I am exhibiting functional thinking. I recognise that the pub is busy and that accidents like this can happen. I can assess that the other customer is genuinely sorry, or even if I think they are not, I may choose not to create a scene and spoil my evening. My thinking process is leading me away from any negative consequences.

If I had chosen the options in route 2, my thinking would be dysfunctional. I think the person has done it deliberately. I am seeing myself as a victim, the apology will be seen as a 'wind up', and I cannot let them get away with it. My thinking is presenting me with negative options, which may result in negative consequences. Much challenging behaviour results from such dysfunctional thought processes. A cognitive behavioural approach aims to promote changes in the ways individuals think and consequently act in relation to trigger events.

DEVELOPING GROUP WORK SKILLS

Many care situations are group situations where you are working not just with one individual but with a group of people. In order to enable people to fulfil their potential in these group situations, it is useful to understand some things about groups, the ways in which they function and how people behave when they are in groups. A group may be defined as a collection of people who have some reason for being together.

Tom Douglas (1978) is a group worker and writer who has promoted working with groups as a valuable way of helping people through problem situations.

I will use the example of a group for young people in a children's home, set up with the aim of enhancing decision-making skills, to illustrate some of Tom Douglas's main points. Here are some of his statements, followed by their relevance in relation to the young people's group:

- ❏ *The more a person needs a group, the more pressure it can bring to bear.* The young people were highly motivated to take control of their lives and the group was seen as an important component in this process.
- ❏ *Groups can begin to repair the deficiencies of naturally occurring groups.* Many of the young people had had little opportunity to talk through problems in family or friendship situations.
- ❏ *A group worker takes the interactions of people in a group to improve the quality of their lives.* The group worker looks at the behaviour and roles of the young people in the group, attempts to enable all members to participate, builds upon the strengths of group members and prevents some members from becoming too dominant and others from remaining too passive.
- ❏ *A group worker can highlight for people what their behaviour is and the consequences of it.* Within the group there is one member who is always playing the fool. The group worker encourages this when it is really helpful and discourages it when it is inappropriate, without posing a threat to the young person.
- ❏ *A group possesses more resources than individuals.* The group discussed what decisions they thought they should be able to make in the home and produced suggestions about meals, outings and holidays which were taken on board by care workers. If they had done this individually, their suggestions would have carried less force and they may not have been able to see the potential for change.
- ❏ *The group worker enables people to feel safe to express themselves.* The group worker gained the respect of the young people by being there every week at the agreed time, by being fair to participants in ensuring that everyone had a say, by handling outbursts of temper calmly and firmly, by emphasising the confidentiality of things said in the group. In this way group members felt safe to express themselves.
- ❏ *A group is like a small society with its own rules and its own behaviour patterns.* Over a period of weeks, members began to look forward to group meetings because they had a sense of belonging to something which was having a positive effect upon their lives. They established a few group rituals, always beginning

with a few jokes and ending with crisps and a drink; different members had different roles in the group and each person had a niche which the others respected. Outside the group, members started to feel more positive about themselves.

Douglas emphasised that working with groups is not easy and that anyone working with groups should try to gain some supervised practice, run a group alongside someone who is already experienced and has skills in this work, and should gain feedback from the group. He suggested that the worker should keep a record of group work, of things which were successful, of thoughts about why some things were effective, other things were not, as a means of building up a group work data bank.

Some of the ideas of W Bion (1968), a psychoanalyst writing before Tom Douglas and probably influential on his thinking, are also interesting in relation to group work. Bion contributed to the development of the use of group therapy in psychiatric hospitals and was very interested in the functions and the dynamics of groups, i.e. what groups achieve and how they work. He advocated the use of groups in creating a living-learning environment. This was a way of getting away from a medical model of health in which staff were the experts and patients the sick, passive recipients of treatment. Bion's emphasis was to use groups to encourage participation by everyone in performing the essential tasks of living. In examining the dynamics of group situations, Bion drew attention to many issues, four of which are:

❏ **The unconscious life of the group** and the members' need for psychological security. Like Douglas, Bion found that the most successful groups were those which individuals needed for their own wellbeing, needs being at both a conscious and an unconscious level.

❏ The notion that individuals carry and express feelings in group situations, not only for themselves but also for the group; also that what is often seen as **individual pathology may be a collective problem**. Individuals can be scapegoated for problems present in a group, a family or an organisation. This is also part of the unconscious life of the group.

❏ Groups have a tendency towards **fight/flight** in the face of difficult issues. This is a process whereby, through what Bion calls groupthink, groups refuse to face difficult issues. They prefer to take the easy route of lightening the conversation, unless an effective group worker can encourage confrontation of issues and a recognition of what cannot, as well as what can, be changed.

❑ The effective group worker creates a **group climate** which is safe and which reinforces the group task. This climate needs to encourage individuals, particularly those who are more shy, to assert their opinions in the face of more dominant people.

ACTIVITY 9.15

Apply each of the ideas of Bion given above to the young people's group used in examining Douglas's ideas.

ADVOCACY

What is advocacy?

The word 'advocacy' derives from the Latin 'advocare', which means 'to call to one's aid'. In general terms, it means someone who 'pleads a case'. Advocacy is about standing up for and supporting a person or group who are at risk of being relegated to the margins of society. Advocacy is a process of working towards natural justice and is encountered in some form every day. Parents stand up for their children, children stick up for their friends. Someone who has to go to a difficult meeting or face a new situation might seek a friend to accompany him or her. In such a situation, the friend is acting as an advocate.

However, there are some people who do not have family or friends or anyone else to help them. They might not understand information which has been given to them, or options which are open to them. They may not have had enough experience or be confident enough to speak up for themselves. In such circumstances, there is a need for someone to be on and at their side, someone to help them stand up for themselves or who can stand up for them. In essence, advocacy means acting as if you were the client, expressing their views as if they were your own. Advocacy can be informal or formal. Butler, Carr and Sullivan (1988) have identified a number of different informal advocate roles. These include spokesperson, neighbour, enabler, defender of cultural and ethnic identity, and friend.

Origins

Contrary to popular belief, advocacy is not a new concept. It has existed throughout recorded history and across cultures, political systems and religions. Different cultures and belief systems have influenced attitudes to advocacy. In the legal system, the right to a legal representative dates from Roman law and has existed in England since the thirteenth century. Over the past 100 years, as notions of human rights have become more established, advocacy has become more widespread and concepts of advocacy have become refined. Trades unions in many countries have provided formal industrial advocacy for almost 100 years. The women's suffrage movement advocated strongly for the rights of women to vote, as a first step towards equal rights. More recent social rights movements – the civil rights movement in America, the anti-apartheid movement in South Africa and the aboriginal land rights movement in Australia – have all helped to popularise ideas of rights. Contemporary rights movements, e.g. those affecting children, older people, and people with disabilities, have all led to a growth in advocacy for these groups.

Many marginalised groups which by definition are excluded from society usually find a voice to represent their cause, for it is believed that by removing the excluding quality, the whole human being underneath will be revealed (e.g. homeless people, or people with alcohol problems). Those groups who are sometimes portrayed as less than human (e.g. criminally insane, or people with a learning disability), have suffered throughout history from society's tendency to question their essential humanity and, therefore, their right to a voice (Gray and Jackson, 2002).

Definition

The definition of advocacy which has enjoyed the widest currency represents the advocate as a valued citizen who is unpaid and independent of human services. He or she creates a relationship with a person at risk of social exclusion, and chooses one or several of many ways to understand, respond to and represent that person's interests as if they were the advocate's own. The key features identified in these definitions of advocacy might be summarised as follows:

- ❏ It is a process of speaking up for or representing a person or a cause.
- ❏ It is partisan: it involves taking sides.
- ❏ It usually involves the rights or entitlements of the client.
- ❏ It happens where someone other than the client has the power to make a decision.
- ❏ It usually happens in a context of conflict.
- ❏ It relies mainly on reasoned argument.
- ❏ It requires the advocate to have a clear mandate.
- ❏ It requires the advocate to minimise any conflict of interest.
- ❏ It requires clear thinking, determination and resources.

(Westhorp and Sebastian, 1997)

Key principles

The Scottish Executive (2000) has indicated that there are certain key principles underpinning 'good' independent advocacy:

- ❏ Advocacy schemes should be firmly rooted in, supported by and accountable to a geographical community or a community of interest.
- ❏ Advocacy schemes should be constitutionally and psychologically independent of local and national government.
- ❏ Advocacy schemes cannot be both providers of a service and advocates for users of that service.
- ❏ Different approaches to independent advocacy are needed; there is no single best model.
- ❏ Advocacy schemes should maintain a clear and coherent focus of effort.
- ❏ Advocacy schemes should undergo regular independent evaluation of their work, and commissioners should provide finance for this.

Independent advocacy

While care workers, social workers, nurses, doctors, teachers and other professionals working for an agency look out for and speak up for the people they serve, they are not and cannot be independent. To be on someone's side, advocates have to be structurally and psychologically independent of the service system. Independent advocates – whether paid or unpaid – can be entirely clear that their primary loyalty and accountability are to the people who need advocates, not to the agencies providing health and social services and not to the government.

Independent advocates do not have the same conflicts of interest as professional workers, who are often expected to make judgements about who is most deserving or most eligible for a service. Because advocates do not have this sort of power over people and do not control access to resources, they are in a better position to see things from the person's point of view rather than the system's point of view. They can focus on representing the interests and wishes of the people who need an advocate and be clear that this is their role.

Professional workers who advocate strongly on behalf of a particular individual or group may be seen as acting unprofessionally or as being critical of their employing organisation. This entails personal risks, and can also put the professional worker in a situation where their views are discounted.

Wolfensberger (1992) has argued that all people have some important needs which can only be addressed by or within a freely given, voluntary relationship, i.e. a relationship in which neither party receives outside motivators or incentives for engaging in the relationship, and especially not payment, because this would degrade the relationship, and reduce or even nullify some or all of its potential benefits.

Different types of advocacy

The tasks and goals of advocacy, advocates and advocacy organisations can extend along a continuum from *individual advocacy* (one advocate working with/for one person), to *citizen advocacy* (where a concerned and committed member of the community acts as supportive advocate with/for an individual), to *peer advocacy* (where an advocate supports a client who shares a common experience or setting with them, e.g. two residents in a nursing home), to *self-advocacy* (where an individual is assisted in an environment of mutual support to gain the confidence and skills they require to advocate effectively on their own behalf), to *collective advocacy* (where a group of people form, or join an existing coalition to undertake actions that advocate for and assist them in meeting their goals), to *systems advocacy* (where an organisation is able to direct its attention and actions towards change at a national level).

Advocacy: conclusions

If the rights of people are to be fully recognised, respected and realised, there will be a continuing need for advocacy services working with and not against all those working in the human services. While there is always likely to be a measure of tension in that relationship, there is no reason why that tension cannot be turned to constructive and creative ends. Failure to do so is not in the interests of actual or potential clients.

Example

Tom, a young man with Down's syndrome and epilepsy, attended a college for further education, where he was enrolled on a social skills course. A new principal had just been appointed and one of his first acts was to call for risk management assessments on all students with special needs attending the college. Tom was informed that in view of his epilepsy and the fact that his class was located on the third floor and that the only means of access was by stair, he would have to withdraw from his class. The risk assessment pointed out that in the event of a fire and Tom having a seizure on the

---

staircase, he might seriously impair student egress and at the same time injure not only himself but also others using the stair. It was recommended that Tom should attend a similar social skills course but at a college in another part of the city. This college was all on one level so that there was no necessity to ascend or descend stairs. Tom expressed his distress to his class tutor who explained that there was nothing she could do.

Tom's family were extremely unhappy at the proposed action of the college and contacted the local advocacy service. Tom made clear to Peter, the advocate, that he did not wish to go to another college, as it would mean losing contact with friends. In talking with Tom and his parents, Peter learned that Tom had had only one seizure in the last five years, that he was on medication and that on the last occasion of a seizure he had forewarning of its occurrence. Peter also learned that in undertaking their risk assessment, the college had not taken into account the infrequency of seizures. Having represented Tom's case to the college, Peter was informed that Tom could remain at college as long as he attended a specially arranged class in a ground floor room with his course tutor on a one-to-one basis. When Peter put this option to Tom, he turned it down, as he did not want to be separated from his friends. He also pointed out that it would be setting him apart from all the other students.

The predicament facing Tom raised a number of questions for Peter, as he learned that all students with a physical disability and/or a neurological impairment affecting mobility were being asked to transfer to another college. Peter contacted the college principal and informed him that his college was acting in a discriminatory manner. The principal replied that he was merely acting in accordance with guidelines issued by the Health and Safety Executive. Peter enquired what would be the position of a student, tutor or principal who broke their leg; would they, too, have to move to another college or be confined to a ground floor location?

Peter then contacted all the further education colleges within the local authority to establish what their health and safety procedures were in relation to students with actual or potential mobility problems. The results of the survey revealed a marked disparity in practice between colleges. As a consequence of the issues raised by Tom's case and the findings of the survey, Peter contacted the education department of the local authority. He pointed out that a significant number of colleges were operating a *de facto* policy of segregation and acting in a way that ran counter to the government's policy of inclusion. Peter suggested that the education department should issue guidelines that would bring an end to such practices.

To the delight and relief of Tom and his parents, a letter was received from the college indicating that Tom could continue to attend the social skills course until the end of the academic year. That delight and relief were short-lived. The letter went on to point out that the college was in the process of undertaking a comprehensive review of its admission procedures and that one possible result of that review was that health and safety considerations might oblige the college to impose restrictions on those it admitted to college courses. Tom's parents showed the letter to Peter who, on reading the letter, smiled. The smile, he explained, arose from the fact this was, in his opinion, a face-saving letter in which the local authority was suggesting that nothing really had changed but actually was conceding defeat. However, Peter stressed that Tom should keep in touch with him and contact him if there were any further problems.

ACTIVITY 9.16

1. If the advocacy service had been directly funded by the education service and you had been in Peter's shoes, would you have pursued this case quite so vigorously?
2. How far was Peter justified in taking this matter beyond just representing Tom's particular concerns? In other words, is an advocacy service entitled to pursue a general issue of concern without the direct instruction of a client?
3. If you had been the advocate in this case, would you have acted differently? If so, why and in which ways?
4. What personal qualities do you think the ideal advocate should possess?

SUMMARY

This has been a long and somewhat varied chapter, looking at many possible tools that can be used in putting care plans into practice.

Whether or not these tools are used will depend on the result of the assessment and care planning process, and decisions shared and made with the service user about the best ways to achieve the content of the care plan. The aim is always to optimise the wellbeing of people, and this may be done through, for example, reducing emotional or physical pain, providing positive care environments, developing networks and circles of support, promoting resilience, promoting spiritual wellbeing, or using some of the other skills of care such as task-centred work, cognitive behavioural work, group work skills or advocacy.

FIVE KEY POINTS

1. Thorough assessment and care planning usually precede decisions about implementation.
2. Person-centred plans involve people as much as possible in ways to implement them.
3. In promoting people's wellbeing, consideration should be given to reducing emotional and physical pain, creating positive care environments, developing networks and circles of support and promoting spiritual wellbeing.
4. A variety of tools is available to enhance wellbeing as plans are put into practice. These include task-centred work, cognitive behavioural work, group work and advocacy.
5. For some people, wellbeing cannot be optimised without advocacy, where someone promotes and supports the needs and wishes of another person as if they were that person.

THREE QUESTIONS

1. What are three things that you should consider when making decisions about how to implement care plans?
2. What are three features that enable you to identify whether a person is likely to be resilient?
3. Under which circumstances may it be helpful to use one of the following:

- ❑ task-centred work
- ❑ cognitive behavioural work
- ❑ promoting spiritual wellbeing
- ❑ group work
- ❑ advocacy?

RECOMMENDED READING

ANGLIN, J. (2002) *Pain, Normality, and the Struggle for Congruence.* New York: The Haworth Press, Inc. An account of a study of group homes for children which is both interesting and a challenge. Lots of original thinking in relation to care work.

CROMPTON, M. (2001) *Who am I? Promoting children's spiritual wellbeing in everyday life; a guide for all who work with children.* Barkingside: Barnardo's. Although written with children in mind, this is a fascinating and detailed examination of spiritual wellbeing with ideas which can be applied to work with any service user group.

GRAY, B. and JACKSON, R. (2002) *Advocacy and Learning Disability.* London: Jessica Kingsley Publishers. Again, although written specifically in relation to one service user group, the ideas have much wider currency. An interesting and informative book.

Figure 9.8

CHAPTER 10

SUPERVISION AND PROFESSIONAL DEVELOPMENT

Peter Laverie

> **The unexamined life is not worth living.**
>
> (Socrates, recorded by Plato, approx 399BC)

By the end of this chapter you should be able to:

- ❑ explain the concept and purpose of supervision in care services
- ❑ describe different forms of supervision
- ❑ understand how to use supervision as a reflective practitioner
- ❑ describe the principles of lifelong learning and continuous professional development.

The content of this chapter provides you with underpinning content and context for all care qualifications. It relates especially to the following units:

HSC23: Develop your knowledge and practice

HSC33: Reflect on and develop your practice

HSC43: Take responsibility for the continuing professional development of self and others

Higher National Supervision unit: Supervision in care settings.

DEFINING SUPERVISION AND ITS PURPOSE

Every care worker, including you, has the right to receive supervision. Those who use care services have a right to receive their help and support from properly supervised staff. This places a responsibility on employers to ensure that appropriate systems of supervision and development are in place and being used effectively. There is also a responsibility on you to make use of supervision opportunities so that you can reflect upon and improve your practice.

So, what is supervision? Is it a method of controlling the workforce; a system of appraisal used to calculate financial reward; a means of assessing suitability for promotion; a vehicle to provide education or training; an administrative task to record holidays and absences; a tool for coordinating teams; a chance to offer emotional support; an opportunity for workers to think about and understand their practice? Supervision is all of these things. Care services cover a broad spectrum of activity including care practice and social work intervention. It is worthwhile trying to define supervision further, as it relates to workers providing these varied services.

Thompson (2002) describes supervision thus:

> Supervision is, in principle at least, a process through which an organisation seeks to meet its objectives through empowering its staff. This involves a range of tasks:
>
> - monitoring work tasks and workload
> - supporting staff through difficulties
> - promoting staff development
> - acting as a mediator between workers and higher management where necessary
> - problem solving
> - ensuring legal and organisational requirements and policies are adhered to
> - promoting teamwork and collaboration.

Thompson has identified a broad range of activities in describing this process known as supervision. It would appear that supervision itself must take different forms. Payne (2000) states that:

> All forms of supervision . . . are supposed to involve an element of assessment of the competence and achievements of the worker by the supervisor.

The provision of care services for the benefit of service users requires a knowledgeable, competent workforce with staff supervision as a means of developing the quality of those services. Supervision involves interacting with care workers in a way that contributes to their individual development and the development of their organisation as a whole.

Coulshed et al. (2001) reminds us of the importance of supervision, pointing out that:

> . . . the greatest portion of the budget in human service organisations is usually spent on staff salaries; thus the ways in which staff are supported and their skills developed can influence the quality of organisational performance as a whole.

With effective supervision three principal objectives are achieved:

- ❑ service users receive a better quality of service
- ❑ care workers feel supported and developed
- ❑ the organisation flourishes.

The functions of supervision

Kadushin (1976) identifies supervision as having three main functions:

1. managerial
2. educational
3. supportive.

While these functions are interrelated, it is important to develop an understanding of each one.

The managerial function refers to the formal organisational relationship between supervisor and supervisee for the purposes of:

- ❑ task allocation
- ❑ administrative duties
- ❑ management of time
- ❑ ensuring legal and policy requirements are being met
- ❑ explaining procedures
- ❑ audit and accountability.

The educational function refers to the developmental processes undertaken in supervision by both supervisor and supervisee:

- ❏ education and training
- ❏ learning opportunities
- ❏ identifying barriers to learning
- ❏ skills development
- ❏ reflective practice.

The supportive function recognises the pressure you may experience when working in care services, and refers to the role undertaken by the supervisor in providing care and support by:

- ❏ providing emotional support
- ❏ identifying protected time and space to enable you to explore difficult issues
- ❏ helping you to understand the impact which your work may be having on you and others.

In addition to these, supervision may also serve other functions such as mediation and collaboration.

What is essential is that both those who provide supervision and those who receive it value the process highly. It is a critical activity, which allows you to reflect and gain a fuller understanding of the quality of your practice. It helps you to question and evaluate organisational policies and objectives. Furthermore, you can be reassured about your roles and tasks, and confirm your commitment and ability as a member of a successful team.

Supervision provides you with the chance to 'have a look' at how you are doing the job with the benefit of another person's eyes and ears. It presents an opportunity to look at and consider other ways of working in a safe environment; to search for new meaning in difficult situations and to discover that there is learning to be gained by engaging in the process.

In selecting a career in care services, which naturally directs you to identify and meet people's needs, a particular helping relationship is established. Supervision should fulfil the role of making sense of that experience – this is known as **reflective practice.**

There is plenty of scope for confusion when using the term supervision, as it is also used to describe different processes. In some areas of industry, for example, it can be used as a generic term for 'first line management' of workers. This is generally said to be carried out by 'supervisors' and is sometimes called 'supervisory management'.

In the context of personal social services, supervision generally refers to situations where care workers meet with an individual who is usually their immediate line manager. This time is spent in a structured way, dealing with a number of issues of concern either to the practitioner or supervisor regarding the service users they work with, the staff team and ultimately their agency or organisation.

Generally this process takes place in a private location and is 'protected time' in the sense that it should not be subject to any interruptions. It should also be a planned and regular occurrence. A record of some sort should be kept of matters discussed, and certain safeguards should exist with regard to the confidentiality of the information contained therein.

Although supervision can take many forms (dealt with in the next section,) it should be:

- planned
- regular
- protected
- encouraged
- recorded
- productive
- valued
- understood
- evaluated.

There are other forms of interaction between managers and staff that may also be described as supervision. One example might be supervision said to be given 'on the hoof', and although this may link with the idea of supervisory management as mentioned earlier, rather than the more formal setting also described, it still has a usefulness and validity. Some managers will argue that it is the only method of supervision they have time for, as they are too busy to sit down with individual staff. While this argument is unacceptable and raises basic questions about their understanding of the supervisor role, the provision of informal supervision, even by peers, has a valuable place in care services and the development of reflective practitioners.

Supervision may be defined as a process of planned interaction with staff for the purposes of sharing information, problem solving, monitoring performance,

ACTIVITY 10.1 Your Experiences of Supervision

Here is an opportunity to reflect on your experiences of supervision either as a student or care service worker.

Take some time to consider the following:

Your designated post		
Type of organisation and services offered		
Length of time in post/placement		
Supervisor		
Supervision	**Planned**	**Actual**
Frequency of:		
Duration of:		
When was your last supervision session?		
Are there any barriers to your supervision taking place?		
Do you contribute to preparing the agenda for these sessions?		
What are the main topics generally discussed?		
Are you happy with your current supervision arrangements?		
What would you change or add to improve your supervision?		

ACTIVITY 10.2 Statutory Functions

Give three examples of statutory functions involving your social service organisation and think how these may be supported and verified in supervision.

Statutory function 1	
Statutory function 2	
Statutory function 3	

You may find it useful to share and discuss your answers with a colleague, or indeed your supervisor.

---

providing training and learning opportunities, offering support and contributing to individual and organisational development.

The work involved in care services tends to be complex and often involves operational and statutory responsibilities and accountabilities. This means that your practice may be subject to scrutiny by a range of agencies, including inspection and registration bodies, judicial and legal agencies and professional standards organisations.

It is of paramount importance that, when you are carrying out a statutory function, you are fully supported in ensuring that this is carried out in the prescribed manner. Supervision serves not only to ensure that the work is being done the way it should be, but also serves as a vital support for you. Supervision is essential to allow the necessary checks to be carried out, but also serves to alert managers to potentially difficult situations arising, and to intervene where necessary.

You need to understand your legal and ethical responsibilities, including the requirements of: care regulations; meeting national occupational and national minimum or care standards; registering and maintaining registration with social services councils; membership of professional associations.

One of the main purposes of professional supervision is to ensure that you understand and carry out your operational and statutory responsibilities. Here are some examples of statutory functions, which may be similar to your own:

1. A social services department carries out assessment of needs for community care service users. This is a statutory requirement

under the National Health Service and Community Care Act 1990.

The assessment forms might be sampled during a supervision session and support offered with any problems.

2.   A voluntary organisation care home for older adults is registered and subject to statutory inspection.

Following inspection, adherence to recommendations and any difficulties in implementation could be checked with staff during supervision.

3.   Under general health and safety legislation, all staff are responsible for ensuring a safe working environment.

In this example, supervision could be used to monitor that all necessary safety checks are being carried out.

The value base

When defining the concept and purposes of supervision, it is essential to consider the value base. In *Understanding Social Work,* Thompson (2000) states:

> At its simplest, a value is something we hold dear, something we see as important and worthy of safeguarding. Consequently, values are an important influence on our actions and attitudes – they will encourage us to do certain things and to avoid certain others. In this way, values are not simply abstract concepts – they are very concrete in the sense that they have a strong influence over what happens. They are a very strong force in shaping people's behaviour and responses to situations. It would be very foolish therefore to underestimate the significance of values . . .

Those who participate in the supervision process, whether care workers, supervisors or managers, must be able to demonstrate both an understanding and practice of an appropriate value base.

Supervision should encourage you continually to question both your personal and professional values and principles, together with those of the organisation. This is a key element in developing reflective practice. Because the world changes, the value base is not written in stone, but develops in response to changing visions and underlying paradigms. The principles of equality and diversity can be

ACTIVITY 10.3 Your Value Base

Consider these questions:

1. What impact do your personal values, principles, interests and priorities have on your practice?
2. How do you know your answer to Question 1?
3. From whom could you receive feedback about your values, principles, priorities and interests?
4. Do you actively seek out feedback on your performance at work? If your answer is yes, how do you go about doing this? If no, why not?

promoted in supervision by the supervisor demonstrating their ability to recognise your uniqueness, and focusing on assisting you to develop your existing strengths. Supervisors who focus on identifying and pointing out weaknesses are wasting potential. In your work you are asked to promote people's rights to choice, privacy, confidentiality and protection. The skilled supervisor, in helping you to reach an understanding of these issues, should be able to demonstrate the boundaries of confidentiality, e.g. in supervision. Who has right of access to supervision records and whose permission is required to access these?

Supervision should be helping you to recognise your sometimes conflicting roles of carer and also agent of social control. During sessions, workers must explore issues of power and empowerment and the effect which these have on service users. Without question, supervision must be used to assist you in developing your understanding of the importance of anti-discriminatory and anti-oppressive practice. It is also sometimes an opportunity for your supervisor to demonstrate how you might develop appropriate strategies to challenge and counter discrimination and inequality. Supervision affords many ways to examine the potential effects of current work practices and how they might be serving to perpetuate disadvantage. Supervisors are well placed to help you see how much of your everyday work might be encouraging or reinforcing feelings of discrimination in service users.

At the beginning of this chapter, your fundamental right to receive supervision was acknowledged. You also have the responsibility to engage fully in the process.

As a care worker, you must take responsibility for understanding how your values, principles, priorities and interests have an effect on your work practice. This is an important part of reflective practice (making sense of your experiences). Feedback can come from many sources, and you should seek this out.

This is a quite separate and distinct responsibility from that of the supervisor, who is required to provide feedback.

Forms of supervision

There are different forms of supervision, which can be delivered formally and informally:

- ❏ individual supervision
- ❏ group/team supervision
- ❏ peer supervision.

While it is generally understood that a more senior, experienced worker delivers supervision, there is nothing to stop effective supervision being undertaken by colleagues or service users. Senior staff, other professionals, work partners, service users and their representatives are all able to provide you with valuable feedback on your performance and service delivery. You can make excellent use of this information to gain further insight and reflect upon your practice.

Individual supervision

Let us first consider individual supervision. On an informal basis, individual supervision takes place all the time. The idea of a new worker being 'shown the ropes' is an old one. Many care workers have had much valuable training from experienced colleagues and, of course, a fair share of poor practice has been transferred too.

Managers and supervisors will often take an informal opportunity to:

- ❏ demonstrate a task
- ❏ offer immediate feedback
- ❏ explain a procedure
- ❏ provide information
- ❏ answer a question
- ❏ analyse a situation.

They may also delegate this responsibility to other staff. As experienced workers, you will seek out this type of advice and support from both colleagues and supervisors. This kind of active learning is crucial to you as a reflective practitioner when developing your skills and understanding. Notwithstanding the many ways in which you may receive informal, individual supervision, it has an important part to play in your development. A well-supported and enthusiastic care team will show evidence of informally supervising each other.

The most common and traditional form of supervision is the planned, formal session between you and your nominated supervisor. Here are some reasonable basic expectations of this form of supervision:

1. **It should occur on a regular basis**
   Supervision sessions should ideally be scheduled on a planned basis. The interval between sessions might vary from one week to one month (or longer sometimes) but whatever interval is defined, it should not be subject to sudden and unexpected variations.

2. **It should be reliable and have high priority**
   Sessions should not be cancelled, postponed or rescheduled without very good reason. Sadly, supervision sessions, especially with staff in positions of little authority, often receive low priority and are the first thing to be affected when 'something important' happens. Remember, supervision is not only your right; it is also a requirement of national regulations and standards.

3. **There should be some form of agenda**
   There should be a way for each of the people who are giving or receiving supervision to contribute and work to an agenda of some sort. This might take the form of pre-printed organisational formats or other forms.

4. **There should be no time pressures**
   Sufficient time needs to be allocated in advance so that there is enough time to explore the items on the agenda in the necessary depth. No one should feel they are being rushed through sessions. At the same time, if both parties know the duration of the session, it can also help to avoid the equally frustrating scenario of endless circumlocution.

5. **It should be confidential**
   The nature and boundaries of confidentiality should be understood. It is a prerequisite in any supervision session. If information shared with someone giving supervision might be shared with anyone else, then the supervisee might have to be reminded about that. Remember, there is no such thing as 'off the record'.

Activity 10.4 Making Sense of Your Supervision

Make some notes of your responses to these questions:

1. How does your supervision compare to the list of basic expectations of supervision?
2. How would you describe your relationship with your supervisor/manager?
3. Do you find supervision a supportive process? If so, why, and if not, why not?
4. Are you actively involved in preparing for your supervision sessions?
5. If you were a supervisor, what would be your strengths in delivering supervision?
6. Which three areas of your practice are you aiming to develop over the next six months?
7. Which aspect of your performance at work least pleases you?
8. How could you make better use of your supervision sessions?

Your answers to these questions will be particular and personal, but you may find them helpful when trying to assess how your supervision is going. Again, if you feel able to, you may find it useful to discuss these questions (and your answers) with your supervisor or another colleague.

Group/team supervision

Perhaps without realising it, group or team supervision is a common feature of care services. It can occur in a number of formats:

- ❑ shift teams
- ❑ staff teams of different grades
- ❑ multi-disciplinary teams
- ❑ management teams
- ❑ specifically organised groups of workers (e.g. new staff).

The use of team supervision can be valuable to the busy or over-stretched manager, in that they can deal with a range of similar issues affecting a whole team rather than absorb time from individual sessions.

What are the advantages of this form of supervision?

- ❑ an effective way of delivering training and development
- ❑ can be used to reinforce good practice across a team
- ❑ assists with interpersonal communication difficulties
- ❑ allows the team to explore common issues
- ❑ workers may feel more supported and therefore able to share more readily
- ❑ the group can pool their expertise and resources to find solutions to difficult problems
- ❑ enables the staff team to consider the impact which they have on the lives of service users as a group.

Some of the disadvantages include:

- ❑ group dynamics come into play and this has to be considered and managed
- ❑ some individual workers may find it more difficult to contribute
- ❑ can reinforce the negative behaviour of sub-groups within the team
- ❑ unnecessary elements of competition can be introduced to the team.

The reflective practitioner endeavours to analyse their performance within the context of the team and elicit feedback from colleagues in this setting. Most personal social services organisations adopt person-centred approaches in the delivery of their services. It is useful to extend the principles of these approaches into what might be referred to as *person-centred teams*. In this case, a well-structured system of individual supervision can be greatly enhanced by reinforcing the value of team members using the vehicle of group supervision.

Team or group supervision can be delivered formally or informally, but it is more efficient if its use is thoroughly planned and prepared. When using this form of supervision, it is important to be clear about who is supervising what. Brown and Bourne (1996) identify the following options:

1. The supervision of individuals within a group/team setting by the supervisor.
2. The supervision of individuals by the group/team.
3. The supervision of the group/team as a whole by the supervisor.
4. The supervision of the group/team by themselves.

They also identify advantages and disadvantages in group/team supervision and summarise them as follows:

Advantages:

- ❏ the opportunity to make use of a wider variety of learning experiences
- ❏ the opportunity for supervisees to share their experiences
- ❏ emotional support
- ❏ safety in numbers
- ❏ opportunity to compare and contrast own experiences and practices with others
- ❏ can help foster team or group cohesion and identity
- ❏ opportunity for supervisor to see supervisees in a different kind of relationship
- ❏ opportunity for supervisor to become aware of potential problems that derive from and relate to the unit/project/team
- ❏ allows for responsibilities, functions and roles of the supervisory process to be separated and delegated among a number of people
- ❏ peer influence may make modification of behaviour more likely
- ❏ supervisees can observe and learn from the supervisor, both directly and as a role model
- ❏ development of confidence and skills in groups may be transferable to work with service users
- ❏ allows a gradual step from dependence on the supervisor, through a lesser dependence on peers, to self-dependence
- ❏ allows greater empowerment through lateral teaching, learning, and support of peers.

Disadvantages:

- ❏ to maintain relevance of discussions to the widest numbers, specific and urgent needs are often discussed only in generalised terms
- ❏ group may stimulate sibling rivalry and peer competition that hinder the supervisory process
- ❏ it is more difficult to incorporate a new appointee into a supervisory group than to provide them with individual support
- ❏ it is easier to hide and opt out of the responsibility to engage in exploration, problem solving, and decision making

- ❏ greater opportunities for critical feedback, which can be inhibiting if confidence is lacking
- ❏ the supervisor is more exposed and requires greater self-assurance than in individual supervision
- ❏ communication and interventions which assist one member may create problems for others
- ❏ while encouraging autonomy, the supervisor may find it more difficult to restore the focus, should the group follow a non-productive route
- ❏ supervisors will have to acquire or refresh their knowledge of group interaction, group dynamics and individual behaviour in the group context
- ❏ the supervisor must focus both on the individual and the group
- ❏ in highly cohesive groups, the pressure to conform to group thinking and attitudes can become counterproductive.

(Brown and Bourne, 1996)

ACTIVITY 10.5 Team List

Can you identify four or five issues from your workplace, which you think could be dealt with productively using a group/team supervision setting?

Peer supervision

Although one or two aspects of peer supervision are mentioned in the previous section, it is a form of supervision in its own right and worthy of consideration. Peer supervision may be a regular activity in which you participate, but perhaps you do not identify it as such. Shift partners, team members and other colleagues will, as a matter of course, offer support, advice and guidance to each other and usually on an informal basis, i.e. not structured or planned.

Workers participate in this form of supervision equally, i.e. there is no supervisor or person fulfilling a hierarchical role. This improves the professional experience and encourages confidence, increases responsibility and promotes an environment of helping and sharing. Given the amount of collaborative practice in which care workers participate, there is a beneficial effect if these practitioners have had an opportunity to understand and develop their authority and autonomy.

Meetings can become more productive if a portion of the agenda is devoted to supervision in general and reflection in particular. Some examples of these meetings might include:

- shift meetings
- project meetings
- multi-disciplinary meetings
- training sessions
- staff meetings
- inter-departmental meetings
- intra-departmental meetings
- multi-agency meetings.

Another form of supervision, which has evolved from the peer group model, is 'tandem' supervision. This is similar to 'mentorship' currently in use in a variety of fields. Tsui (2005) explains this model:

> *Tandem* supervision occurs when two frontline [social] workers, one with professional experience and the other relatively junior, consult with each other apart from the peer group. They are like two wheels, big and small, of a classic tandem bicycle. Both are steering in the same direction. In professional practice, both are practitioners, and neither is designated the supervisor. In tandem, they meet occasionally and informally to discuss their assignments and working experiences. Tandem members arrange to go on vacation at different times so that they can cover each other's work, thereby exposing themselves to learning opportunities. However, tandem members are not accountable for each other's job performance. The main objective is to share professional knowledge and skills.

Although it would be unfair to expect new or inexperienced workers to participate in offering advice and guidance, they would benefit from having a helping relationship 'in tandem' with a more skilled professional. However, there are numerous possibilities for supportive partnerships between colleagues where they can give critical feedback, discuss decision-making processes, share feelings and learn from each other.

Peer supervision helps to build trust and confidence and, if used appropriately, allows workers to challenge each other in a less inhibited way than if a supervisor or manager were present. Similarly, emotional support and encouragement can be offered and perhaps more readily accepted, without the possibility of increased feelings of anxiousness or vulnerability, were more senior staff to be present.

Evidence of a well-structured and managed care service will include not only formal, individual supervision but a variety of peer supervision activities, which demonstrate a supportive and helping team.

THE REFLECTIVE PRACTITIONER

Throughout this chapter there have been several references to 'reflective practice' or 'the reflective practitioner'. An essential aim for you is to develop your skills in reflective practice. Both formal and informal supervision in all their forms play an important part in that development.

Skilled care practitioners are active learners who think about, analyse and improve their practice. So what does this process of 'reflecting on practice' mean? When delivering services for and with service users in collaboration with colleagues and other agencies, you can be confronted with many relationships, situations and experiences, which require reflection in order to:

- ❑ make sense of the experience
- ❑ gain a fuller understanding
- ❑ explore what was happening
- ❑ analyse your actions and reasons for them
- ❑ examine your feelings
- ❑ review the outcomes of behaviour
- ❑ compare with previous experiences and situations.

You can then use this information, or be assisted to use it, to build more skilled and knowledgeable approaches for your future practice. The reflective process is continuous: see Figure 10.1.

The opportunity for reflection cannot rest with the provision of supervision; you must develop the skill of self-reflection, which will become an important tool while working. Although the traditional process of reflection takes place after an experience or situation, the delivery of care services sometimes demands the ability to 'think on your feet'. This is referred to as reflect-in-action rather than reflect on action. Schon (1983) describes it as follows:

> The practitioner allows himself to experience surprise, puzzlement, or confusion in a situation which he finds uncertain or unique. He reflects on the phenomenon before him, and on the prior understandings, which have been implicit in his behaviour. He carries out an experiment which serves to generate both a new understanding of the phenomenon and a change in the situation.

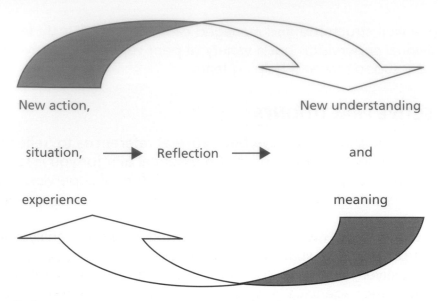

Figure 10.1 The reflective process

ACTIVITY 10.6 Evaluation Challenge

How many synonyms can you think of for the word '**evaluate**'?

Your challenge is think of more than 60! Here are a few to begin with: *assess, ponder, calculate . . .*

Schon expressed the view that practitioners build up a catalogue of experiences and reactions to those experiences like a repertoire they can draw upon: a central feature of reflective thought. In building a menu of experiences and understanding, you will have undertaken a great deal of evaluation as part of your reflection.

The process of reflection

Self-evaluation, or assessing your own practice, can be a difficult process. Where to begin, what to consider, how to do it, are the questions which new and often more experienced workers are faced with.

Let us assume that you are beginning the process of reflection in relation to a piece of work you have undertaken recently with a service user. Consider this series of questions as a model of reflection:

1. What was I trying to achieve?
2. Did I achieve it?
3. How do I know this?
4. How well did I achieve it?
5. What did I learn from the experience?
6. How did I feel about the work?
7. Who else can give me feedback?
8. What would I change?
9. What do I need to learn for the future?
10. In which other situations can I apply my new understanding?

This question model can be applied to teams and groups of staff as well as individual workers. The evaluation process is part of reflective practice and systems of quality assurance. Supervision itself is a form of quality assurance and quality improvement. Its delivery develops the worker, the team, the agency, but, most importantly, it raises the standards of care services provided.

THE ROLE OF THE SUPERVISOR

It is worth considering the role of the supervisor in relation to the process by which workers are managed, receive feedback and are supported in their practice. Supervision has been identified by Kadushin (1976) as having three main functions:

1. management
2. education
3. support.

It is important to remember that the supervisor is fulfilling a different role from that of the worker. The supervisor is likely to be receiving supervision from a superior and will have performance and organisational demands, which may lead to different priorities from those of the worker. The supervisor will be aiming to perform effectively as a manager. Martin and Henderson (2001) emphasise the importance of improving managerial (and supervisory) effectiveness:

> Managerial effectiveness is a measure of the extent to which the results one sets out to achieve are achieved. However, just achieving what you have set as targets is not enough in itself. It is very important that the targets that you set are ones that will really add value to the area of work for which you are responsible.

. . .It is also interesting to consider whether service users would be entirely happy with your current approach to reviewing effectiveness. Staff may all be working very hard, but are they achieving the high quality of service delivery that everyone would like to be part of? Effectiveness is not easy to pin down because it has to be considered in relation to the ever-changing needs and expectations of service users.

The supervisor will be concerned with the development of both the individual and the organisation of which your practice is one small part.

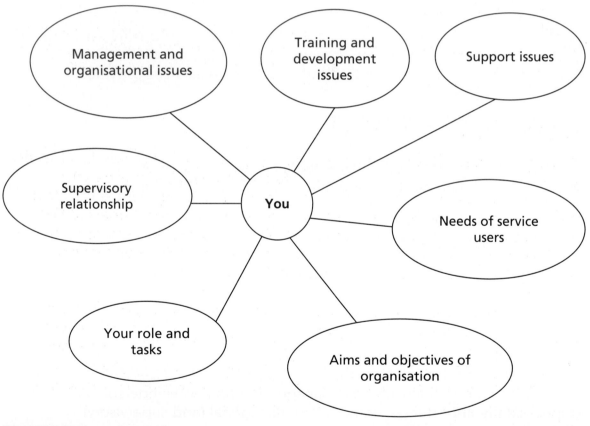

Figure 10.2 Mind map of supervision

ACTIVITY 10.7 Mind Map of Supervision

Construct a mind map, which details your supervision, using the information provided in Figure 10.2.

Having expressed your right to receive supervision, the responsibility to use supervision must also be stressed. It will therefore be necessary for you to understand the following:

- ❏ your role
- ❏ the supervisor's role
- ❏ the needs of service users
- ❏ organisation/agency aims and objectives
- ❏ priorities for practice
- ❏ the quality of relationships with other team members
- ❏ communication skills.

While the supervisor will identify or should be identifying areas for you to develop, and offering support in this, part of your role is to establish a positive and effective relationship which promotes this work. Understanding supervision includes understanding your role and those of service users, colleagues, supervisor, managers and organisation.

PROFESSIONAL DEVELOPMENT

As part of professional development, both at personal and professional levels, you should understand the concept of **lifelong learning**. Alongside your childhood and adulthood experiences of formal education sits the idea that learning is always taking place and this process never stops. Rogers (2002) identifies the system of institutions which aim to provide learning opportunities as too narrow a definition of education, preferring to include all forms of learning. He explains the idea of 'learning throughout life':

> As we shall see in more detail later, learning is an activity in which we take part all the time in the course of everyday living. It is the process by which we face, cope with and use our experience. Throughout our lives we face situations in our work, in our domestic settings and in our wider relationships that were not conceived of when we were at school or college, and they all call for new learning.
>
> We need to learn to meet the changing demands of our various occupations, whether heart surgeon, historian or handicraft expert. All the tasks we engage in, whether they comprise paid employment or work in the home, call for new knowledge, new skills and new attitudes at various stages.

Rogers's explanation clearly relates to the essential features of reflective practice, in that you are learning all the time and must consider your experiences in order to gain understanding and meaning. Also, your roles and tasks in the delivery of care services will change, as will the needs of service users, thereby demanding new learning, skills, and action. Supervision plays an important part in identifying and providing new learning opportunities.

The workforce in care services is regulated, and you are or will be subject to the requirements of formal registration in line with other professions. Social service councils recognise these changing demands on the skills and training of the workforce and, in addition to setting the appropriate qualifications levels for care services, they establish and quantify the continuous professional development requirements needed to maintain registration.

Continuous professional development requirements are designed to ensure that service users are cared for by appropriately trained and experienced staff, and that the correct standard of care provided is maintained and improved. Logically, supervisors should have training in giving supervision, as should you in making use of it.

While the law requires registration of the workforce and organisations must adhere to these requirements, there is still a responsibility for each worker to assess and identify their training and development needs along with their supervisor. It is not possible to excuse yourself from the professional responsibility to engage in active learning throughout your working life.

SUMMARY

This chapter has attempted to define and explain supervision, and, more importantly, to emphasise its importance not merely as a tool of appraisal, but also as a living, working and continuous process in which you must actively and enthusiastically engage. There has to be recognition from employers that they have a legal and moral responsibility to provide you with appropriate supervision. Supervision exists to manage, organise, develop and support you in order that your skills and practice are of the highest standard to meet the needs of those who use care services.

FIVE KEY POINTS

1. You have the right to receive supervision and the responsibility to make use of it.
2. Supervision should be a regular, planned, protected activity, which offers training and development, support, feedback on performance, and makes you accountable for what you do.
3. You should understand the various forms of supervision which can help you and others with your work.
4. As a reflective practitioner, you are trying to gain a fuller understanding of your practice by making sense of your experiences.
5. You must be committed to the idea of lifelong learning and participate fully in programmes of professional development as required.

THREE QUESTIONS

1. What are the main purposes of supervision?
2. Identify the different forms of supervision and how each might be used effectively in your work place or organisation.
3. Describe what is meant by reflective practice in the context of delivering care services.

RECOMMENDED READING

THOMPSON, N. (2002) *People Skills*, 2nd edn. Hampshire: Palgrave MacMillan. This is an excellent book which should be read by all practitioners. The author explains superbly the task of working with people effectively.

TSUI, MING-SUM (2005) *Social Work Supervision. Contexts and Concepts.* California: Sage Publications. This publication provides a very informed and detailed explanation of supervision and will be of great interest to those who receive and give supervision.

CHAPTER 11

THIS CARING BUSINESS

George Baker

This chapter invites you to:

- ❏ expand your horizons
- ❏ look again at the notions of reflective practice and critical thinking
- ❏ look at the passion and the power of care practice
- ❏ use recommended texts to extend your conceptual thinking.

The content of this chapter provides you with underpinning content and context for all care qualifications.

INTRODUCTION

Learning anything new is a bit like climbing a mountain: it is hard work, best done in small stages, and sometimes you feel like quitting. But the view when you reach the top usually makes it all worthwhile! As you move towards the end of your course, you will hopefully see things differently now compared to when you started, with new perspectives and new understanding. The process has probably changed you a bit too. If the world is not quite the way you thought it was, then maybe you are not the way you thought you were either!

You are a little more reflective and a little bit better informed now about work in the field of care and possibly even the world in general. You have grown in both competence and confidence. You have maybe achieved this with the support of others including family, friends and colleagues, but I am sure you may also have encountered some obstacles along the way. Workmates might have been jealous and partners might have felt ignored or threatened. But these minor irritations aside, it has been more than worthwhile, and you should feel proud of your achievement.

If we take our mountain analogy a little further, then as you stand on the summit and look around, you may just see some more peaks in the distance, and guess what? Having climbed one, you might just have developed an appetite for more. And why not? You have not only developed a taste for learning, you have also developed many of the necessary skills. In a metaphorical sense, you have the boots now, so why not use them some more?

In a sense, think of reading this final chapter on the top of your mountain. Its aim is to help you to ask some important questions about how you might best use your new skills, and develop a sense of perspective about your place in the field of care and its place in the wider world. It also looks at some of the pitfalls you might encounter along the way. In addition, it might also serve to encourage you to climb some of those distant tops!

This chapter invites you to ask questions about what you are doing. It builds upon the ideas outlined in Chapter 10 about being a reflective practitioner, and looks at the notions of reflective practice and critical thinking from a slightly different perspective. It also returns to the concepts of passion and power, value base and relationships, to remind you of their importance. The chapter contains references to textbooks, some of which are also recommended for further reading.

DEVELOPING THE HABITS OF CRITICAL THINKING AND REFLECTIVE PRACTICE

One of the difficulties of working with people is that no one has yet developed the manual with the answers to all the difficulties and problems you might encounter. Plumbers may be able to turn to the plumbing manual and builders to the architect's plan when they are stuck, but for those of us in the people professions, the book with all the answers has not yet been written. While there are manuals of good practice and codes of conduct which can act as guidance and benchmarks, the very nature of what we are trying to achieve and the number of factors which can influence outcomes, mean essentially that such a totally encompassing complete guide to practice never can be.

Some workers in the field of human services are turning to ideas from chaos theory to help them understand these complexities. Chaos theory concerns the unpredictability of large systems, where the smallest of changes in one single factor can ultimately result in massive changes in the whole system. Because of the almost infinite number of factors involved, it is impossible to predict the effects of changes in individual factors on the larger system. The classic explanation concerns the effect of a butterfly flapping its wings as it flies from a tree in the Amazon rain forest, which sets up a tiny air current which contributes to other currents which ultimately result in a hurricane in the Atlantic ocean. Chaos theory tells us that the weather can only be successfully predicted in a very general way for no more than about four or five days, even with the use of massive supercomputers. It also helps to explain the unpredictability of human actions or the ultimate effect of interventions by care workers. (For a good explanation of chaos theory, see Wikipedia, 2004.)

Because of the difficulties outlined above, it becomes necessary to work in a way in which you are constantly developing your own understanding and skills by reflecting on what you get right and, equally importantly, what you get wrong. In order to do this effectively, you need to receive good feedback from the people you are working with and you also require to be honest in your assessment of your own performance. This is the basis of reflective practice, and is a habit which you should build into your own work practice. Do not worry, this does not mean writing an actual reflective log after everything you do, but it does mean being rigorous in your evaluation of your approach and actions in every intervention and situation.

Some people think that experience alone leads to the development of wisdom ('I've been doing this job for 30 years, son!'). It does not! How many people do you know who make the same mistakes over and over again, such as those who finally manage to struggle out of bad relationships with abusive partners only to find themselves in fresh relationships with brand new abusive partners? The little equation below is a good way of considering this question.

Experience *does not equal* Wisdom

Experience + Reflection *equal* Wisdom

Along with the development of reflective practice, you should also be developing the skill of critical analysis. This essentially requires that you do not always accept things at face value and are curious about reasons why. Often truth and real meanings are found behind barriers erected to hide and disguise them, and you will not find them unless you are prepared to be both critical and analytical. You might be good at this already! You know very well for example that your partner's response of 'I'm fine' when you asked how they were feeling is not necessarily a totally honest response. You might sense too that government statements do not always tell the real story – 'Unemployment reaches record low point', 'Tractor production up by 150 per cent' or 'Social workers to blame in rising crime figures'; or that newspaper headlines do not always tell the truth. The origins of a recent headline, 'Asylum-Seekers to Get Free Driving Lessons' were eventually discovered to relate to a report that two individuals who had been given formal refugee status and therefore allowed to live in the UK, had been given driving lessons as part of their employment training for new jobs.

Messages might contain sub-messages; people might have hidden agendas. When you sharpen your skills of critical analysis, you become better equipped to pick these things up. A good starting approach is to challenge statements with questions such as 'Who says, and why?'

Noam Chomsky (2001) puts it well when he says 'Think for yourselves. Do not uncritically accept what you are told . . .' He goes on to add, interestingly for those of us involved in care work, '. . . do what you can to make the world a better place, particularly for those who suffer and those who are oppressed.'

THE PASSION AND THE POWER

Passion

The work you do with people is not easy. It could be argued that most of you who work in this field at whatever level came to it for a particular reason, or indeed a number of connected reasons. These might include a general desire to do good, a quest for social justice, political beliefs, a wish to give something back (often after being the recipient of human services yourself), an aspiration to make changes, or some other reasons which might not be too clear. Whatever the motivation, the best workers across the spectrum of care tend to be driven by an energy or passion for what they do. They have what was referred to in Chapter 4 as oomph. People without this passion fail to make much impression on anything or anybody.

This passion creates an enthusiasm to work in a way which makes things happen. A colleague once had a poster above his desk which said 'There are only three kinds of people in this world – those who make things happen, those who watch things happen and those who wonder what happened!' I am sure you would agree that the best care workers should belong to the first category! But how can you maintain this passion and enthusiasm in the face of a whole range of organisational constraints, competing demands on your time, and often phenomenal levels of personal stress?

You have to work hard to maintain the initial passion and idealism which you brought to this work. John O'Brien, philosopher, teacher and a leading speaker in the inclusion movement says, 'You choose to work in this field with passion because you are moved by a set of issues and these issues essentially reflect questions that live within you'. He borrows some ideas from American authors on leadership, Ron Heifetz and Marty Linsky (2002), and makes the connection that the qualities they identify as necessary in the field of effective leadership are equally essential for all workers in this field. The three most essential qualities he names are innocence, curiosity and compassion. At first sight these seem strange qualities for leadership or effective human service workers, but further analysis illustrates some important points.

The quality of innocence allows you to see things which others do not because they think they know all the answers. The quality of curiosity means that you will always maintain doubt, so that you will always be open to changing realities and never blinded by your own certainties. The quality of compassion means that you might just understand the effect of your actions on, and what you might be asking from, others.

The real value in this approach is the insight which it offers into what happens when things do not work out as planned or, as John O'Brien says, when people

Quality	Becomes . . .	Dressed up as . . .
Innocence	Cynicism	Realism
Curiosity	Arrogance	Authoritative knowledge
Compassion	Callousness	The thick skin of experience

Figure 11.1 Qualities

'lose heart'. When this happens, these qualities may become transformed into their virtual opposites. Because nobody would dare to claim these as their own, they become dressed up as what might appear to be desirable attributes as outlined in the figure below.

You might find evidence of this transformation in individuals or the organisations you work for. Sometimes you might discover this disguised cynicism, arrogance and callousness in those who claim to be the hardened experts in their field. You might be surprised at how easy it is to become like this – often people will say it is the only way to survive. Cynicism, arrogance and callousness represent safe ways of going about business but they essentially suffocate the essence of what we should be doing to protect, promote and assist in the act of living.

Power

Moving on from ideas about passion, remember what has been said in this book about power and think about it a little more. As care workers you are powerful people, although it might not always feel like that! You essentially exercise two types of power – state power and personal power. You exercise what is essentially state power through carrying out your mandatory duties or statutory elements of your roles – examples might include undertaking community care assessments, working to a professional code of conduct (as demanded by statute) or even limiting the freedom of young people in your care. In doing so, you are acting in accordance with relevant legislation, although sometimes the borders become fuzzy around the application of relevant statute.

I once worked in a large institution which was designed essentially to provide total institutional care for people who were at that time labelled as 'mentally subnormal'. The physician superintendent boasted proudly that while there were over a thousand people incarcerated in this institution, only 27 people were compulsorily detained under the relevant 'section' of the Mental Health Act. 'What happens if someone tries to leave?' I naively asked. 'Why,' he replied, 'we section them, of course'.

One way of analysing the use of personal power in the relationship between the care worker and the service user is to use the work of French and Raven to examine different types of power. This framework is more generally used to examine power in management situations, so we will try to give some relevant examples from both areas.

French and Raven (1960) identified five types of power which they described as follows.

Reward power

The leader or care worker is seen as having the capacity to reward people. For a worker, this might be by the allocation of good shifts, by praise, by access to promotion or by letting you leave early. In a care setting, a care worker might be perceived as having the ability to reward people by prioritising their case, making sure their interests are best represented, or something as simple as positive feedback on how they are doing.

Coercive power

The leader or care worker is seen as having the power to inflict punishment of some sort. From the perspective of the worker, this might be by allocating the lousy shifts, public humiliation, blocking chances of promotion or losing your overtime sheet. Sadly too, some service users may perceive care workers as holding this sort of power over them. They fear they may be punished by withholding of services (of which sometimes the care worker may be the sole provider), by being ridiculed or even by being abused. In situations where the balance of care and control is towards the control end, such as people detained in secure accommodation, there is a great danger in overuse of coercion as a sole means of directing people. It does not take much to tip the balance to bullying and abuse.

Referent power

People follow leaders who exhibit this type of power, sometimes called charismatic power, essentially because they want to be like them. There is an essential difference between people who manage and people who lead, and the difference is often because of the charismatic power that real leaders can exhibit. This points out the necessity for care workers to go about their business in a way which might serve as a good example to those whom they might wish to influence. It may also illustrate a difficulty in this field of work where, although we may have a surfeit of managers, good leaders might be a bit thin on the ground! (We will return to this theme later in the chapter.)

Position power

This type of power is essentially related to the position in the hierarchy or organisation which the person occupies. Position power is basically *authority* and is related to the person's power to control an element of resources belonging to the organisation or to the legal powers to act attached to their position. There is potential for much confusion around understanding the nature of this type of power, which is examined below.

Expert power

This type of power is derived from people's perception that an individual knows more about a particular subject than they do. Thus we expect our managers to understand more about how things work than we do, and in most cases they do. Service users might expect care workers to be experts in the field of particular legislation, know how systems work, understand some of the problems they face and so on. Workers who appear incompetent will not be able to exercise any influence at all.

It is essential in understanding the nature of power that you realise that it is based on people's perceptions:

The power that you have is the power that people perceive you to have.

Some people make the mistake of confusing power and authority. They might believe that having authority automatically confers personal power on them.

Example

Sheila was a care worker in a residential establishment. She was a good worker who, after achieving the necessary qualifications and experience, was eventually rewarded by a promotion to first line management. After going out on Friday night with her colleagues to celebrate, she came back to her new post on Monday morning with her new business suit and attaché case. As part of the management team now, she intended to have little contact with service users and was concerned with the much more important matters of directing staff in their duties and making sure no one was shirking. As the days went by, she became increasingly frustrated at staff who seemed to have little respect for her new power and indeed appeared to subvert everything she tried to do.

What Sheila perhaps failed to appreciate was that personal power has to be built up. It is not always automatically attached to position power (authority). French and Raven's concepts are useful in helping us to understand some of the finer points about the application of different types of power. They point out, for example, that over-reliance on one type of power alone will ultimately become counter-productive. The leader who relies totally on reward power and gives out favours all the time, or the leader who is dependent only on coercion as a means of gaining what they want, perhaps by constant bullying, is ultimately going to fail. Good leaders operate from a number of different power bases.

Power might be defined as the capacity to influence outcomes. Many of the people we work with might be seen as relatively lacking in power and dependent on us to help make things happen. The power imbalance between worker and service user might be pretty substantial, but a number of other factors come into play at this point. One of these factors is related to the notion that all power generates resistance, and that even the most apparently powerless people can still exercise influence.

This idea of generative power was developed by Michel Foucault, a French philosopher who wrote much about how power was used in different ways to control society. In *The History of Sexuality* (Foucault, 1978), he tells the story of how a young boy in care was initially chastised for the sin of masturbation and then punished more and more severely for re-offending. Foucault asked why it should be necessary to exercise so much energy in punishing what was a harmless act. He suggested that cause and effect have been reversed. It was necessary to punish the boy essentially to show who was in charge, and the resistance generated perpetuated this need.

This notion might help to illustrate the reason why institutions often have a dazzling array of what appear to be petty rules and regulations. They are primarily necessary to remind people of exactly who has the power and control. Consider any such rules which might exist in the organisation in which you work, try to identify those which do not seem to serve any useful purpose, and think about the reason for their existence.

If you are interested in discovering more about the use of power in everyday work or indeed life situations in general, I would recommend 'The 48 Laws of Power' by Robert Greene (1998). This is a wonderful little handbook which distils ideas about power from people who were experts indeed in its use, such as Machiavelli and Mao Tse Tung, in a very tongue-in-cheek fashion. Some examples of the laws are quoted below and I let you work out their possible meaning and relevance on your own!

Always Say Less Than Necessary

Never Outshine the Master

Do Not Build Fortresses to Protect Yourself, Isolation Is Dangerous

Remember that the main reason for understanding power is the importance of using it wisely, not misusing it, and being able to share it with and, where appropriate, hand it over to, service users.

GETTING THE BALANCE RIGHT – THE VKS MODEL

In order to become a well-rounded competent care worker at any level, it is necessary to have a balance between three major elements – the value base, knowledge and skills. This balance is shown in the figure below.

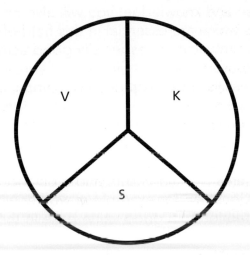

Figure 11.2 The VKS model

Each of these three components plays a vital part in ensuring that you are able to carry out your responsibilities in a competent and sensitive fashion.

Value base

The idea of a sound value base has been covered elsewhere in the book, especially in Chapter 2. It is hard to overstate the importance of attention to this, for it forms the very bedrock upon which good practice is built. At times you will find yourself facing difficult decisions and be unsure about which course to follow. This is where you should be able to compare your possible courses of action against your professional value base, in order to help guide you to the ethical course to follow. In this way, your value base acts as a sort of compass to show in which direction you should be heading.

Knowledge

Your knowledge base consists of your awareness and understanding of all the various subjects which you have studied and pieces of practice which you have learned from your career to date. Workers in the field of care are required to develop a very wide knowledge base drawn from a variety of related subjects which might include psychology, sociology, social policy, law, technical aspects of work and so on. An analogy for your knowledge base is to think of it as a sort of map which can show you where you are and where you can go.

Skills

In addition to value base and knowledge, you will also be required to develop a very wide range of skills which are essential in this field of work. These might include such skills as communication, especially good active listening to help you understand what service users may be trying to tell you; counselling skills to help you support individuals; skills in developing and maintaining supportive relationships, and perhaps more specialised skills of intervention and assessment. The best analogy for these skills is that they are a sort of tool box that you can reach into to select the most appropriate tool for the situation.

Each of the above elements is vital in itself, and a balance between the three is also hugely important. Consider, for example, a worker who has all the required knowledge and pays attention to a good value base in their work, but lacks a range of skills such as the ability to communicate with service users or build meaningful relationships with them. This will seriously limit their effectiveness as a practitioner. A knowledgeable worker with great skills in relating to clients who fails to pay any attention to the value base could even be considered dangerous.

There are increasing requirements for workers to undergo regular professional development as part of their continuing registration, but good workers will be continually increasing their knowledge, developing their skills and refining their values anyway. You should take every opportunity you can to work on these areas.

THE CENTRALITY OF RELATIONSHIPS – MAKING CONNECTIONS

The ability to build meaningful and respectful relationships with people is one of the most important skills which you can develop. At times this will be very difficult – you may be working with people who have experienced abuse and whose experience of relationships has always been negative, or who might have the greatest difficulty making themselves understood, or who may be just too angry to listen. But without taking time to build relationships you cannot expect to make any sort of connections and, if you cannot connect with people, you will not be able to help them.

This is not about persuading people to like you. It is about using all of your wide range of skills to engage meaningfully with people. The young adult with behaviour problems might be trying to tell the people around him something by his behaviour which he cannot articulate in any other way. The only way to achieve anything is to start to build a relationship. Similarly, the older woman with severe depression is not going to share anything with you until you start to build bridges. If you follow this sort of approach, a degree of trust and a willingness to communicate will often follow. Remember too that the inability to speak does not mean an inability to communicate – 'Just because I cannot speak does not mean I do not have anything to say!'

FINALLY . . .

At the start of the chapter you stood on top of a mountain looking around and thinking about how you might best now set about this task of care practice. As you reach the end, you might think it is becoming a little misty! Be assured, however, that the information you have looked at in this chapter and in this book should be useful in helping you to see things a little more clearly. Neither be overwhelmed at the complexity of this business of social care nor be seduced by simple answers. Most of all, enjoy the challenges of this difficult but ultimately extremely rewarding field of work.

RECOMMENDED READING

FOUCAULT, M. (1978) *The History of Sexuality*. London: Random House. This is a fascinating book which explores ideas about sex and power. Not for the faint-hearted, though!

GREENE, R. (1998) *The 48 Laws of Power*. London: Profile Books. A wonderful book available in both full and condensed versions. Full of ideas and methods about how to use concepts of power to achieve what you want.

HUTTON, W. (2002) *The World We're In*. London: Little Brown. A comprehensive exploration of a range of dilemmas facing the UK today. Especially strong on the analysis of recent tendencies to follow the lead of the United States of America in many areas.

ZELDIN, T. (1998) *An Intimate History of Humanity*. London: Vintage. A brilliant book which explores the different types of relationships which have existed throughout different phases of history. Well worth reading if you are interested in the nature of relationships that we all experience.

GLOSSARY

Abuse The violation or neglect of those unable to protect themselves, to prevent harm from happening, or to remove themselves from harm or potential harm by others.

Acceptance Taking people as they are without judging them; an absence of rejection.

Accidents Unforeseen major and minor incidents where an individual is injured.

Adolescence The stage of development between childhood and adulthood; usually seen to begin with puberty and to end with responsibility and independence.

Advising Telling others how they might act, feel or think rather than letting them decide for themselves.

Advocacy Actively promoting and representing the cause of another; speaking on behalf of someone as if speaking as that person.

Ageism Discrimination applied to or experienced by people because of their age. This term is applicable both to older and young people.

Agency An establishment or organisation providing a service to service users.

Anti-discriminatory practice Practice which acknowledges, understands and challenges the many negative effects of discrimination.

Anti-oppressive practice Acting against abuses of power in order to empower people.

Assessment An exploration of service user needs as part of the process of care, in order to enable the service user to reach a quality of life which is as good as can be; the basis for planning.

Attitude The way in which something is viewed in an evaluative way; an habitual mode of regarding anything. Attitudes affect the way people behave.

Behaviour How people conduct themselves. The way they do things themselves and in their relationships with others.

Belief An opinion or conviction which is held to be true, often without any sort of proof.

Body language Non-verbal communication expressed through the position, attitude and expression of the body, or parts of the body, e.g. the way in which you sit; the degree of eye contact.

Care/formal care Caring for people in society, other than self or family, in an agency whose codes of practice are dictated to and guided by legislation, policy and professional ethics.

Care plan An agreement arising from an assessment about which needs are to be met, how they are to be achieved and how problems are to be dealt with.

Choice Promoting choice means giving different options, real options, from which the service user can select as independently as possible.

Client The recipient or user of a service. Although 'service user' is the term used in this book, client is still an accepted term in care practice and counselling.

Cognitive development The gradual unfolding and increase in complexity of thought and intellectual processes during the life cycle.

Communication Communication occurs whenever people receive and/or give messages which they regard as significant. It can be verbal, non-verbal or symbolic.

Community A network of people who are linked, usually by sharing a geographical locality; may also refer to those linked by occupation, ethnic background and/or other factors.

Community care Providing the services and support which people need to be able to live as independently as possible in their own homes or in 'homely' settings, rather than institutions.

Confidentiality Maintaining the right to privacy of information; not divulging personal information without consent.

Congruence Being genuine; ensuring that your verbal and non-verbal behaviour give the same messages.

Counselling A process which aims to help people help themselves through communication to make better choices and become better decision makers.

Culture The way in which people live, lifestyle, values; can also be seen as consisting of all the messages received from society about what is good, bad, desirable, undesirable etc.

Development Gradual unfolding; increase in complexity involving change and movement. Human development can be physical, intellectual/cognitive, emotional, social and spiritual.

Deviance Behaviour of individuals or groups which is outside the socially defined normal limits of behaviour.

Disablism Discrimination applied to, or experienced by, people with physical/or learning disabilities.

Discrimination The process whereby some groups or individuals in society treat others less favourably than themselves, based upon prejudice and stereotypes.

Emergency Immediate and threatening danger to individuals and others.

Empathy Putting yourself in someone else's shoes and attempting to imagine how he or she feels.

Empowerment Enabling people to take control of their lives; gaining the power to make decisions and choices.

Equality of opportunity The belief that everyone should get an equal chance to access the opportunities in society.

Ethnic group A group with a long shared history and a cultural tradition of its own. Other important characteristics may be common geographic origin, language, literature and religion.

Ethics A branch of philosophy that studies morality, moral problems and moral judgements.

Ethnocentrism Prejudicial assumptions made in theorising and explaining human behaviour and aspects of society, which favour one or some groups over others; may lead to accounts which make false assumptions and which are biased.

Feminism Sets out to explain the position of women in society; to focus attention upon how women have been subordinated and oppressed and how this can be changed.

Gender The term used to describe socially constructed differences between men and women. Sex refers to biological differences.

Genetic The influence of genes, which are inherited from parents and determine everything from eye colour and body shape to some illnesses, e.g. haemophilia.

Hazard Something with the potential to cause harm.

HNC Higher National Certificate.

Holistic care Care which sees the whole person in a social situation and attempts to satisfy physical, intellectual, communication, emotional, cultural, spiritual and social needs.

Homophobia The fear of people who are homosexual, often displayed through discriminatory actions.

Ideology A set of beliefs and ideas that are held by a group, e.g. the ideology of the Scottish Nationalist Party or the Conservative Party.

Implementation Putting plans into effect; carrying out what has been agreed upon in the planning process.

Inclusion See 'Social inclusion'.

Institution A part of society which has regular and routine practices, regulated by social norms.

Institutional discrimination The routine, day-to-day, ingrained discrimination which exists in any of the different institutions in society.

Institutionalisation Becoming dependent upon the routines and narrow confines of an institution, resulting in such characteristics as apathy, lack of initiative and inability to make personal plans.

Keyworker A worker who is allocated to work more closely with a service user than other workers, who has a coordinating role with that service user within the agency.

Labelling Attaching a (usually negative) name to acts or conditions which then becomes a 'master status', e.g. labelling people as deviant, neurotic or difficult.

Learned helplessness A decline in the desire and ability to do things beyond what may be expected in relation to a person's state of health, usually because too much assistance is being given.

Legislation The law; Acts of Parliament.

Marginalisation Literally means to 'place at the edge' and refers to the process whereby some groups are forced to live outside the mainstream of society and denied opportunities to participate as full citizens.

Modelling Demonstrating behaviour, feelings or thoughts to others which may, if adopted, improve the quality of life for the service user.

Monitoring Ongoing evaluation; keeping a check on what you are doing to ensure that it meets objectives.

Nature/nurture debate Refers to dispute about whether nature (inherited characteristics) or nurture (the environment, socio-economic factors and socialisation) determines behaviour and development.

Normalisation Affording all citizens the same rights and opportunities to develop and contribute to society in ways which are socially valued; developed predominantly as an attempt to promote the aim of integrating people with a disability fully into society.

NVQ National Vocational Qualification; awarded at different levels upon successful completion of a detailed assessment of practice competence by an approved workplace assessor.

Oppression Abuse of power by a group or an individual over a less powerful group or individual, with the effect that those less powerful are denied their rights.

Patriarchy The dominance of men over women in society.

Prejudice A strongly held negative attitude or set of attitudes based not upon fact or reason but upon traditional beliefs, lack of understanding and/or stereotypes.

Principles The practical manifestation of values; the first, most important things.

Psychology The study of mind and behaviour.

Record A written account of significant information including decisions, incidents, feelings, actions and monitoring of the implementation of assessments/plans.

Relationship Being connected in some way with another; a helping relationship is characterised by empathy, genuineness and unconditional positive regard.

Residential care The provision for need in a registrable home. Care Commissions are responsible for the inspection of these homes using National Service Standards.

Respite care A temporary period, usually spent in a supported, residential environment, in order to give carers a break and/or provide help and a change for those in need of care. It can also be used as an opportunity for assessment or reassessment.

Rights The valid claims that individuals have, e.g. to be respected, to have privacy etc.

Risk The likelihood of harm or hazard potential being realised.

Role play Enacting behaviour in simulated settings or imagination.

Scapegoats Individuals or groups of people who have been inaccurately and unjustly targeted as being responsible for a problem.

Self-concept A personal judgement of worthiness expressed in the attitudes which you hold towards yourself.

Self-esteem A sense of your own worth. This can be a positive or negative evaluation of yourself.

Service user One who receives or avails him or herself of help or assistance towards fulfilling need and/or improving the quality of life, sometimes also called a client or resident.

Sexism Discrimination applied to or experienced by people on the basis of their sex and/or gender.

Siblings Brothers and sisters.

Social class People in the same or similar socio-economic circumstances. Socio-economic differences result in differences in wealth, power and life chances.

Social exclusion The prevention of some people/groups from taking a full and valued part in society, e.g. those who are marginalised because of poverty or disability.

Social inclusion Describes the idea of taking positive steps to assist and include people who have traditionally been excluded from society; includes treating everyone as a valued member of society and facilitating participation in that society.

Socialisation The process or way in which people learn the culture of their society.

Society Usually, but not always, the country or nation-state, defined in terms of language, laws, education, religion.

Sociology The study of societies and the analysis of social relationships as constituted by social interaction. No single definition is satisfactory because of the diversity of sociological perspectives.

Status Position in society or social institution; what a person is; it can also mean the prestige associated with that position.

Statutory Provided by or connected with central or local government.

Stereotype A fixed, general, over-simplified and usually negative image of what a particular individual or group is like because of the possession of certain characteristics, e.g. the false 'stereotypes' of all gay men being promiscuous, or all people from a particular city being mean.

Stigma A distinguishing mark or characteristic which is both noticeable and regarded as objectionable by some individuals or groups. Stigmas have the power to spoil a person's social and personal identity.

Summarising Making statements which say briefly what you or another person has been saying; may include feedback from you.

Support Giving encouragement, help, understanding, warmth, whatever is needed, to another.

SVQ Scottish Vocational Qualification; awarded at different levels upon successful completion of a detailed assessment of practice competence by an approved workplace assessor.

Symbolic communication Messages, behaviour and actions which represent something else, e.g. an unwelcoming physical environment says 'we do not care about you'.

Team A group of people who work together to achieve the philosophy and goals of their agency.

Transitions Changes from one life state to another which people undergo during their lives, e.g. marriage, loss of a partner, retirement.

Value That which is desirable and worthy for its own sake.

Voluntary organisation A not-for-profit, non-statutory organisation; often a charity.

References

ADAMS, J. et al. (1977) *Transition: Understanding and Managing Personal Change.* London: Martin Robinson.

ADAMS, M. et al. (2000) *Readings in Diversity and Social Justice.* New York: Routledge.

AHMED, S. (1986) 'Black children in a day nursery, some issues of practice' in S. Ahmed, J. Cheetham and J. Small (eds) *Social work with Black Children and their Families.* London: Batsford.

ANGLIN, J. (2002) *Pain, Normality, and the Struggle for Congruence.* New York: The Haworth Press, Inc.

ARBER, S. and GINN, J. (2004) *Ageing and Gender: Diversity and Change.* University of Surrey: Centre for Research on Ageing and Gender (CRAG).

BARR, A. et al. (2001) *Caring Communities: A Challenge for Social Inclusion.* York: YPS.

BAYLEY, J. (1999) *Iris – A Memoir of Iris Murdoch.* London: Abacus.

BELBIN, R.M. (1993) *Team Roles at Work.* Oxford: Butterworth-Heinemann.

BERESFORD, P. (2004) 'Pointless Policy', *Community Care,* 8 January 2004.

BERESFORD, P. (2003) *Shaping our Lives Conference speech.* London: Shaping our Lives, National User Network.

BERESFORD, P. and BRANFIELD, F. (2004) 'Shape up and listen', *Community Care,* 4 November 2004.

BEVERIDGE, SIR W. (1942) *Social Insurance and Allied Services.* London: HMSO.

BIESTEK, F.P. (1961) *The Casework Relationship.* London: George Allen and Unwin.

BION, W. (1968) *Experiences in Groups.* London: Tavistock.

Bradford Social Services Department, Community Health NHS Health Trust, Bradford Interfaith Centre (2002) *Spiritual Wellbeing: policy and practice.* Leeds: NIMHE.

BRADSHAW, J. (1972) 'The Concept of Social Need', *New Society,* 30 March 1972.

BRAYE, S. and PRESTON-SHOOT, M. (1995) *Empowering Practice in Social Care.* Maidenhead: Open University Press.

BROWN, A. and BOURNE, I. (1996) *The social work supervisor: supervision in community, day care and residential settings.* Philadelphia: Open University Press.

BROWN, H. and CRAFT, A. (1989) *Thinking the Unthinkable.* London: fpa Education Unit.

BUTLER, K., CARR, S. and SULLIVAN, F. (1988) *Citizen Advocacy: a powerful partnership.* London: National Citizen Advocacy.

Chambers (2003) *Chambers Paperback Dictionary.* Edinburgh: Chambers Harrap.

Child Protection Audit and Review (2002) *It's everyone's job to make sure I'm alright.* Edinburgh: Scottish Executive.

CHOMSKY, N. (2001) *9–11: Noam Chomsky.* New York: Seven Stories Press.

CHOWDHURY, R. and WORLEY, A. (2003) *An NOP survey on disabled people's experiences of access to goods and services in Britain.* London: DRC.

Circles Network (2004) *Annual Report April 03–March 04.* Rugby: Circles Network.

CLOUGH, R. (1996) *The abuse of children in residential care.* Surbiton: SCA.

CLOUGH, R. (2004) 'Recording', *Care and Health*, July 2004.

COATES, C. (2004) 'My Practice', *Community Care*, 12 August 2004.

Commission for Racial Equality (1996) *Roots of the Future*. London: CRE.

Community Care Magazine (2001) 'Behind the Headlines', *Community Care*, 4 October, 2001.

Community Care Magazine (2001) 'Prisoner of the Past', *Community Care*, 19–25 April 2001.

Community Care Magazine (2004) 'She won't let us help her', *Community Care*, 22 July 2004.

Community Care Magazine (2004) 'Uncharted Territory', *Community Care*, 22 July 2004.

Community Care Magazine (2004) 'Valuing people fails to halt prejudice', *Community Care*, 25 November 2004.

Community Care Magazine (2004) 'Viewpoint', *Community Care*, 28 October 2004.

Community Care Magazine (2004) 'Wheels for all', *Community Care*, 5 August 2004.

CORBY, B. (2000) *Child Abuse, towards a knowledge base*, 2nd edn. Buckingham: Open University Press.

COULSHED, V. and MULLENDER, A. (2001) *Management in Social Work*, 2nd edn. Hampshire: Palgrave.

COULSHED, V. and ORME, J. (1998) *Social Work Practice*, 3rd edn. Basingstoke: BASW Macmillan.

COWLING, V. (ed) (1999) *Children of Parents with Mental Illness*. Melbourne: Australian Council for Educational Research Ltd.

CPAG (2001) *An end in sight? Tackling child poverty in the UK*. London: CPAG.

CPAG (2004) *Annual Report*. London: CPAG.

CRE (2004) *CRE report reveals racism in football management*. www.cre.gov.uk

CRITTENDEN, P. and AINSWORTH, M. (1989) 'Child Maltreatment and Attachment Theory' in D. Cicchetti and V. Carlson (eds) *Child Maltreatment*. Cambridge: Cambridge University Press.

CROMPTON, M. (1998) *Children, Spirituality, Religion and Social Work*. Aldershot: Ashgate.

CROMPTON, M. (2001) *Who am I? Promoting children's spiritual wellbeing in everyday life; A guide for all who work with children*. Barkingside: Barnardo's.

CROMPTON, M and JACKSON, R. (in press) *Spiritual Wellbeing of Adults with Down's Syndrome*. Southsea: Down's Syndrome Education Trust.

Daily Express (2001) 'Doctor didn't quiz child with 128 injuries', *Daily Express*, 13 October 2001.

DALRYMPLE, J. and BURKE, B. (1995) *Anti-Oppressive Practice: Social Care and the Law*. Buckingham: Open University Press.

DALY, M. (ed.) (2001) *Care Work: the quest for security*. Geneva: International Labour Office.

DANIEL, B. and WASSELL, S. (2002) *The School Years: Assessing and Promoting Resilience in Vulnerable Children 2*. London: Jessica Kingsley Publishers.

DAVIES, M. (2002) *The Blackwell Companion to Social Work*, 2nd edn. Oxford: Blackwell Publishing.

DAVIS, L. (1992) *Social Care, Rivers of Pain, Bridges of Hope*. London: Edward Arnold.

DECALMER, P. and GLENDENNING, F. (1997) *The Mistreatment of Elderly People*. London: Sage.

Department of Education and Skills (2004) *Every Child Matters*. Norwich: TSO (The Stationery Office).

Department of Health (1989) *Caring for People*. London: HMSO.

Department of Health (2001) *Valuing People*. Norwich: TSO.

DICKENS, C. (1999) *Nicholas Nickleby*. London: Penguin Popular Classics.

DICKENS, C. (2004) *Oliver Twist*. London: Penguin Popular Classics.

DOUGLAS, T. (1978) *Basic Groupwork*. London: Routledge.

DOWIE, C. (1988) 'Adult Child/Dead Child', in *Plays by Women* (first produced in 1987). London: Methuen.

EOC (2004) *Facts about men and women in Great Britain*. www.eoc.org.uk

FARNSWORTH, V. (2003) 'How I helped an Inquiry', *Community Care*, 26 June 2003.

FEINBERG, J. (1973) *Social Philosophy*. Englewood Cliffs: Prentice Hall.

FINKELHOR, D. and KORBIN, J. (1998) 'Child Abuse as an international issue', *Child Abuse and Neglect*, vol. 12, 3–23.

FLAHERTY, J. *et al.* (2004) *Poverty: The Facts*. London: CPAG.

FONAGY, P. *et al.* (1994) The Emanuel Miller Memorial Lecture 1992: 'The theory and practice of resilience', *Journal of Child Psychology and Psychiatry*, vol. 35, no. 2, 231–57.

FOUCAULT, M. (1978) *The History of Sexuality*. London: Random House.

FRENCH, R. and RAVEN, B. (1960) 'The Bases of Social Power', in D. Cartwright and A. Zander (eds) (1960) *Group Dynamics*. New York: Harper and Row.

GILLIGAN, R. (1997) 'Beyond permanence? The importance of resilience in child placement practice and planning', in *Adoption and Fostering*, vol. 21, no. 1, 12–20.

Glasgow City Council (2001) *City of Glasgow Multi-Agency Procedures for the Protection of Vulnerable Adults*. Glasgow: Glasgow City Council.

Glasgow City Council (1997) *Language Matters: A Guide to Good Practice*. Glasgow: GCC.

GOFFMAN, E. (1968) *Asylums*. Harmondsworth: Penguin.

GORDON, S. *et al.* (ed) (1996) *Care giving*. Philadelphia, University of Pennsylvania Press.

GRAY, B. and JACKSON, R. (2002) *Advocacy and Learning Disability*. London: Jessica Kingsley Publishers.

GREENE, R. (1998) *The 48 Laws of Power*. London: Profile Books.

GSCC (2002) *Code of Practice for Social Care Workers*. London: GSCC.

HACKETT, S. (2004) 'Children who Abuse', *Community Care*, 21 October 2004.

HARRIS, J. and Craft, A. (1994) *People with Learning Disabilities at risk of Physical or Sexual abuse*. London: Bild.

HEIFETZ, R. and LINSKY, M. (2002) *Leadership on the Line*. Cambridge: Harvard Business School Press.

HENDERSON, R. and POCHIN, M. (2001) *A Right Result? Advocacy, Justice and Empowerment*. Bristol: The Policy Press.

HENG, S. (2003) 'The Simon Heng Column', *Community Care*, 29 July 2003.

HMSO (1995) *Disability Discrimination Act*. London.

HMSO (1948) *Education Reform Act (England and Wales)*. London.

HMSO (1998) *Human Rights Act*. London.

HMSO (1990) *National Health Service and Community Care Act*. London.

HMSO (1976) *Race Relations Act*. London.

HORWATH, J. and LAWSON, B. (eds) (1995) *Trust betrayed?* London: National Children's Bureau.

HSE (2001) *Handling Home Care*. Norwich: HMSO.

HSE (2001) *Health and Safety in Care Homes*. HSG220. Norwich: HMSO.

HUTTON, W. (2002) *The World We're In*. London: Little Brown.

INGHAM, I. (ed) (2003) *Gogaburn Lives*. Edinburgh: Living Memory Association.

JAY, M. and DOGANIS, S. (1987) *Battered: The Abuse of Children*. London: Weidenfeld and Nicolson.

JUKES, A.E. (1999) *Men who Batter Women*. London: Routledge.

KADUSHIN, A. (1976) *Supervision in Social Work*. New York: Columbia University Press.

KAHAN, B. (1994) *Growing up in Groups*. London: National Institute for Social Work.

KANT, I. (1964) *Groundwork of the Metaphysics of Morals*. New York: Harper and Row.

KEEGAN, G. (2002) *Higher Psychology: Approaches and Methods*. London: Hodder & Stoughton.

KERR, D. (2004) 'Grief and Crime', *Community Care*, 13 May 2004.

KENWORTHY, N., SNOWLEY, G., GILLING, C. (eds) (2002) *Common Foundation Studies in Nursing* (3rd edn.). London: Churchill Livingstone.

KING, M.L. (1963) 'Letter from Birmingham Jail, Alabama' quoted in E. Knowles (1997) *The Oxford Dictionary of Phrase, Saying and Quotation*. Oxford: OUP.

KINSELLA, P. (1993) *Supported Living – A New Paradigm*. Manchester: National Development Team.

KOHLER, T. (2000) *Savannah Citizen Advocacy*. Edinburgh: SHS.

KUBLER-ROSS, E. (1989) *On Death and Dying*. London: Routledge.

LAMING, LORD (2001) *The Victoria Climbie Inquiry*. Norwich: HMSO.

Lord Chancellor (2001) *Code of Practice for the Freedom of Information Act*. www.pro.gov.uk/recordsmanagement/CodeOfPractice.htm

LUKES, S. (1974) *Power: A Radical View*. London: Macmillan.

MARTIN, V. and HENDERSON, E. (2001) *Managing in Health and Social Care*. London: Routledge.

JAY, M. and DOGANIS, S. (1987) *Battered: Story of Child Abuse*. London: Weidenfeld and Niclolson.

MALCOLM X. (1964) speech at Militant Labor Forum, New York, 29 May 1964.

MARRIOTT, A. (1997) in R. Decalmer and F. Glendenning (eds) *The Mistreatment of Elderly People*. London: Sage.

MASLOW, A. (1954) *Motivation and Personality*. New York: Harper.

MCLEOD, E. and BYWATERS, P. (2000) *Social Work, Health and Equality*. London: Routledge.

MCPHERSON, SIR W. (1999) *The Stephen Lawrence Inquiry*. Norwich: The Stationery Office.

CHRISTINE MEYER (2004) www.family-futures.org.uk. Edinburgh: SHS Trust.

MILLER, J. (2000) *Care in Practice for Higher Still*. London: Hodder and Stoughton.

MILLER, J. (1996) *Social Care Practice*. London: Hodder and Stoughton.

MORRAN, D. and WILSON, M. (1997) *Men who are Violent to Women*. Lyme Regis: Russell House Publishing Ltd.

MANT, B., DEMARASSE, R. *et al.* (1991) *Person-Centred Development*. Rugby: Communitas Publication.

MURRAY, P. and PENMAN, J. (1996) *Let our children be*. Sheffield: Parents with Attitude.

MURRAY PARKES, C. (1998) *Bereavenent Studies of Grief in Adult Life*. London: Penguin.

NELSON-JONES, R. (1988) *Practical Counselling and Helping Skills*. London: Cassell.

NEWMAN, T. (2003) 'Protection Racket', *Community Care*, 30 January 2004.

Nursing and Midwifery Council (2002) *Code of Professional Conduct*. London: NMC.

O'BRIEN, J. (2002) Scottish Human Services Trust Conference. Edinburgh: Herriot Watt University.

O'BRIEN, J. and LOVETT, H. (1992) *Finding a Way Toward Everyday Lives: The Contribution of Person-Centred Planning*. Harrisburg: Pennsylvania Office of Mental Retardation.

PARKER, R. *et al.* (1991) *Looking after Children: Assessing Outcomes in Child Care*. London: HMSO.

PARROTT, L. (1999) *Social Work and Social Care*. London: Routledge.

PARTON, N. (1985) *The Politics of Child Abuse*. London: Macmillan.

PATEL, N. *et al.* (eds) (1998) *Visions of Reality: Religion and Ethnicity in Social Work*. London: CCETSW.

PAVEZA, G. *et al.* (1992) 'Severe family violence and Alzheimer's disease: prevalence and risk factors', *Gerontologist*, vol. 32, no. 4, 493–7.

PAYNE, M. (2000) *Teamwork in Multi-Professional Care*. Hampshire: Palgrave.

PEARL, J. (2004) 'Be Honest with Me', *Community Care*, 26 August 2004.

PEARPOINT, J. *et al.* (1993) *PATH: A workbook for planning positive, possible futures.* Toronto: Inclusion Press.

PEARSALL, J. (ed) (2001) *Concise Oxford Dictionary.* London: BCA.

PERCY, G. (1995) in J. Horwath and B. Lawson (eds) *Trust Betrayed.* London: NCB.

PITHER, C. (2004) *Cognitive behavioural approaches to chronic pain.* www.wellcome.ac.uk

PRITCHARD, J. (ed) (1999) *Elder Abuse Work.* London: Jessica Kingsley.

PRITCHARD, J. (2001) 'Forewarned is forearmed', *Community Care*, 9 August 2001.

RAMON, S. (ed) (1991) *Beyond Community Care.* Macmillan in association with Mind publications.

REID, W. and EPSTEIN, L. (eds) (1977) *Task-Centred Practice.* New York: Columbia University Press.

RITCHIE, P. *et al.* (2003) *People, Plans and Practicalities.* Edinburgh: SHS Trust.

ROGERS, A. (2002) *Teaching Adults.* Berkshire: Open University Press.

ROGERS, C. (1991) *Client-centred Therapy.* London: Constable.

ROGERS, J. (1990) *Caring for People, Help at the Frontline.* Milton Keynes. Open University.

SANDERSON, H. *et al.* (1997) *People, Plans and Possibilities.* Edinburgh: SHS Trust.

SCHON, D. (1983) *The Reflective Practitioner. How professionals think in action.* London: Temple Smith.

SCA (2002) *Introduction to Care Planning.* Surbiton: SCA.

SCA (2002) *SCA Handbook.* Surbiton: SCA.

Social Care Institute for Excellence (SCIE) (2004) *Position Paper 3: Has service user participation made a difference to social care's services?* London: SCIE. (www.scie.org.uk)

Scottish Executive (2000) *Independent Advocacy: a guide for commissioners* Edinburgh: Scottish Executive Publications.

Scottish Executive (2001) *National Care Standards – care at home.* Edinburgh: The Stationery Office.

Scottish Parliament (2002) *Scottish Parliament Official Report*, 2 May 2002. Edinburgh: The Scottish Parliament.

SHEERAN, P. (2004) *How images of smokers, drinkers and drug takers affect young people's own life styles.* www.ersc.ac.uk, 13 October 2004.

Skills for Care and Development/Skills for Health (2004) *Health and Social Care National Occupational Standards.* Leeds: Topss.

Social Care Association (2000) *Handbook.* Surbiton: SCA.

SMALE, G. *et al.* (1993) *Empowerment, Assessment, Care Management and the Skilled Worker.* London: National Institute for Social Work.

SRC (1993) *Training Package in Residential Care.* Glasgow: SRC.

STAUNTON, H. (ed) (1996) *The Complete Works of William Shakespeare.* Ware, Hertfordshire: Wordsworth Editions Ltd.

STEVENSON, O. and PARSLOE, P. (1993) *Community Care and Empowerment*. York: Joseph Rowntree Foundation in association with *Community Care*.

STEWART, I. and VAITILINGAM, R. (2004) *Seven Ages of Man and Woman: A look at Britain in the second Elizabethan era*. London: ERSC.

SWINTON, J. (2001) *A Space to Listen: meeting the spiritual needs of people with learning disabilities*. London: The Foundation for People with Learning Disabilities.

WOOD, J. (1998) 'Jewish issues in social work education' in Patel N. *et al.* (1998).

TAYLOR, B. and DEVINE, T. (1993) *Assessing Needs and Planning Care in Social Work*. Bury St. Edmunds: Arena.

TESTER, S. (2004) *Feeling 'at home' enhances the quality of life for older people in care homes*. www.ersc.ac.uk, 27 February 2004.

The Stationery Office (2004) *Children Act*. Norwich. TSO.

The Stationery Office (1998) *Data Protection Act*. Norwich: TSO.

The Stationery Office (2001) *Freedom of Information Act*. Norwich: TSO.

The Stationery Office (2002) *Freedom of Information (Scotland) Act*. Edinburgh: TSO.

The Stationery Office (2000) *Race Relations Amendment Act*. Norwich: TSO.

THOMPSON, N. (2003) *Promoting Equality*. Basingstoke: Palgrave Macmillan.

THOMPSON, N. (2002) *People Skills*, 2nd edn. Basingstoke: Palgrave Macmillan.

THOMPSON, N. (2000) *Understanding Social Work*. Hampshire: Palgrave.

TOSSELL, D. and WEBB, R. (1994) *Inside the Caring Services*, 2nd edn. London: Edward Arnold.

TSUI, Ming-Sum (2005) *Social Work Supervision. Contexts and Concepts*. California: Sage Publications.

UKHCA (1998) *The Home Care Worker's Handbook: The essential guide to care in the Home*.

UN (1989) *The UN Convention on the Rights of the Child*. London: UNICEF.

UN (1948) *The Universal Declaration of Human rights*. Geneva: UN Human Rights Commission.

UPIAS (1976) *Fundamental Principles of Disability*. London: Union of Physically Impaired Against Segregation.

WADDELL, H. (2004) 'Unspeakable episodes', *Community Care*, 28 October 2004.

WARD, A. (1993) *Working in Group Care*. Birmingham: Venture Press.

WARDEN, J. W. (2003) *Grief Counselling and Grief Therapy: A handbook for the Mental Health Practitioner*. London: Routledge.

WATERHOUSE, SIR R. (2000) *Lost in Care*. London: Department of Health.

WILLIAMS, M. (2004) 'Overcoming the Inner Critic' in The Wellcome Trust (2004) *Talking Heads: Cognitive Behaviour Therapy comes of Age*. London: The Wellcome Trust.

WITCHER, S. (2004) 'Live and let Live', *Community Care*, 12 February 2004.

WESTHORP, G. and SEBASTIAN, A. (1997) *Introduction to Advocacy Module*. South Australia: Disability Action Incorporated.

Who Cares? Scotland (2003) *Let's Face It*. Glasgow: Who Cares? Scotland.

WOLFENSBERGER, W. (1972) *The Principle of Normalisation in Human Services.* Toronto: National Institute on Mental Retardation.

WOLFENSBERGER, W. (1972) *A Brief Introduction to Social Role Valorisation as a High Order Concept for Structuring Human Services.* Syracuse: Syracuse University.

WOOD, J. (1998) 'Jewish issues in social work education' in Patel, N. *et al.* (1998).

WYLD, C. (2002) 'Stress and strain of moving', *Community Care*, 18 April 2002.

ZELDIN, T. (1998) *An Intimate History of Humanity.* London: Vintage.

Website references

www.ageconcern.org.uk

www.barnardos.org.uk

www.bbc.co.uk

www.family-futures.org.uk

www.healthandsafetytips.co.uk

www.hse.gov.uk

www.lib.gcal.ac.uk/heatherbank/contact.html Heatherbank Museum of Social Work

www.nch.org.uk

www.shapingourlives.org.uk

www.sheffield.gov.uk

www.unison.org.uk/safety/index.asp

http://users.ox.ac.uk/~peter/workhouse/Barnsley/Barnsley.shtml

http://en.wikipedia.org/wiki

Index